the shadowlands
of conduct

American Governance and Public Policy Series
Series Editor: Barry Rabe, University of Michigan

the shadowlands of conduct

ETHICS AND STATE POLITICS

BETH A. ROSENSON

Georgetown University Press
Washington, D.C.

Georgetown University Press, Washington, D.C.
© 2005 by Georgetown University Press. All rights reserved.
Printed in the United States of America

10 9 8 7 6 5 4 3 2 1   2005

This book is printed on acid-free, recycled paper meeting
the requirements of the American National Standard
for Permanence in Paper for Printed Library Materials
and those of the Green Press Initiative.

A previous version of chapter 5 appeared as Beth Rosenson,
"Against Their Apparent Self-Interest: Authorization of Independent
Legislative Ethics Commissions, 1973–1996," *State Politics and Policy
Quarterly* 3, no. 1 (Spring 2003): 42–65.

Library of Congress Cataloging-in-Publication Data

Rosenson, Beth A.
The shadowlands of conduct : ethics and state politics / Beth A. Rosenson.
        p. cm. – (American governance and public policy)
Includes bibliographical references and index.
ISBN 1-58901-045-0 (pbk. : alk. paper)
1. Political ethics–United States–States–History–20th century.   I. Title.
II. Series.
JK2445.E8R67 2005
172'.0973–dc22   2004023163

contents

figure, tables, and sidebars

figure

text tables

appendix tables

sidebars

preface

Political ethics is in one sense a perennial concern, dating back to the beginnings of government. However, the ethics of public officials has become a subject of increasing attention in recent years. The question of how to prevent politicians from engaging in corrupt or other unwanted activities has only become more urgent in today's era of low public trust. In the United States, questions about the ethics of politicians cut a wide swath, touching upon the behavior of executives, legislators, judges, and public administrators at all levels of government.

This book is animated by an interest in the laws that have been enacted to promote higher standards of conduct for one particular group of public officials, namely lawmakers. Legislatures are a linchpin of representative democracy. Especially at the state and local levels, lawmakers are arguably closer to the people than chief executives, judges, and other public servants. The challenge of preventing the pursuit of private financial gain from corrupting their judgment is therefore a critical one. One solution is to rely on voters to throw out unethical politicians. Another approach, which is the main subject of this book, is to enact laws proscribing certain kinds of behavior. Why has the latter approach become increasingly important in the United States? Where did the modern "ethics movement" come from? What factors have catalyzed the passage of ethics and financial disclosure laws that are the source of both praise and criticism? Why have some states adopted stronger ethics laws than others?

I first became interested in the subject of political ethics in the early 1990s, while working as a reporter and editor for a community newspaper chain in the Boston suburbs. The cities and towns where I covered city government had experienced more than a few incidents involving corrupt public officials, which had led to a sense of cynicism among the citizens of these communities. I found myself wondering what types of laws might be enacted to prevent such self-serving behavior by state and local politicians. Having studied comparative politics as an undergraduate, I was interested in understanding how policies and politics varied across settings, in this case in how corruption and good-government laws might differ across the American states. When I returned to school to complete my Ph.D., this project became a natural outgrowth of my two central interests in the control of political corruption and comparative state politics.

Although there is substantial scholarly work on anticorruption legislation passed during the Progressive era and after Watergate, I discovered in the early stages of my research that the states had also taken important strides between the two periods, specifically in the two decades preceding Watergate. In addition to representing an untold and interesting story, these pre-Watergate laws are important for two reasons. First, they reflect the role of the states as "laboratories of democracy" whose innovations are later picked up by the national government. Second, the pre-Watergate efforts laid the foundation on which the more well-known post-Watergate ethics statutes at the state and national level have been built. To understand where ethics laws are now and where they are likely to go in the future, it is essential to understand their origins. The book provides a historical narrative of the legislative ethics laws enacted by the states from 1954 to 2004. In so doing, it offers explanations for the circumstances of the laws' varied passage across the states, and also for the gaps and loopholes that are built into them. A key argument of the book is that even "strong" ethics laws, upon further examination, often turn out to contain significant limitations. The interests and concerns of legislators themselves are an important reason for these limitations, as the book details. Reformers may take heart from the story told here regarding how ethics reform is passed despite the obstacles to its success, but the book also contains a cautionary tale about the limits of political reform and how legislation may fall short of reformers' expectations.

The research here is presented in a way that requires no knowledge of formal statistical methods, although I use such methods—along with detailed case studies–to answer the question of why states vary in their ethics laws and ethics enforcement mechanisms. The aim is to reach both political scientists and others with theoretical or practical interests in the subject of legislative ethics in particular, and in political reform more generally. The text therefore uses "Key Influences" boxes to highlight the results that are statistically significant. The multivariate regression analyses that underlie these results are presented in the appendices for those who want to examine the findings in greater detail. The methods used are discussed briefly in the text, but detailed discussions of the models and measures used are reserved mainly for the endnotes and appendices.

acknowledgments

This project was a long time in the making, and therefore my debts are numerous. The first set of debts dates back to my years at the Massachusetts Institute of Technology, where I did my doctoral research. Charles H. Stewart III supported me early on in my somewhat unorthodox interest in legislative ethics. Along with Steve Ansolabehere and Daniel Kryder, the other members of my dissertation committee, he sharpened the questions I was asking and the way I presented my argument. MIT also provided funding for field work in New York and the opportunity to present what was very much a work in progress. Some of the data were difficult to obtain, and I particularly appreciate the assistance of Robert Stern of the Council on Governmental Ethics Laws, as well as the help of numerous librarians at MIT, the Massachusetts State House Library, and the New York State Library.

At the University of Florida, numerous colleagues were helpful during the writing of this book. Rich Conley, Larry Dodd, David Hedge, Larry Kenny, Richard Scher, Daniel Smith, and others read different chapters and gave useful feedback. As department chairs, Michael Martinez and Les Thiele also provided important support. The book was also greatly strengthened by comments given during presentations at the American Political Science Association, Midwest Political Science Association, Northeastern Political Science Association, New England Political

Science Association, Florida Political Science Association, and the University of Florida.

Chapter 5 was published in somewhat different form in *State Politics and Policy Quarterly*. Christopher Mooney, the editor of the journal, provided extensive and invaluable suggestions that improved not only that particular chapter, but also the general argument I wanted to make.

I also thank Gail Grella and Barry Rabe of Georgetown University Press for excellent editorial assistance and, more importantly, for constantly communicating their belief that I had an important and interesting story to tell. Thanks are also due to Alan Rosenthal, an extremely dedicated and helpful reviewer, and to a second anonymous reviewer of the manuscript.

On a personal level, I am grateful for the emotional support of my parents, Joan and Larry Rosenson, and my twin brother Jon Rosenson. I was also sustained during this long process by the love and support of my old friends Carolyn Bess, Jeanne Madden, Heidi Mintz Massefski, and of my newer friends, most of them colleagues in Gainesville, Florida. I could not ask for a better environment, intellectually and personally, than the political science department to which I belong. My husband Duane Bernstein was sometimes more enthusiastic about the book than I was, and his entire family also provided cheerleading and emotional support, even if they couldn't tell you what the book is about to save their lives. My son Graham Dustin Bernstein, now two, showed little interest in this project besides shredding and eating pages of it as they came out of the printer, but I am grateful for his presence in the latter stages of writing. May he and his new brother Avery live to see a world in which both politicians and regular citizens behave ethically.

one

Setting the Stage: Legislative Ethics and the Process of Ethics Reform

In January 2004, the *Providence Journal* reported that three state legislators had worked as consultants for the drugstore chain CVS. One, Democratic Senate president William Irons, received $70,000 in commissions for serving as an insurance broker to CVS over a twenty-four-month period, only a year after having led an effort to defeat legislation opposed by the company. A second, Democratic senator John Celona, chair of a committee overseeing the health care industry, acknowledged being paid $1,000 a month as a consultant to CVS when a bill opposed by CVS died in his committee. A third, Republican representative William McManus, a business analyst for CVS, was also named in an ethics complaint charging him with conflict of interest in speaking against a bill to allow the sale of medications imported from Canada.

Although it was not illegal for these Rhode Island legislators to work for private companies in addition to serving as lawmakers, state law required them to disclose those relationships, which they did not. The media reports suggested that the legislators' ability to serve the public was compromised by their ties to the company and that hiding those ties represented a breach of the public trust.

Not only journalists but also lawmakers worried about the implications of the revelations for the legislature's public image and ability to serve its representative function. One Democratic state senator asked, "Why didn't they come out and tell the public of this hidden agenda?"

Another Democratic state senator suggested, "There can be unfortunate results when members of the part-time General Assembly serve two masters—the citizens in their districts and their regular, full-time jobs." The CVS scandal fueled calls for new ethics legislation, including a proposal introduced on January 27, 2004, by Senate president Joseph A. Montalbano to reinstate a total ban on the acceptance of gifts by lawmakers and other public officials. The ban had been repealed in 2000 and replaced with a $450 annual limit on gifts from each lobbyist.[1]

Rhode Island is not alone in recent years with regard to controversies involving charges that state legislators had reaped private financial benefits from their jobs as public servants or had conflicts of interests stemming from their activities outside the legislature. In Tennessee in 2003, state senator John Ford faced accusations that he and his ex-wife had spent $2,200 in state funds on FedEx packages for their personal use, including one from Neiman Marcus. In Washington in late 2003, a state senator who was also a partner in a vineyard was criticized for her votes favoring wineries. A Wisconsin legislator was under fire in February 2004 for working as a consultant to a construction company that had recently been awarded a generous contract by the state.[2] Though it was not illegal for these part-time legislators to work in the private sector, the potential damage to their ability to fairly represent the public was called into question.

The issue of legislative ethics was also front-page news in New York in 2003 and 2004. In March 2003, Democratic state assembly member Gloria Davis was sentenced to ninety days in jail for taking a $24,000 bribe from a Bronx contractor to whom she steered state business. Her case touched off additional revelations about another contractor who had given her free rides to the state capital; the second contractor represented a company that did business with the state prison system. The company was revealed to have kept a "petty-cash book" documenting payments to state lawmakers that went beyond the $75 limit on gifts. These gifts included a $200 plane ticket for one assembly member, and Valentine's Day chocolates and a fruit basket for other lawmakers, each valued at over $100.

These revelations led to calls for an overhaul of the state's ethics laws by watchdog groups such as Common Cause and the League of Women Voters and by Republican governor George E. Pataki. Among the proposed changes to the law, still being urged as of January 2004, were a ban on all gifts and junkets given to lawmakers and top policymakers. Advocates also recommended the creation of an independent ethics commission to oversee the state legislature, to replace the existing enforcement body—composed of eight legislators—described by one observer as a "snoozing, toothless lapdog."[3]

As of February 2004, a number of states had taken recent action in the area of conflict-of-interest legislation, or were considering the enactment of new laws. Illinois, for example, passed a new ethics law in November 2003 in response to a federal corruption investigation of Democratic governor George Ryan that began in the late 1990s. The governor and former secretary of state was accused of having taken over $167,000 in gifts and cash for himself and his family in exchange for granting government contracts to state vendors and landlords. Ryan was ultimately charged with nineteen counts of racketeering, mail and tax fraud, and lying to federal investigators, and he stepped down from office after one term. The scandal in essence forced a state that had historically turned the other cheek when it came to policing political corruption to take action.

Among other things, the new law limited gifts from a lobbyist to a legislator or other public official to $75 per day in food and beverages and $100 per year total in gifts; outlawed golf and tennis perks that lobbyists had showered on politicians; required the posting on the Internet of financial disclosure statements; and set up a new system of ethics officers and inspector generals to oversee both the executive and legislative branches of state government. Common Cause of Maryland was also urging in February 2004 that state legislators place their own statements of economic interests online for easy public access following revelations that a cable television lobbyist had tried to entice lawmakers on a cruise while they were attending a legislative conference in San Francisco.[4]

States looking to change their legislative ethics laws are not always looking to strengthen those laws, however. Some lawmakers in Iowa as of January 2004 were looking to relax the limit they had placed a decade earlier on their own acceptance of gifts worth over $3 from individuals with an interest in legislative actions. One legislator, a critic of the existing law, suggested that such a limit was "insulting" and that it was absurd to argue that "a legislator can be influenced by a meal or drink." Under existing Iowa law, lobbyist-financed meals involving only a small group of legislators and lobbyists are not allowed, while events to which all lawmakers are invited are. The main impact of the limit, said the legislator, had been to "stifle the social life at the Statehouse."[5]

The problem of how to regulate potential conflicts between legislators' private financial interests and their public duties is thus very much on the agenda of both the media and policymakers today. Even in Nebraska, which had not experienced any recent political scandals, an ethics "refresher" course was held for lawmakers in January 2003 to familiarize new legislators with the state's ethics laws. The idea of the seminar, said one state legislator who supported the idea, was "to make sure people know the law and also that they develop a mindset of asking themselves: 'Am I doing the right thing?'"[6] It therefore appears that there is a growing concern within the states about how to prevent legislators from misusing their public positions and obtaining questionable financial benefits for themselves, or at least about how to sensitize legislators to these issues.

This concern, as the above cases make clear, is not simply about bribe taking. Many of the stories in today's news alleging unethical legislative behavior do not involve charges of outright bribery or the existence of a direct payoff in exchange for legislative action. Instead, the behavior that is the subject of increasing media attention is often more nebulous and falls into the domain of "conflict-of-interest law." The central claim is that legislators in some cases are being unduly influenced in their decision making by the financial benefits they reap, even if they do not engage in an explicit exchange of cash for action.

State legislators today are criticized for a host of practices, which include going on vacations that are financed at least in part by lobbyists, receiving honoraria for speaking before trade associations with an interest in legislation, using state aides and state planes to conduct private business, and joining lobbyists' firms after they leave office. Such activities have become increasingly subject to regulation, as the scope of legally acceptable behavior has been progressively narrowed through conflict-of-interest laws. Yet as this book details, there is considerable variation in the ways that state governments have sought to control such behavior. Some states have enacted a wide range of laws restricting various types of legislative conduct, while others have put in place only minimal restrictions.

This book focuses on the precise ways in which the states have sought to regulate potential conflicts of interest involving legislators. Two central questions guide the chapters that follow. The first is why lawmakers, despite their well-known dislike of ethics laws, nevertheless enacted many such laws in the second half of the twentieth century. The second question is why states differ in the extensiveness of their legislative ethics regulations and in how they enforce their ethics laws. Whereas most books on legislative ethics focus on Congress, this book uses the variation that exists among the fifty states to understand the circumstances under which legislators will restrict their own behavior or engage in self-regulation.

The book thus illuminates the conditions that facilitate the passage of ethics laws and, more generally, the passage of laws that pose a threat to the political and economic self-interest of lawmakers and that lawmakers would prefer to avoid. As such, the findings are relevant more generally to the study of political reform that involves legislative self-regulation, such as laws restricting patronage and nepotism, campaign finance reform, and term limits.

In comparison with the professions of medicine and law, state legislatures were relatively late in developing codes of ethics for their members.[7] The focus here is on states' action with regard to ethical self-regulation during the years 1954 to 1996. During this time, the states went beyond existing bribery statutes, which deal with blatant quid pro quos, to enact a wide range of laws aimed at behavior in what Governor Thomas Dewey of New York, in 1954, called the "shadowlands of conduct."[8] Such conduct is characterized by *potential* and *apparent* conflicts between legislators' private interests and their public duties.

New York was the first state to enact a general ethics law that set standards to guide and restrict the behavior of public officials, including legislators, in 1954. Since then, most other states have followed New York's lead and enacted a range of laws that delineate improper conduct for legislators. These standards, enshrined in statutes and in legislative rules, restrict legislators from accepting certain things of value (e.g., gifts and honoraria), from representing clients before state agencies, from working as lobbyists after leaving office, and from using public facilities and equipment for private purposes. Most states today also require public financial disclosure for legislators and other public officials.

Furthermore, from 1973 to 2002, approximately half the states established independent commissions to enforce their legislative ethics regulations. This delegation of the authority to police ethics to an outside agency is particularly interesting in light of the fact that the U.S. Congress has kept that authority solely within the purview of its legislative ethics committees. Why state legislators have gone beyond Congress and established such commissions is one of the questions this book addresses.

Although state legislative conflict-of-interest regulations have coincided with and in some cases followed from federal legislation, in important ways the states have *led* the federal government in the timing and strength of their restrictions on legislators and their enforcement mechanisms. In doing so, they have in certain respects exceeded the efforts of Congress in a policy realm that many analysts see as vital to the health of democracy.[9] The importance of ethics policy to the functioning of democratic government highlights the need to understand how and why ethics laws vary across legislatures, the central topic of this book.

Why Legislative Ethics Matters

Corruption and political ethics are important topics in the study of politics because they bear upon fundamental questions of representation and governmental performance. Since the Watergate scandal of 1972, there has been a renewed interest in the topics of political ethics and corruption, or what is sometimes called "public integrity."[10] Watergate involved a range of questionable behavior that went beyond the break-in to Democratic Party headquarters at the Watergate complex in which President Richard Nixon was implicated and which gave the scandal its name. Other issues raised in the impeachment charges against the president included allegations of domestic surveillance of Nixon's enemies, illegal campaign contributions, the sale of ambassadorships in exchange for campaign contributions, and obstruction of justice.

Watergate is widely believed to have led to a decline in public trust. As such, it is an example of the more general principle that corruption or unethical political behavior matters because it influences the public's perceptions of government in a negative way.[11] Public trust is an important pillar of a healthy democracy. Mistrust can lead to political apathy and to diminished political participation. Most generally, unethical behavior, specifically decision making based on financial interests rather than the merits of the case, diminishes the quality of representation provided by legislators and chief executives.[12]

Corruption also matters from an economic perspective because it generates inefficiencies and appears to reduce economic growth. Corruption can lead to expenditures of public resources that may be unwise or undesirable. Countries that are corrupt tend to stagnate economically.[13] Finally, unethical behavior is argued to benefit the "haves"—wealthy corporations and individuals—more than the "have-nots" and to divert limited resources away from those citizens who may need them the most.[14] For all these reasons, then, unethical behavior by legislators is something that can affect the very fabric of democratic government and can have very real political and economic consequences.

Without sufficient attention to ethics, Dennis Thompson argues, legislatures will fail to serve their central purpose in a democratic society. Thompson argues that we should care about legislators allowing their autonomous judgment to be corrupted because when they make policy decisions based on the possibility of private gain, they fail to live up to the ideal of deliberative democracy promoted by the founding fathers. Thompson therefore suggests that legislators should follow basic principles such as considering policies on their merits, treating citizens and colleagues fairly, and publicly accounting for their actions. Ethics laws may help further these principles—particularly the first and third; they may increase public confidence in government; and they may have beneficial effects on the legislative process.[15]

Yet there is no shortage of ethics law detractors, who argue that in a number of different ways, modern ethics laws go too far. The central crit-

icism is that even well-intended ethics laws can have harmful consequences for the functioning of the legislature. For example, it is argued
that the process of raising and investigating ethics charges can make legislatures a more unpleasant place to serve and can complicate the development of consensus among legislators, particularly across partisan lines.
Others suggest that ethics regulation can paradoxically have negative
effects on public perceptions of government officials as frequent ethics
allegations lead citizens to mistrust both ethical and unethical politicians
and public administrators.[16] Mackenzie, for example, criticizes the "ethics
culture" that is at the root of modern ethics regulation as one "rooted in
distrust, in the notion that every public official and every candidate . . . is
suspect." Along somewhat different lines, Maletz and Herbel argue that
conflict-of-interest laws in effect aim too low by defining political ethics
too narrowly, leading not to an "ethics of aspiration or excellence" but to
a "trivialization of ethics."[17]

Finally, ethics laws are often argued to have a deterrent effect on the
recruitment and retention of otherwise qualified legislators. One claim is
that the laws, particularly financial disclosure requirements, violate legislators' privacy. Also, it is argued that mandatory disclosure and restrictions on outside income make people less likely to run for legislative office
and more likely to leave voluntarily once elected.[18]

Despite these claims and concerns about ethics laws, there is little systematic research demonstrating whether the alleged effects—both positive and negative—actually occur in reality.[19] One reason it is hard to
judge the effects of ethics laws, particularly at the state level, is that we still
do not know much about the content of these laws and how they vary
among legislatures. There is simply not much information available about
the nature, number, and distribution of ethics restrictions across the
American political system.

More generally, there is not a clear understanding of how and when
these restrictions were put in place. Anechiarico and Jacobs point out that
there is "no systematic scholarship devoted to explaining why (laws regulating) government ethics became stricter" during the second half of the
twentieth century in the United States and abroad. Maletz and Herbel
similarly state, "There seems to be no clear and definitive explanation for
the upsurge in concern for [political] ethics [that we see today]," although
they note that it is "frequently suggested that this development owes something to the Watergate crisis."[20]

This book provides evidence for the claim that Watergate indeed catalyzed the passage of ethics laws. But it also demonstrates and details the
ways that state ethics regulation preceded Watergate by nearly twenty
years. More generally, the book highlights the common factors that

explain the passage of state legislative ethics laws across different periods
of time, both before and after Watergate.

The Puzzle in Brief

The main question that guides this book is why legislators have enacted
ethics laws that seem to threaten their economic and political well-being,
and which many believe are insulting and demeaning. Ethics laws typically restrict legislators' relationships with businesspeople, potential
clients, lobbyists, and others, in the name of preventing such relationships
from swaying their decision making. Laws restricting the collection of fees
for speechmaking or representing legal clients before state agencies and
postgovernment employment opportunities limit lawmakers' ability to
earn outside income.

This situation poses a direct threat to legislators' economic well-being,
which may be particularly detrimental to lawmakers from states where
official salaries are low. Scholars know that at least part of legislators' resistance to ethics laws is rooted in economic self-interest. For example, legislators who earn large amounts of honoraria are more likely to oppose
limits on honoraria than those who do not. Lawmakers who are attorneys
are more likely than other lawmakers to oppose restrictions on lawyer-
legislators representing clients before state agencies.[21] One of the key
reasons why legislators oppose ethics regulation, then, is the threat it represents to their economic status.

Ethics laws also pose a potential threat to legislators' political security.
Aggressive journalists, such as the investigative reporters from the *Boston
Globe* mentioned above—as well as other legislators—sometimes use
ethics laws to harm legislators' political careers. In addition to the economic and political ramifications of ethics laws, some legislators find the
very idea of ethics regulation to be demeaning, an "insult to their
integrity." In legislative debates over ethics reform, two stances are typical. First, members commonly assert that only legislators themselves, not
laws or outside agents, should be the arbiters of legislative ethics. Some
go even further and assert that ethics comes from the heart and cannot be
promoted by statutes or legislative rules. As Frank Glinski, a Democratic
state senator voting against a 1964 ethics proposal in New York, put it, "I
have the Ten Commandments and I have my integrity and as far as I am
concerned, that is enough."[22]

Second, legislators often charge that ethics regulation is merely a symbolic way of appeasing misguided journalists, reformers, and the public.

Much less frequent is the speech that argues for the benefits of new legislative ethics laws. Conversely, legislators have shown greater willingness to pass laws regulating the executive branch. New York, for example, bars executive branch officials but not legislators from accepting honoraria from interest groups. Indiana, New York, South Carolina, and other states have independent commissions to enforce the state's ethics laws for the executive branch, but they leave enforcement of the laws with regard to legislators up to the legislators themselves.

Thus many lawmakers generally view new legislative ethics laws as undesirable, unnecessary, and something to be avoided if possible.[23] In this sense, ethics laws are not unlike campaign finance reform, term limits, or other self-regulating policies. The conditions of their enactment are interesting because legislators appear to be acting against their own economic and political self-interest and to be doing something they would rather not be doing and seem not to truly believe in.

Furthermore, ethics policy is not something that legislators *must* enact on a regular basis, as is the case with education, transportation, or tax policy. Indeed, during the period studied here, 1954–96, legislators in most states enacted new ethics laws no more than once a decade, and often much less frequently (see appendix A). Between 1954 and 1996, no state enacted legislative ethics laws on more than five occasions. Three states—North Dakota, Vermont, and Wyoming—did not pass any legislative ethics laws during this forty-three-year period, and six states enacted ethics laws only once. Most states enacted new laws on only two or three occasions. For example, Alabama first enacted a conflict-of-interest law that covered legislators in 1973 and then waited twenty-two years to strengthen that law. Missouri first enacted a legislative ethics code in 1978 and did nothing again until 1991.

Given these features of ethics legislation—the threat it poses to legislators' economic and political interests, and the fact that legislators do not have to consider it on a regular basis as they do other types of policies—how is it that ethics laws come to be enacted? We know that some states have indeed enacted significant self-regulatory measures over the past half-century. Consider New York, which today has strong disclosure laws for legislators, a relatively strong gift restriction, a two-year "revolving door" limit on legislators becoming lobbyists after leaving office, and a ban on lawyer-legislators representing clients before state agencies. Other states, such as Kentucky, Massachusetts, and Texas, also have relatively broad ethics laws that cover a range of activities.

Why did these states enact tough laws despite the seemingly reflexive resistance of legislators to such regulation? Conversely, why did states such as Minnesota, Montana, and New Hampshire enact relatively weak regulations for legislators? Table 1.1 illustrates the wide variation in the stringency of states' legislative ethics laws as of December 1996. The scores for each state are based on an ethics law index that I constructed, which has six main components. Points are given for six types of legislative ethics restrictions: (1) a basic ethics code, (2) limits on honoraria, (3) limits on gifts from lobbyists, (4) postgovernment employment restrictions, (5) limits on representation of clients before state agencies, and (6) mandatory financial disclosure.

A state that scores 0 points has no ethics restrictions in any of these categories. A state that scores 6 points (slightly below the average score for the data set) has several different restrictions in place. An example of such a combination would be a basic ethics code, a numerical limit on honoraria, a two-year postgovernment employment limit on legislators working as lobbyists, and a restriction on lawyer-legislators representing clients before state agencies. All states that score 7 points or above have restrictions in at least four of the different categories. Appendix A provides a detailed explanation of the scoring for the different components of the index and the years when different restrictions were enacted in each state.

This book examines why state policymakers have enacted both weak and strong legislative ethics laws. What factors have facilitated and hindered their passage? Under what circumstances have lawmakers overcome their underlying disinterest in this type of legislation?

The limited research on ethics policymaking suggests that it may be fundamentally different from other types of policymaking.[24] Yet legislative ethics policy also seems on its face to bear some similarities to other more common regulatory policies. For example, it regulates economic activity, even if the target of the regulation is legislators rather than businesses or citizens. As such, the same factors that influence the willingness of policymakers to regulate in areas such as welfare and taxation policy—such as ideology—may come into play. Also, ethics policy, like other policies to reduce the influence of special interests, is generally popular with the public.[25] As such, it may also be influenced by the same factors that influence the adoption of other popular legislation.

Political scientists have not systematically explored the question of whether the forces influencing ethics policy adoption differ from those influencing other policies. One limitation of the existing scholarly work on ethics policy is that it focuses primarily on individual cases of successful reform. Another limitation is that existing research has focused virtu-

Table 1.1 Stringency of State Legislative Ethics Laws, 1996

State	Ethics Score	State	Ethics Score
Kentucky	10.5	Indiana	6.0
South Carolina	10.0	Michigan	6.0
California	9.5	West Virginia	6.0
Florida	9.5	Nebraska	5.5
Texas	9.5	New Mexico	5.5
Connecticut	9.0	Minnesota	5.5
New Jersey	9.0	Virginia	5.5
Pennsylvania	9.0	Arizona	5.0
Wisconsin	9.0	Oregon	5.0
Iowa	8.5	Utah	5.0
Illinois	8.5	Georgia	4.5
Maryland	8.5	Hawaii	4.5
New York	8.5	Kansas	4.5
Ohio	8.5	Colorado	4.0
Oklahoma	8.5	Delaware	4.0
Alabama	8.0	Maine	4.0
Arkansas	8.0	Montana	4.0
Massachusetts	8.0	Mississippi	3.5
Alaska	7.5	North Carolina	3.0
Rhode Island	7.5	New Hampshire	3.0
Tennessee	7.5	Idaho	1.0
Louisiana	7.0	South Dakota	1.0
Missouri	7.0	North Dakota	0.0
Washington	7.0	Vermont	0.0
Nevada	6.5	Wyoming	0.0

Note: Minimum, 0; maximum, 10.5; mean score, 6.12; standard deviation, 2.77. Scores are based on a state's ethics restrictions for legislators in six categories: (1) basic ethics code, (2) honoraria limits, (3) gift limits, (4) limits on representation of clients before state agencies, (5) postgovernment employment limits, and (6) financial disclosure requirements. Higher numbers indicate more stringent restrictions. An explanation of the scoring system can be found in appendix A.

Sources: State conflict-of-interest statutes and legislative rule books (see appendix A).

ally exclusively on ethics reform in the post-Watergate period, and even more specifically on reform in the 1990s.[26] This book looks at both successful and unsuccessful reform efforts, and it also examines ethics policymaking across different eras. This allows for greater generalization about ethics policymaking and the factors that contribute to the enactment of new ethics laws.

Approaches to Understanding Legislative Ethics Reform

This book applies both qualitative and quantitative methods to the study of legislative ethics. In-depth case studies of ethics reform efforts in three states in three different decades provide some preliminary explanations of why legislators enact ethics laws and highlight the way that ethics reform unfolds as a process over time. Quantitative analysis of ethics reform in forty-seven states over a fifty-four-year time frame, divided into smaller subperiods, allows for rigorous testing of the theories explored by the case studies. The multimethod approach of the book allows us to examine ethics reform as a process and to take advantage of the rich variation in states' ethics policies in order to understand why this process is more successful in some cases than in others.

In seeking to explain why legislative ethics reform is enacted or not enacted and how the content of states' laws varies, I draw upon five main streams of literature or research approaches to the question of why and how legislative ethics reform is enacted: (1) case studies of reform in particular states; (2) cross-state analysis of why states vary in their legislative ethics laws; (3) case studies of public interest groups concerned with good-government reform; (4) research on earlier political reform efforts; and (5) the "new institutionalism," which pays particular attention to the effects of institutional structures on the decisions made by political actors.

In the first category, one case study examines legislative support for and opposition to ethics regulation in Massachusetts in the 1970s. Bradbury argues that in the wake of a major legislative scandal, liberals and non-power-holders in both houses of the legislature, along with the public interest group Common Cause, spearheaded substantial ethics reforms, including financial disclosure requirements and the establishment of an independent ethics commission. The main opponents of this reform were legislative leaders. Loftus asserts that a similar pattern held in Wisconsin in 1974, when liberal, non-power-holding legislators pushed forward a major ethics law.[27]

At the aggregate, cross-state level, several recent works address variation in states' efforts to regulate legislative ethics. These accounts also aim to identify the key political actors in the reform process and their interaction. In a series of papers, Marshall Goodman and his colleagues use quantitative analysis, case studies, and surveys of legislators to explain why some states had stronger ethics laws than others in the mid-1990s and to identify the factors that facilitated the passage of these laws.[28]

One important contribution of this work is that the authors conduct case studies of three states and survey legislators in twenty states in order to elucidate the process of legislative ethics reform and highlight who the key actors were. Their central argument is that ethics legislation is driven primarily by scandals and the media. Reform is a "reactive defense" to negative media publicity. The earlier papers of these authors also suggest that higher compensation is associated with the existence of certain legislative ethics regulations. But their later work contradicts this conclusion.[29] The inconsistency of these findings points to a need for further research to clarify the question.

These authors also suggest that political culture, which might be thought to influence ethics legislation, does not matter. There are a number of other potential explanatory factors they do not consider, for example, party competition and ideology. This book considers a wide range of potential explanatory factors that have been suggested by prior work, as well as ones that have not been explored previously in a systematic way.

Rosenthal also considers state legislative ethics laws in the mid-1990s. He concurs with Goodman's assessment of recent state ethics legislation as a scandal-driven process. His focus is on laws passed in the late 1980s and early to mid-1990s; his narrative and conclusions are based on informal interviews with legislators from states in which significant ethics legislation was enacted during the 1990s and secondary-source accounts of reform in various states. His assessment of state ethics laws, however, is based primarily on states with strong laws. Thus we do not learn much about why some states have enacted weak ethics laws or no laws at all. Still, his argument about the central role of scandal in the ethics reform process is important.[30] This book probes for a more general influence of scandal that he suggests existed in some states in the 1990s and shows that scandal was indeed a critical explanatory factor over a longer time horizon.

Another useful literature for developing theories to explain the success and failure of state legislative ethics reform is the literature on modern public interest group activity. Several scholars have written about Common Cause, the nation's biggest good-government group, and other groups with an interest in ethics in government, such as the League of Women Voters and Ralph Nader's Congress Watch. Their research suggests that good-government reform is driven by a particular ideology and mindset. In his case study of Common Cause, McFarland argues that the group's membership draws predominantly from upper-middle-class professionals who typically hold liberal beliefs. McCann and Berry similarly place modern good-government advocates within a broader category of "public interest liberalism."[31]

McCann also points to the "moralistic tendencies" of the good-government movement, or what he calls an "almost obsessively moralist" and "morally self-righteous" posture. This moralistic worldview has important parallels with the worldview of Progressive era reformers, who Hofstadter argues were motivated in large part by the concern about "moral degeneration." Mowry similarly suggests that the Progressives were guided by the belief that "behind every political question was a moral question."[32] The modern ethics movement appears to fit into the Progressive reform tradition to the extent that it is driven by a moralistic worldview.

The emphasis on the moralism of modern ethics-in-government reformers connects to contemporary debates in the state politics literature on the role of political culture in shaping political outcomes. This literature derives from Daniel Elazar's *Cities of the Prairie*, in which he categorizes states based on their dominant political cultures—moralist, individualist, and traditionalist. Elazar, and later research using his typology, suggest that moralistic states have a lower tolerance for corruption.[33] This book examines how this might lead to a link between moralistic culture and the enactment of legislative ethics laws.

For a more historically informed perspective on modern ethics reform in the fifty states between 1954 and 1996, studies of previous political reform movements in the United States are also illuminating. The ethics reform movement in the second half of the twentieth century is similar to earlier reform efforts in that it shares the goal of reducing the influence of "special interests" on legislators and other public officials. Historians and political scientists looking at earlier political reform efforts have focused primarily on Progressive era legislation, such as the establishment of direct democracy mechanisms, campaign finance regulation, and civil service reform. The body of work on political reform both during and before the Progressive era emphasizes the contributions to reform success made by political actors such as governors, outside reform groups, and some legislators, as well as the positive influence of party competition.[34]

These works on political reform also highlight the obstacles to reform posed by certain political actors. For example, analysts of Progressive era reform in the states suggest that institutional power-holders (majority party members who held positions in the legislature such as speaker or committee chair) tended to oppose or block reform efforts. Many analysts of anticorruption reform at the state and national levels prior to the 1930s also assign a central role to scandal and the media as key catalysts to reform.[35] This book explores the extent to which parallels exist between earlier political reform efforts and the modern ethics-in-government reform movement, for example, with regard to the role played by legislative leaders, governors, and the media. The aim is to see whether there are important continuities between good-government reform before and after the last half of the twentieth century.

The literature known as the "New Institutionalism" is also useful for generating theories to explain the failure and success of ethics reform in the states. A basic insight of the new institutionalist literature is that institutions both reflect and at the same time shape the preferences of political actors who make decisions within them.[36] Institutions, by structuring incentives and opportunities, play a central role in determining political outcomes. A major accomplishment of the New Institutionalism has been to restore traditional political institutions such as legislatures to the central place they occupied in political science before the behavioral revolution of the mid–twentieth century. Institutions are again seen as important structuring agents whose features shape the behavior of the individual political actors embedded within them.

Of particular relevance to the research question of this book is how the legislative institution itself may shape legislators' behavior on ethics policy. Weingast and Marshall and Shepsle argue that structural features and procedures of legislatures—such as committee organization, leadership organization, and the rules of debate and amendment—shape the parameters of possible political outcomes.[37] This book explores whether certain characteristics of legislative organization influenced the success and extent of state legislative ethics reform. In particular, it considers whether members' positions in the institutional hierarchy shaped their attitudes toward ethics reform, and whether higher legislative compensation influenced states' propensities to enact stronger ethics laws. Compensation is recognized as having an important influence on state legislative behavior, for example, with regard to turnover and electoral competition. At the national level, congressional ethics reforms have been linked explicitly to pay raises on several occasions, for example, in the 1850s, in 1977, in the early 1980s, and in 1989.[38] As suggested above, findings about the influence of legislative compensation on *states'* ethics policies are inconclusive. This book analyzes whether a consistent relationship can be found between increasing official salaries and ethics regulation at the state level.

In addition to examining how features of legislative organization may influence state ethics policy, this book also considers the potential influence of *outside* institutions on the success or failure of ethics reform. It argues that the media serve as a critical institution linking scandal to reform, not just through "objective" reporting of scandals as they occur but also by taking up the cause of reform and putting pressure on legislators to adopt stronger rather than weaker new ethics laws. In other words, it suggests that the media are far from neutral in the reform process.

The book also considers the role of the initiative process, an electoral institution that is argued to have played an important role in various political reform efforts over the past few decades, such as legislative term limits and campaign finance reform. I examine whether the availability of a direct democracy option to bypass legislators' resistance to ethics reform increased the likelihood that states would enact strong ethics laws and authorize independent commissions to enforce the new laws.

Overview of the Book

Chapter 2 presents three case studies in order to explore some initial hypotheses about why legislative ethics reform fails and why, under different circumstances, it succeeds. The three settings are California in the 1960s, Massachusetts in the 1970s, and New York in the 1980s. The findings from these case studies help guide the statistical analysis of later chapters by providing plausible explanations for variation in reform success. The chapter also looks closely at the actions of key political actors on ethics reform to explain where the impetus and the obstacles to reform come from.

Chapter 3 focuses on early innovation in state legislative ethics regulation during the pre-Watergate years from 1954 to 1972. The chapter provides a quantitative analysis of variation in states' efforts during this period. Seven explanatory factors for the variation are considered: culture/ideology, party competition, scandal/corruption, economic self-interest, policy diffusion, direct democracy, and preexisting laws. The influence of scandal is emphasized, and the contributing influence of other factors is identified. And by looking closely at the language of some of the early state codes, the chapter also provides insight into the controversies that are at the heart of the concept of ethics regulation. The limited nature of these early ethics laws—the gaps and loopholes that characterize even the ostensibly strongest laws—is highlighted. This theme of gaps and loopholes in coverage is developed throughout the book and provides an important clue to explaining the puzzle of why legislators are willing to enact laws they claim to despise.

Chapter 4 carries the quantitative analysis of chapter 3 into the post-Watergate period, focusing on the years from 1977 to 1996. The same factors for explaining variation in the enactment of ethics laws prior to Watergate are considered here. As in chapter 3, the argument stresses the central role played by scandals in the ethics reform process, even as it explores the way in which the nature of scandal changes over time.

Chapter 5 focuses on the enforcement side of ethics regulation. States with strong laws do not necessarily have strong enforcement mechanisms; content and enforcement of the laws may diverge. This chapter therefore explores the variation in states' willingness to authorize independent ethics commissions to enforce the laws. It also highlights the ways that legislators have sought to limit the capacity of even the strongest enforcement bodies. As with the content of the laws, gaps and loopholes in enforcement in even the ostensibly "toughest" states blunt the laws' impact and make them an acceptable form of self-regulation to legislators. Chapter 6 summarizes the general argument of the book and speculates on the effects of the laws and on what the future holds for legislative ethics regulation in the states.

two

Three Case Studies: Initial Explanations of Ethics Reform Failure and Success

In California, a proposal to establish the state's first legislative ethics code—which included a restriction on gifts from lobbyists and limits on lawyer-legislators representing clients before state agencies—was introduced in the 1961–62 and 1963–64 sessions. It failed to make it out of committee in either house of the state Legislature. The code was ultimately enacted in July 1966, along with a 166 percent pay raise for legislators. In Massachusetts, proposals for a law establishing mandatory financial disclosure and an independent ethics commission were introduced every year between 1972 and 1976, but these also died in committee. In the 1977–78 legislative session, reform succeeded—disclosure was enacted and an independent commission was set up. Finally, in New York, an ethics reform proposal that failed in 1985 and 1986 was enacted in 1987. The law strengthened existing financial disclosure requirements for state lawmakers and limits on lawyer-legislators' activities. The pattern in all three cases of initial failure followed by later success allows us to address the general question: Why does ethics reform fail sometimes but succeed other times?

This chapter presents three case studies, based on the three cases described briefly above, of the process of legislative ethics reform. The case studies are used for an initial exploration of several major theories about the failure and success of ethics reform. As suggested above, the cases are drawn from three states in three different decades: California in the 1960s, Massachusetts in the 1970s, and New York in the 1980s. Because a "within-case methodology" is used, there are in effect six observations: three outcomes represent failure to enact reform, and three outcomes represent successful reform.[1] At the end of the chapter, I also consider—albeit in a more cursory fashion—the case of Vermont, which represents a continued failure to enact legislative ethics reform.

The questions asked of each case flow from three theories about the failure and success of ethics reform. These theories center on the potential contribution of scandal, legislative compensation, and party competition to the ethics reform process. I also explore the role of legislative power-holders and governors in the ethics reform process. Finally, in constructing a narrative of the reform process for each case, I also look for other factors beyond those incorporated in the standardized questions asked of each case that may also help explain why failure occurs sometimes and success other times.

Three methods are used in combination here. The first method—structured, focused comparison—singles out specific aspects of a case for investigation and applies standardized questions to each case. The second, congruence procedure, compares observed values of the outcome we want to explain—in this case, ethics reform success or failure—with the observed values of the factors that are expected to be associated with different outcomes. The final method, process tracing, focuses on the decision process itself as it unfolds in time: the stimuli actors attend to, the behavior that occurs, and the interactions of different actors and institutions. The sources used for the structured focused comparison, congruence procedure, and process tracing were newspaper and secondary-source accounts of reform, legislative histories that tracked the progress of bills through state legislatures, and gubernatorial papers that highlighted the involvement—or noninvolvement—of chief executives in the reform process.[2]

Explaining Why Ethics Reform Fails and Succeeds

The result we want to explain (the dependent variable) is the failure or success of ethics reform. Failure is defined as a reform proposal not being enacted, and success is the passage of the same or very similar legislation. For California, the period of failure is from 1961 to 1964. For Massachusetts, it is from 1972 to 1976. For New York, it is from 1985 to 1986. The period of reform success is defined as the biennium during which reform passed: 1965–66 in California, 1977–78 in Massachusetts, and 1987–88 in New York. For each case, I ask several standard questions and measure each of the factors that potentially explain success versus failure for the base period of reform failure and then for the period of reform success.

Three main theories about reform success versus failure arise in the literature that deals with anticorruption regulation in general and the regulation of legislative ethics in particular. First, several political scientists have argued that the successes of the ethics-in-government movement in individual states since the late 1980s can be traced in many cases to scandals. Analysts of earlier anticorruption efforts in American history similarly argue that scandals involving legislators, and the attendant media coverage of unethical behavior, helped catalyze a range of political reforms at both the state and national levels, ranging from campaign finance regulation to direct democracy reforms to bribery laws.[3]

Scandals are generally hypothesized to catalyze reform through the mechanism of media attention. According to research on agenda setting, scandals can help bring reform proposals to a more central position on the policy agenda.[4] I therefore pay close attention to how the media covered both scandals and the reform proposals that preceded and followed them.

A second theory is that higher legislative compensation can facilitate ethics reform. Sacks suggests this was the case for the American states during the 1960s and 1970s. Goodman, Holp, and Rademacher make a similar argument for certain types of ethics regulation during the 1990s.[5] There is evidence that increasing legislators' official pay can have a positive effect on their willingness to accept limits on their outside income. One such example is the U.S. Senate in 1983, when senators voted to limit honoraria to 30 percent of their salaries and simultaneously raised those salaries by 15 percent. The same strategy of linking limits on honoraria to a pay raise was used again in the U.S. Congress in 1989, when both houses banned the practice of accepting fees for speechmaking.[6] Whether this pattern holds at the state level is unclear, though, because recent evidence suggests that professionalized states that paid their lawmakers relatively high salaries did not have stronger legislative ethics laws.[7]

A third theory is that interparty competition may facilitate the passage of legislative ethics laws. Several scholars argue that intense electoral competition in the late nineteenth and early twentieth centuries contributed to the passage of civil service legislation, campaign finance regulation, and other Progressive era reforms.[8] Parties vying for electoral support in a closely competitive environment, according to this reasoning, are more likely to pass popular laws that can help increase their vote margins. These scholars argue that national and state parties that were in danger of losing control of the executive branch and one or both houses of the legislature were more likely to enact legislation that would appeal to the general public. Ethics laws are a classic type of popular legislation that parties can use to expand their base of support or to mobilize existing support.[9]

Finally, in exploring the role of legislative leaders and governors in the ethics reform process, I draw on theories about the role of these actors in earlier reform efforts. It is sometimes argued that legislative power-holders—speakers, Senate presidents / majority leaders, and committee chairs—have historically resisted these efforts, such as those by state-level reformers to require campaign finance disclosure and limit campaign contributions and spending during the Progressive era. The reason is that the aim of such laws was to "rewrite the rules of the game . . . or destroy special privilege,"[10] something those who enjoyed special privileges or perks were apparently unwilling to do. Bradbury makes a similar argument about the strong opposition of legislative leaders in the Massachusetts House and Senate in the 1970s to ethics reform. But other work by Rosenson and by Loftus has found that top legislative leaders, majority party members, and committee chairs sometimes come out strongly in support of ethics reform, for example, in New York in the 1960s or Wisconsin in the 1970s.[11] Thus the evidence on the role of legislative power-holders is mixed and calls for more in-depth study.

The role of governors in the ethics reform process is also potentially relevant to explaining reform failure versus success. Governors hold a unique position in state politics and have significant influence over the political agenda, because of their high visibility and informal power. Research suggests that governors played a central role in promoting anticorruption legislation during the Progressive era. Conversely, one study found that although governors played an important role in the success of some state ethics reform efforts in the 1990s, in general they did not have an influential role, according to a majority of legislators surveyed.[12]

One specific way that governors may affect the political agenda is through their electoral campaigns. Two authors argue that Progressive governors in states such as California, Iowa, and Wisconsin made reducing corruption and increasing government accountability part of their campaign platforms in the early 1900s.[13] Once elected, they fought for and won enactment of the legislation they had promised.

Governors' motives for doing this are likely to be a mix of genuine conviction and political expediency. Running on an anticorruption platform and enacting anticorruption laws helped Progressive governors expand their political bases by appealing to the public's interest in cleaner government that was not the captive of special interests. We might also expect chief executives to be stronger supporters than legislators of legislative ethics reform because of competition between the two branches. It is logical that executives should be more enthusiastic about reforms targeted at their main competitor for power than legislators themselves. Governors can even be expected to support ethics laws that cover the executive branch as well as the legislative branch, because of the traditional role of executives as guardians of the greater public interest—in contrast to the traditional role of legislators as representatives of more narrow, particularistic constituencies.[14]

To explore the potential contribution that these various factors made toward reform failure and success, five standard questions were asked of all three cases.

Scandal

The first question was whether there were there any significant political scandals reported by the major state newspaper. "Scandal" is defined as an event featuring a reported charge of a conflict between a public official's (or officials') private interests and public duties. Included in this category are indictments and convictions for bribery, political extortion, and embezzlement, and investigations or reports (by law enforcement agencies or by state government itself) of patterns or incidents of corruption. These incidents must involve legislators, the governor, and other statewide officials, because these are the most important public officials for the purpose of understanding state ethics regulation. Scandals are measured for a given year beginning two years prior to that year and running through the first six months of that year. Data came from the *New York Times Index* for all states and from the three major newspapers for each state (the *Los Angeles Times, New York Times,* and *Boston Globe*). Two additional newspapers were used for Massachusetts (the *Boston Herald* and the *Boston Phoenix*).[15]

Put simply, scandals involving legislators should facilitate reform. This should be especially true with regard to scandals that implicate members of the legislative leadership. Such scandals should provide a powerful impetus to reform because advocates can most easily use them to link legislative ethics as a problem to ethics reform as a solution. Scandals involving governors should also be important because of the governor's central role in state politics, but not as important as those involving legislators. The media can be a powerful tool to link scandal to reform; attention will be paid to how this linkage happens, if indeed it does occur.

Compensation

The second question was whether there were there any increases in legislative compensation during the period of reform success compared with the period of reform failure. The fact that compensation may vary over the period of failure—which is more than two years in California and Massachusetts—is taken into account. Compensation is measured as the real biennial salary for legislators, not including allowances for travel.[16]

The question of what amount of change in legislative compensation would be expected to affect the likelihood of ethics reform success is difficult to answer a priori. As a preliminary hypothesis, I expect that changes in compensation over 25 percent are expected to be associated with ethics reform success, while smaller increases should not make a difference.

Party Competition

The third question was whether the partisan balance of power in the state changed from the period of reform failure to that of success. Interparty competition is measured in two ways: first, by the number of seats held by the majority and minority party in each chamber, and second, by which party controls one or both legislative chambers and the executive branch.[17]

Again, it is difficult to specify a priori when changes in party competition will matter and what size change is necessary to make a difference in the likelihood of reform success. We can make some initial predictions, however. First, a switch in one party's control of either chamber of the legislature or the executive branch should contribute more to the likelihood of reform success than a simple change in the number of seats held by each party in either chamber. Second, if there is more than a five-seat difference between the parties in the upper house and more than a ten-seat difference in the lower house, the situation is not highly competitive and should not be associated with an increased likelihood of reform success. But if a party loses at least ten seats in either chamber in a given election, this is a substantial change in party competition that may enhance the prospect of reform success. The last two conditions are admittedly arbitrary distinctions. In the quantitative analysis of later chapters, the data are allowed to "speak for themselves" in terms of the level of party competition that may be associated with ethics reform success.

Legislative Leaders and Governors

Finally, the fourth and fifth questions concerned the positions and actions of the governor and key legislators. I consider a range of legislative power-holders. These include the speaker of the House and the Senate president / majority leader, as well as committee chairs, particularly of the committees that had jurisdiction over the ethics bills. The guiding question is: Did any of these actors take a conspicuous stand for or against reform during the period of reform failure and/or the period of success? What actions, if any, did they take to push reform forward or to hold it back? Was there any evidence that their actions contributed to the fate of reform proposals? Table 2.1 shows the hypothesized effects of the factors that are expected to influence reform failure and success.

Why These States?

Before the findings of the three cases are presented, a brief discussion of the case selection criteria is in order. All three states examined here are large, urban states with liberal citizen and elite ideology and relatively aggressive print media.[18] Holding these background conditions relatively constant allows us to focus on the potential impact of the other variables of interest—namely, scandal, compensation, and party competition. Second, information about the introduction and passage of legislation in those cases was relatively accessible compared with other potential cases,

Table 2.1   Predicted Effects of the Explanatory Factors on the Success or Failure of Ethics Reform

Factor	Predicted Direction of Influence
Scandal / Media coverage	+
Legislative compensation	+
Party competition	+
Governors	+
Legislative power-holders	
Speakers / Senate presidents	?
Committee chairs	?

and good newspaper accounts of ongoing ethics reform efforts were available. The *Los Angeles Times*, *Boston Globe*, and *New York Times* all reported extensively on the ethics reform process in these states. Finally, because the three cases come from three different decades, any findings that are consistent across the cases will not be subject to the charge of period-specificity. Our findings can be generalized over a broader time frame than if we only looked at cases from one decade, as do most recent case studies of state ethics reform. Later chapters examine several shorter sub-periods. Distinctions can then be made about factors that may matter in one period but not another.

The cases were also chosen to conform to the following pattern. In each case, a certain ethics reform proposal was introduced in a given year, but it was not enacted (either during that year or over a period of several years). After a period ranging from one to five years, the same or similar proposal was enacted. This raises the question of how past failure may affect future success, a concern addressed in the discussion section at the end of the chapter and explored further in later chapters.[19]

California, 1961–66: Reforming Ethics and Modernizing a Legislature

On July 7, 1966, the California Legislature adopted a conflict-of-interest bill by a vote of 22–8 in the Senate and 66–1 in the Assembly. The bill, part of a broader constitutional revision package, went before the voters as a referendum item that November and was approved by a 2:1 margin. It had several provisions. First, it contained general prohibitions against a legislator engaging in "any activity which is in substantial conflict with the proper discharge of his duties in the public interest," accepting outside employment that "he has reason to believe will . . . impair his independence of judgment," and disclosing, for pecuniary gain, confidential information acquired in the course of doing his job.[20] It also contained more specific provisions, such as a limit on lawyer-legislators representing clients for compensation before certain state agencies, with two exceptions: the Workers' Compensation Appeals Board and Commissioner of Corporations. Additionally, it established a permanent, joint legislative ethics committee, composed of three members from each house, to investigate alleged violations of the new law. Finally, the bill included a legislative pay raise that increased members' annual salaries from $6,000 to $16,000, an increase of 166 percent.

Assembly speaker Jesse Unruh's (D-Inglewood) claim that "this is as tough a conflict-of-interest statute as there is on the statutes books anywhere in the country, and perhaps tougher" was something of an exaggeration.[21] Although it was true that the California law set a new standard with regard to limiting representation by lawyer-legislators before state agencies, other states had already enacted ethics regulations that were absent from the California statute. For example, New York already had a revolving door provision for legislators that said they could not become lobbyists until two years had passed. Also, a number of other states—such as Arizona, Florida, and Illinois—by 1966 already required public disclosure of certain financial interests; California would not do so until 1974. Still, the law represented an important step for the state of California. For the purposes of this chapter, it was a major leap forward with reference to a recent failed effort: Virtually identical conflict-of-interest proposals had been put forward in both the state Assembly and the state Senate during the previous two biennial sessions. The sponsors of these bills were Alvin Weingand (D-Santa Barbara) and Sen. Jerome Waldie (D-Antioch) in the Senate and Frank Lanterman (R-La Canada) in the Assembly. In each chamber, the bills died in the Governmental Efficiency Committee without coming to a vote.

Why did these proposals fail in 1961–62 and in 1963–64 but succeed in the 1965–66 biennium? What made legislators willing in 1966 to swallow what some saw as a bitter pill?[22] The first factor to consider is the role of scandal. In the period of reform failure and the two years immediately preceding it—1959–64—no major corruption scandals involving legislators, the governor, or other statewide officials were reported in the *Los Angeles Times* or *New York Times*. In March 1965, however, a legislative scandal broke. Assemblyman Lester A. McMillan (D-Los Angeles), who had served twenty-three years in the Legislature, was indicted and charged with seeking a $10,000 bribe to prevent the routing of a freeway.[23]

In July, McMillan was acquitted. The judge accepted the defense contention that the legislator, who was also an attorney, had offered simply to represent eight businessmen in his private legal capacity before a state agency. Interestingly, the case was not covered extensively by the *Los Angeles Times*. There were only a handful of articles on the indictment and the trial itself.[24] In the few articles that did appear, both the media and the acquitted legislator responded to the scandal by coming out in favor of ethics reform. Both McMillan himself and the judge made public statements that the case highlighted the need for an ethics code to regulate conflicts between legislators' private interests and their public duties. Judge Joseph Wapner also pointed out that legislators worked only part time and therefore earned relatively low salaries. Their part-time status and poor pay, he argued, meant that legislators except the independently wealthy had to rely on outside employment to support themselves, which led to conflicts of interest that might otherwise be avoided: "People hire legislators to go before courts and boards because they can exert influence. . . . Since the public hasn't decided to do anything about it, it places the members of the Legislature in a terrible position."[25]

The judge therefore urged that legislative salaries be raised to alleviate the problem of legislative conflicts of interest. McMillan himself commented: "There's a great need for conflict of interest laws in this state, but first the people will have to decide to pay their representatives on a full-time basis and pay them a large enough salary so it would not be necessary to practice law on the side."[26]

Despite McMillan's acquittal, then, the case had important repercussions for the Legislature and for the ongoing legislative efforts to enact a conflict-of-interest law. Even before the case went to trial, it prompted the *Los Angeles Times* to take interest in the issue of conflict of interest. Prior to this, the newspaper had given absolutely no attention to legislative ethics reform proposals. In June 1965, however, the paper assigned three reporters to interview every legislator regarding his or her financial interests. The reporters also conducted an independent investigation of the issue, tapping other sources in an attempt to obtain additional information. A special twelve-page section of the *Times* on September 15 detailed the outside income, both earned and unearned, and the campaign contributions of all thirty-nine senators and eighty members of the Assembly. All but three provided information to the paper voluntarily. One of the three was Assemblyman Willie Brown (D-Sacramento), who as speaker years later would sometimes receive criticism for setting a poor ethical example. The article emphasized the point that many of the forty-seven legislators who were attorneys had represented clients before state agencies. One lawyer-legislator was quoted as saying, "There is more opportunity for an attorney to have a conflict of interest than other legislators because it can be hidden in the attorney–client relationship."[27] The article suggested that at least one legislator's autonomy had been compromised by his representation of a construction company before a state agency at the same time as he was introducing a bill that would have benefited that specific company. Further, it quoted another legislator who admitted that some of his legal clients wanted him to represent them before state agencies because of his public position.

In addition, the *Times* piece noted that many legislators held stocks in savings and loan associations and banks chartered by the state. The suggestion was that this had led to favorable legislative action regarding the financial institutions. The article pointed to the existence of many troubling potential conflicts of interest that needed to be regulated, and it suggested that legislators' low pay was a major factor contributing to these conflicts. An editorial four days later took up the cause of regulating legislative conflicts of interest through new legislation: "Having six times unsuccessfully tackled the issue in recent years, [lawmakers] must succeed on the seventh."[28]

Thus the McMillan case appears to have sparked the state newspaper of record's interest in legislative ethics and in the reform legislation that had already been proposed. The scandal led to a shift in the media's agenda and in the legislative agenda, consistent with an agenda-setting model of politics. From 1961 to 1964, the media paid scant attention to the problem of legislative ethics and to the relevant proposals that had been sponsored in the Legislature. In 1965 and 1966, after McMillan's indictment, the *Times* began devoting more of its news coverage both to the subject of legislative conflicts of interest and to pending proposals for reform. The paper also began to use its editorial page to promote a code of ethics for legislators and a pay raise, described as the "cart" to the ethics code's "horse." It also reported favorably on New York's 1964 ethics law, recommending that California follow New York's example, in particular by placing a two-year ban on lobbying by former legislators and requiring detailed financial disclosure.

The *Times* continued to play the role of reform booster when the Assembly and Senate began seriously considering ethics legislation in 1966. Late in the process, when a conference committee worked to iron out differences between the more pro-reform Assembly and the more conservative Senate, the *Times* gave sustained front page coverage to the committee negotiations and also railed against the attempts of the legislators to water down the Assembly bill. In an editorial titled "Bad 'Compromise on Ethics,'" for example, the *Times* attacked the attempt by some members of the conference committee to wipe out the provisions that made violation of the new law a misdemeanor and conspiracy to violate the law a felony: "Some legislators at Sacramento apparently can't see the forest for the trees. . . . If those pressing the compromise get it through the Senate, they will have won a battle. But they will have also lost the war.[29]

What about party competition and control of state government during the period of ethics reform failure and reform success? In the 1961–62 biennium, the Senate and Assembly were majority Democratic, 28–11 and 46–33, respectively. Democrat Edmund Brown was governor. In 1963–64, the Democrats maintained unified control, with Brown serving a second term. Although the Democrats lost two seats in the Senate in the 1962 election, their numbers increased by six in the Assembly. After the 1964 election, the Democrats were still at the helm of state government, having lost just one seat in the Senate and three in the Assembly in the 1964 election. Thus no significant change in party competition occurred from the time of reform failure to success that could conceivably have contributed to the reform success in 1966. Although the Democrats did lose a few seats in the Legislature between the two periods, they still maintained a significant advantage in both houses (25–14 in the Senate and 49–31 in the Assembly). These margins cannot accurately be described as intense party competition comparable to the situation argued to have helped facilitate earlier political reforms such as federal civil service reform in the nineteenth century. The 1883 Pendleton Act, which inaugurated the national civil service system, was passed during the third-party system, the "most competitive electoral era in American history," in which the two parties alternated control of the national legislature.[30] In California in 1966, by contrast, Democrats had been and continued to be solidly in control of the Legislature, and their control was substantial compared with the control of other state legislatures at the time.[31]

Is there any evidence that increased compensation played a role in the success of ethics reform in 1966? A legislative pay raise was a crucial feature of the ethics package enacted by the Legislature in July. When legislators voted in favor of the conflict-of-interest measure, they were also voting to raise their salaries by 166 percent each year. Members' annual compensation had been stuck at $6,000 in constant dollars since 1955; an increase to $16,000 per year or $32,000 for the biennium was a considerable jump. Sacks argues that this increase was significant, in particular because it made the limit on outside employment of lawyer-legislators (who composed 39 percent of the Legislature) more palatable. The pay increase, he suggests, made these legislators more willing to swallow a major restriction on their capacity to earn outside income by representing clients before the state.[32]

As mentioned above, this linkage has been demonstrated in other settings, notably the U.S. Senate. In an earlier study, I show that a 15 percent pay raise moved some members from opposition to support for honoraria limits and those who switched tended to be members who earned a significant amount in honoraria.[33] We do not have a similar record of votes in California on ethics bills with and without a pay increase because there was never any vote on a bill without a raise. However, it is plausible that the same dynamic was at work with attorneys there. Recall the *Times*'s suggestion that many lawyer-legislators derived a significant portion of their

income from business before the state. For these legislators, the pay raise
is likely to have been an important factor that made the proposed representation limit more acceptable. Looking at the final vote in the Senate on
July 7, attorneys were no less likely to vote in favor than nonattorneys.[34]
Thus there is some evidence that the pay raise may have increased these
members' willingness to accept limits on their outside income. In the
lower house, only one of sixty-seven members voted against the final bill,
so clearly lawyer-legislators were willing to accept ethics restrictions coupled to a pay raise there as well.

What about the role of legislative leaders and the governor? Recall that
from 1961 to 1964, legislators in both houses introduced conflict-of-interest
proposals that went nowhere. During these years, Democrats controlled
both the legislative and the executive branches. The governor was
Edmund Brown. What was the position of Brown, a liberal Democrat who
was first elected in 1958? He beat Richard Nixon in the gubernatorial election of 1962 that yielded Nixon's famous comment to the press, "You won't
have Nixon to kick around anymore." In contrast to Nixon, Brown had a
much less adversarial relationship with the press; he was known for self-
deprecating quips such as "this is the worst disaster to hit California since
I became governor." Brown was an outspoken leader who questioned the
wisdom of capital punishment both during and after his terms as governor,
and was not afraid to raise taxes to finance services he felt were important.
His political passions were wide-ranging, encompassing the development
of public education, transportation, and utilities. Up to 1965, however, they
did not include ethics regulation. During the period of reform failure from
1961 to 1964, his annual State of the State addresses show that Brown never
once mentioned legislative ethics during those years.[35]

Beginning in 1965, however, the governor began to speak out in favor
of legislative ethics reform, both in his inaugural address and in other public addresses. On February 5, for example, he spoke before a group of California newspaper publishers and "solicited their support in developing a
code of ethics for legislators coupled with a pay raise for the lawmakers."[36]
After the Legislature took no action on a code of ethics in 1965, Brown
called it into special session in March 1966 to consider two subjects pertaining directly to the Legislature itself: conflicts of interest and institutional modernization.[37] Why did he do this? One possible reason is that
he wanted to be able to work with a more modern, efficient Legislature—
one that met annually, had greater member stability due to higher
salaries, and was less beholden to outside interests. These factors conceivably would make it easier for him to win enactment of his ambitious

policy proposals, such as increasing state support for higher education and developing California's natural resources.

This belated gubernatorial attention to legislative ethics may have helped bring reform to the forefront of the political agenda. The literature on agenda setting suggests that the governor has a unique role to play.[38] Because of the visibility of the office and his access to the media, the chief executive is positioned to take a leadership role in the policymaking process. This high visibility, according to two scholars, "means that the issues highlighted by chief executives draw the attention of the media and consequently the public."[39]

Brown's decision to call a special legislative session to address legislative modernization and conflicts of interest appears to have been part of a broader movement focused on making the Legislature a more effective institution. At the time, California's Legislature was "reasonably typical of other states. Legislators were poorly paid, met only part of every year, had inadequate offices . . . haphazard procedures, and . . . very few professional staff." Some legislators, notably House speaker Jesse Unruh, began advocating a salary increase in order to "attract brighter, better educated people" and more minorities to the Legislature.[40]

Unruh, a Democrat who became speaker of the Assembly in 1961, was an ambitious politician who would later run unsuccessfully for governor against Ronald Reagan in 1970 and become state treasurer in 1974. As a reformer on several different fronts—he authored a consumer protection bill and a civil rights bill in 1959—Unruh was also a strong advocate for his institution, arguing that legislators needed to be paid more in order for the Legislature to become a more effective body.[41] Under his leadership, in 1963 the Legislature adopted a concurrent resolution establishing an independent Constitutional Revision Commission to consider the merits of a salary increase and examine how increasing staff might improve the Legislature. The commission made its initial report to the Legislature in February 1966 and recommended both a salary increase and a code of ethics for legislators. This report from an independent, gubernatorially appointed commission gave legitimacy to the twin causes of legislative ethics regulation and increased legislative compensation. These would go before the voters as Proposition 1A, a constitutional amendment question on the November ballot, assuming that it was first passed by the Legislature.

Accounts of the 1966 constitutional amendment, then, suggest that Speaker Unruh was a major supporter of a pay increase and of a code of ethics for legislators. What was the position of other legislative power-

holders on reform? It has been suggested that they did not actively support reform efforts in the years of reform failure. But once proposals for
reform were propelled to the front of the agenda and became the subject
of active debate, how did institutional power-holders react? Accounts of
the progress of the ethics proposals in both houses suggest two things: the
main obstacles came from some key committee chairs, and the going was
more difficult in the Senate. After the conflict-of-interest bill passed the
House in June 1966, it came under attack in the Senate Finance Committee, where it had been sent after being approved by the Governmental
Efficiency Committee. Senate Finance Committee chair George Miller, a
Democrat, expressed unequivocal displeasure with the code: "Is there
anyone in the audience who can demonstrate any need for this? The California penal code already had 15 sections covering legislative corruption
(relating to bribery), he argued, so no new laws were needed."[42] He also
criticized the pay raise that was linked to the code, saying he opposed a
full-time Legislature. A majority of the twelve committee members dis-
agreed with both arguments, however, and passed the bill on a voice vote.

When the bill went to the Senate floor on June 30, Miller introduced
an amendment to delete a requirement contained in the House bill that
barred legislators from having "any interest, financial or otherwise direct
or indirect, or engag[ing] in any business or transaction or professional
activity . . . which is in substantial conflict with the proper discharge of
(their) duties." In putting forward the amendment, Miller attacked the *Los
Angeles Times* and other newspapers for their "innuendo" about legislative
integrity—highlighting the fact that the proposed legislation was in part
a response to reporting about legislative conflicts of interest—and again
objected to the proposed creation of a professional legislature. The Senate voted unanimously in favor of the weakening amendment and then
passed the entire package by a 27–6 vote. This set off a battle between the
House and Senate, as Assembly Speaker Unruh publicly attacked the
amendment, and James Mills (D-San Diego), author of the final constitutional revision package in the Assembly, also called it unacceptable. The
Times came out behind Unruh and Mills, referring to the Senate's "emasculating" amendment and urging in an editorial that the deleted language
be restored or the bill dropped entirely.[43]

Several days later, a Senate–Assembly conference committee agreed
to restore the deleted section, bringing the Senate bill back in line with the
Assembly version. Although the vote in the Assembly was 66–1, it was
much closer in the Senate: 22–8. Twenty-one votes were needed for passage because it was a constitutional revision measure. Of the eight voting
no, four were Democrats and four were Republicans. Three of the four

Democrats were in relative positions of power.[44] One of the Democrats, Reapportionment Chair and Rules Committee member Stephen Teale, stated tartly in casting his "no" vote, "I don't think I want to prostitute myself to a group of newspaper publishers—who couldn't stand a conflict-of-interest bill in their own business—just to get a pay raise."[45]

Overall, then, the position of legislative power-holders on reform was mixed. Some powerful committee chairs opposed it and one, the Senate Finance Committee chair, tried to substantially weaken the language contained in the Assembly bill. Conversely, Assembly speaker Unruh took a strong stand in favor of a code of ethics. Bell and Price call Unruh the "leading proponent of Proposition 1A," the ethics and pay raise measure that went before the voters in November 1966. They argue that Unruh "campaigned tirelessly the length and breadth of the state championing the measure."[46] Unruh's interest in ethics legislation, however, seems to have been a byproduct of his more fundamental interest in modernizing and professionalizing the Legislature. Newspaper accounts suggest that Unruh viewed the executive branch as his main competitor for power. Hence, it is not surprising that he supported legislative modernization, of which ethics reform was only one component, to increase the power of the Legislature so it could compete better with the governor in determining public policy. Further, the fact that Unruh was a Democrat may have affected his motivation to advocate a pay raise, if we accept Fiorina's argument that higher salaries lead to higher representation of Democratic legislators.[47]

To the extent that Unruh understood the calculations made by Democrats and Republicans about alternative careers and the asymmetric impact of higher salaries on the two parties, his interest in a pay raise may have been partly animated by the belief that it would disproportionately benefit his party. Finally, it seems that he was more interested in the pay raise than in ethics regulation, but he accepted the latter to gain the former. This is suggested by Unruh's actions during the campaign for Proposition 1A. Bell and Price report that the speaker "persuaded lobbyists to join in the campaign ("take a lobbyist to lunch" became a legislative theme) by warning them that their failure to support 1A with political campaign contributions would long be remembered.[48]"

To summarize the key findings of the California case, two of the three factors that were considered varied significantly between the period of reform failure and success. Between the two periods, there was a scandal involving a veteran legislator and a major legislative salary increase. The scandal appears to have helped move legislative ethics to the front of the legislative agenda, with the print media playing an important role in the process. Yet interparty competition did not seem to be important.

There were no significant changes in interparty competition between the two periods. The role of legislative power-holders was mixed, with some powerful committee chairs opposing reform while others, notably the speaker, supported it. The governor also took a strong and unequivocal stand in favor of legislative ethics reform during the period of reform success after not having advocated reform during the period of reform failure. Gubernatorial support may have helped facilitate reform success both by swaying voters on the referendum and by putting pressure on the Legislature to pass—albeit by a narrow margin in the Senate—the constitutional revision measure.

Massachusetts, 1972–78: Scandal and the Threat of a Ballot Initiative

On May 30, 1978, the Massachusetts Senate voted to accept a conference committee ethics bill. This bill mandated extensive financial disclosure by legislators and other public officials, limited gifts from lobbyists to legislators, restricted lawyer-legislators' appearances before state agencies, and established an independent ethics commission with jurisdiction over legislators and substantial powers. The Senate vote was a voice vote with no debate. The next day, after two hours of debate "dominated by speeches of praise," the Massachusetts House voted 215–12 to accept the conference committee report.[49] On June 5, Democratic governor Michael Dukakis signed the bill into law. Although the final leg of the journey appeared to be smooth sailing, it actually followed a hard-fought campaign, particularly in the Senate. Further, before this victory, ethics reform proponents had endured years of inaction in both chambers.

Massachusetts first enacted ethics regulations covering legislators in 1961 and 1962. These laws, pushed by Governor John Volpe, a Republican, made the state one of the early pioneers in addressing conflicts of interest. The 1961 law was especially innovative for the time, containing a limit on gifts and a requirement for disclosure of financial interests. However, the Legislature (called the General Court) repealed the provision the following year. By the time the 1970s rolled around, Massachusetts lagged behind many other states with regard to mandatory financial disclosure. From 1972 to 1976, at least thirteen legislators and Common Cause put forth a variety of proposals that would have required financial disclosure, established an independent ethics commission, and restricted gifts from lobbyists. None of these bills ever came to a vote on the floor of either house; all were buried in committee in both the House and Senate.[50]

In 1977, legislators finally addressed the issue of legislative ethics by considering a number of proposed changes to the legislative rules. Included among the successful rules changes of 1977 were (1) the establishment of new House and Senate ethics committees; (2) a requirement that the new committees formulate a financial disclosure requirement; and in the House only, two additional regulations: (3) a restriction on lawyer-legislators' appearances before state agencies; and (4) a $35 limit on the value of individual gifts from lobbyists to legislators.[51]

These rules changes in the House and the more limited changes in the Senate represented a significant step in regulating legislators' behavior. But reform elements inside and outside the Legislature wanted to see the changes codified in law and the disparities between the House and Senate rules eliminated. From a good-government perspective, the 1977 rules changes were only a partial success because they could be repealed or changed more easily and less publicly than a statute if either chamber simply failed to approve them at the start of a legislative session (which is what happened with the U.S. House of Representatives in 2003, when the rules governing gifts were watered down).

In addition, reform advocates such as the state Common Cause chapter felt that the *content* of the rules changes was lacking; for example, they wanted an independent, gubernatorially appointed commission, like those that had recently been established in other states. This commission would take over enforcement of the substantive ethics restrictions and replace the House and Senate clerks as repository of the financial disclosure reports. Thus an independent body, not legislators themselves, would control the release of disclosure information to interested citizens, public interest groups, and the media. The commission could also fine those who failed to file or filed false information.

I therefore define the period of reform success here as the 1978 enactment of the financial disclosure and ethics commission law, because this represents truer success from the vantage point of reform advocates. The period of reform failure is defined as the two biennial sessions, 1973–74 and 1975–76. The basic question is: After years of inaction by legislators, what explains the success in 1978? What can we learn from the process by which disinterest in legislative ethics regulation changed to support, restoring Massachusetts to a position of relative strength among the states in terms of its legislative ethics laws?

The first potential explanatory factor to consider is scandal. During the years when reform proposals failed to make it out of committee, the three major Boston newspapers that covered state politics (the *Boston Globe*, *Herald / Evening Herald*, and *Boston Phoenix*) reported no major political scandals involving legislators or the governor.[52] Although Watergate had placed political ethics on the national agenda, corruption in the state of Massachusetts was still an issue simmering below the surface. There were a variety of low-level scandals involving municipal officials, and two state officials from the state bureau that oversees public works faced extortion charges in 1974. But no major scandals involving the Legislature or executive branch appeared in the print media. The head of the Federal Strike Force on Organized Crime and Racketeering in New England, in a 1971 address to other law enforcement agents, suggested that corruption pervaded Massachusetts government. Said Edward F. Harrington, "There are certain individuals on all levels (of government) in the state of Massachusetts who are on the take. However, what we know and what we can prove is a little different. The strike force has been unable to develop a witness with respect to the information we have."[53]

In 1975, Governor Dukakis said in an interview that he had "inherited a corrupt system" but then withdrew his charge several days later, saying he had "no evidence of corruption."[54] Thus there was a general sense that corruption existed but that it was hard to demonstrate conclusively. Allegations by reform elements outside and within the Legislature, for example, that legislators were being paid to pass favorable laws for the racetrack industry, were not backed up by official reports or investigations. In this climate, it is not surprising that little support gathered around the reform programs introduced at the State House from December 1972 to 1976 by Common Cause, another reform group called Citizens for Participation in Political Action, and their legislative backers.

In 1974 over two dozen legislators signed on as cosponsors of Common Cause's omnibus ethics bill—centered on financial disclosure and an independent commission—and the Legislature held public hearings. But members of the Joint State Administration Committee, which held the hearings, were unenthusiastic. "How far are we going to let the people run the government? Maybe we should just do away with elections," said Representative Thomas McGee (D-Lynn), a committee member and House majority leader.[55] The financial disclosure / ethics commission bill, along with eleven other financial disclosure bills filed in 1974, were all discharged to the speaker-controlled Rules Committee, where they languished without coming to a vote. In July 1975, House Majority Leader McGee became the new speaker. Under his rule that year and through the middle of 1976, the House responded even more harshly to various ethics reform proposals. For example, in late 1975 two disclosure bills and one disclosure/commission bill received adverse committee reports as opposed to no report at all.[56]

In July 1976, however, the political landscape shifted when a scandal of major proportions broke. The *Boston Globe* and other papers reported that a federal grand jury was probing two state senators, Majority Leader Joseph DiCarlo (D-Revere) and Assistant Minority Whip Ronald MacKenzie (R-Burlington), on extortion charges. The senators were charged with trying to obtain money from a New York consulting firm, under threat of a harmful legislative committee report regarding the construction of the Boston campus of the University of Massachusetts. The legislators were indicted later that year and went on trial in February 1977. On February 25, a jury found MacKenzie and DiCarlo guilty on all eight counts of the indictment. MacKenzie resigned his seat in April, but DiCarlo refused to resign. He was expelled April 4, the first expulsion in the history of the state Senate.[57]

Analysts of the MacKenzie-DiCarlo convictions concur that they played a central role in the success of ethics reform proposals pending in the General Court. Bradbury calls the trial the "spark in the long smoldering ethics reform movement in Massachusetts," and she quotes veteran State House reporter Robert Turner of the *Boston Globe*: "Many will remember that there has been a lot of talk about policing the Legislature for years, but very little was done until two senators were convicted."[58] The bipartisan scandal, involving a big fish from each legislative chamber, led to a barrage of media attention to the problem of legislative corruption and arguably helped set the agenda for ethics reform in Massachusetts.

What about legislative compensation in the periods of ethics reform failure and success? During the years 1973 to 1976, when ethics reform was languishing in committee in the House and Senate, biennial compensation in constant dollars was $25,376. Legislators received a pay raise in April 1977, several months before they enacted new ethics rules and a year before they passed the comprehensive ethics law. The 17.7 percent raise brought real biennial compensation to $29,879.[59] Secondary-source accounts and newspaper accounts did not emphasize this factor as contributing to the success of ethics reform, in contrast to the California case.[60] Still, it is plausible that the pay raise one year prior to the passage of the 1978 ethics law made legislators somewhat more willing to accept various limits on outside income, mandatory financial disclosure, and a strong ethics enforcement mechanism.

What of party competition? During the early part of the period of reform failure, 1973–74, the state had a Republican governor, Francis Sargent. In the 1974 election, he was defeated by Democrat Michael Dukakis. In the 1973–74 biennium, the Democrats controlled both the Senate and the House, 32–8 and 184–51. In the 1974 election, they gained a total of seven seats in both houses, so in 1975–76 they dominated the Senate 33–7 and the House 190–45. The 1976 election enhanced their strength by an additional three votes total, increasing Democratic control of the Senate to 34–6 and of the House to 192–44. From the period of reform failure to reform success, then, competition between the two parties actually *declined.*[61] State government became unified under Democratic control with Dukakis's election, and the Democrats tightened their grip on the General Court, picking up two seats in the Senate and eight seats in the House. The fact that reform succeeded under conditions of increasingly Democratic control contradicts the hypothesis that ethics reform success may be enhanced by increased interparty competition.

What role did the governor and the legislative leadership play? During the period of reform failure, neither governor made ethics regulation a priority. In his annual address in January 1973, Sargent said he would push for the reorganization of state government, eliminating state agencies and cutting, but said nothing about governmental ethics. In his first inaugural message in January 1975, Dukakis talked about the need to improve public transportation, economic development, and health care. The next year, in January 1976, he promised a balanced budget and again set economic development as a priority. He also called for a reorganization of the court system, but he said nothing about a need for legislative ethics reform.[62]

Dukakis's 1977 State of the State address emphasized job creation, property tax relief, and judicial reform. Again, ethics reform went unmentioned. Later that year, in April, Dukakis pointed in a public address to nearly thirty bills he wanted the General Court to pass, giving priority to balancing the budget and overhauling the court system. He did not mention the proposals for financial disclosure and an independent ethics commission that had been filed by Common Cause and sympathetic legislators.[63]

In 1978, the year the ethics law passed, Dukakis still showed no strong commitment to ethics reform. In his State of the State speech, he sounded themes similar to those of the year before, calling for court reform and property tax relief, and also an increase in local aid. His silence on ethics reform continued even when Common Cause forced the issue onto the agenda in December 1977. As suggested above, Common Cause was determined to see the recently adopted legislative rules enshrined in law and to establish an independent commission and a revolving door limit for legislators. After gathering the requisite number of signatures—55,644 (over 95,000 were collected)—the group filed an initiative petition with the secretary of state on December 7. The petition was referred to the joint

State Administration Committee, and April 5 was set as the date for a public hearing. The House and Senate were required by law to vote on the measure without amendment by May 3. If by that deadline the Legislature failed to act or rejected the petition, Common Cause could "complete" the petition by filing an additional 9,274 signatures by July 5, which would place it on the November ballot for a direct vote by the citizens of Massachusetts. The House voted 199–28 in favor of the initiative petition, while the Senate rejected it 28–7.[64]

Dukakis could have spoken out in support of the initiative proposal in his January 1978 State of the State address—only one month after Common Cause had filed its petition—but he chose not to. When the General Court held hearings in April 1978 and debated both the Common Cause petition and a Senate substitute, Dukakis was, in the eyes of one observer, "curiously silent" on the subject.[65] It was only when a conference committee began meeting in late May that the governor finally spoke out on the matter. The Senate conferees opposed certain financial disclosure requirements contained in the House bill, and Dukakis came down on the Senate side. Dukakis and Senate conferee Chester Atkins expressed concern that disclosure for executive branch officials, particularly those at the middle management level, could make it hard to recruit good people to office. The governor also worried out loud about how disclosure might affect his ability to recruit citizens to serve on unpaid state boards and commissions. Even though his main concern seemed to be the potential effects of disclosure on the executive branch, the governor still had nothing positive to say about disclosure for legislators.[66]

Thus Dukakis did not speak out publicly in favor of any aspect of the ethics bill in 1978. Had he been a strong supporter of the Common Cause petition, there were a number of opportunities on which he might have taken a stand. One was when the petition was filed. Another was when the Senate tried to delay the petition by requesting a Supreme Judicial Court advisory opinion on the constitutionality of the proposed legislation. Common Cause, the Senate Ethics Committee, and the attorney general all submitted briefs on eight questions regarding the petition's constitutionality. On May 27, the State Supreme Court ruled that only one provision of the Common Cause petition was unconstitutional: the one barring legislators from being seated until they had filed a financial disclosure statement. It upheld the constitutionality of financial disclosure, saying it served a "compelling state interest"; and of an independent ethics commission, saying it did not violate the constitutional separation of powers. More generally, it said the proposed law did not violate any right to privacy.[67]

The ruling was not a surprise; these questions had already been liti-
gated with similar results in other states such as Michigan. No financial
disclosure requirements or independent commissions had been over-
turned on the basis of claims like those made by the Senate Ethics Committee. With a judicial consensus that ethics laws similar to the proposed
Massachusetts law were constitutionally sound, Dukakis need not have
worried much about the issue of constitutionality. At the very least, he
might have spoke out in favor of the general *principles* behind ethics
reform, if not the specific proposal under consideration. His only public
comments on the existing reform proposals expressed concern about the
potential impact on executive branch recruitment. He did not mention
any potentially positive impact of the laws, though he could have offered
the common arguments that ethics laws will increase public trust or benefit the economy by reducing corruption. Contrary to the common perception of Dukakis as an advocate of clean government and of proper
government processes, then, his role in the passage of the 1978 ethics law
was negligible. In contrast to California, where Governor Brown took a
strong stand in calling for ethics reform, Dukakis was not a key player in
the Massachusetts case.

What about the position of top legislative leaders on financial disclosure and an independent commission? In 1977, House Speaker Thomas
McGee had fought against many of the ethics rules changes, although he
was outnumbered on many of those votes by reformers from his own
party who allied with members of the minority party. With regard to the
1978 ethics bill, McGee faced additional pressure, this time from Common Cause wielding the threat of an initiative petition that was virtually
certain to succeed at the ballot in November.[68] McGee still remained
steadfast in his opposition to legislative ethics regulation, but his opposition in this case manifested itself more as petulant behavior than in the
use of concrete blocking tactics. For example, when the House held hearings on the Common Cause petition on May 1, McGee had his majority
leader preside in his place to show his displeasure. When the House voted
on May 31 to enact the financial disclosure and ethics commission law,
McGee again refused to preside over the vote, delegating that task to a
lieutenant; he also refused to vote himself.

The speaker's other actions reflected a similar distaste for ethics legislation combined with a reluctant acceptance of the legislation's eventual
success. His choice of conferees to the Senate–House conference committee illustrates this position. They were John Murphy, a trusted member of his leadership team and chair of the powerful Committee on Bills
in the Third Reading; Sherman W. Saltmarsh, a Republican known for

working with the Democratic leadership; and Democrat Robert Cerasoli, one of the ten original signatories to the Common Cause initiative petition and a longtime supporter of ethics reform. Thus he picked two legislators who could be expected to resist efforts to strengthen the existing proposal, but also one strong advocate of reform. McGee and the House leadership may have been marginally more supportive of the initiative petition than they had been of the ethics rules changes because, this time around, it was an election year. Though still unenthusiastic about reform, they did not want to appear to be holding it back right before an election.

Fewer Senate members were up for reelection in 1978 compared with members of the House, so the electoral imperative did not weigh as heavily on them. Still, Senate President Harrington's strong opposition to ethics reform manifested itself in several ways. He led the drive to have the Senate Ethics Committee challenge the Common Cause initiative petition. When that failed and the state Supreme Court ruled the petition constitutionally sound, Harrington then used parliamentary maneuvering to substitute the Senate Ethics Committee bill for the Common Cause petition. This move forced Common Cause to collect extra signatures to bring the proposal to the ballot. The Senate substitute, sponsored by Ethics Committee chair Chester Atkins, was weaker than the Common Cause–House bill in several respects, particularly regarding exemptions to financial disclosure. This substitute passed, and a conference committee was called to hammer out differences between the two chambers.

On May 16, Harrington chose as his three appointments to the conference committee three men who had "publicly expressed disapproval of the initiative petition."[69] One of the three made an announcement that same day that he would not run for reelection and took the opportunity to attack financial disclosure as a hindrance to the recruitment and retention of good public officials. Thus Harrington's conference appointees, even more than those of the House speaker, reflected an oppositional stance toward ethics reform.

The House and Senate conferees made a number of compromises that reflected the Senate's demands that the initial Common Cause proposal be watered down. Disclosure would include trusts but not inheritances, and spouses and dependent children of public officials would only have to report the source, not the amount, of their economic interests. The Senate also won exemptions for disclosure of home mortgages, educational loans, alimony and child support obligations, and debts owed to relatives. Finally, the House conferees acquiesced in the Senate demand that three members of the proposed five-member ethics commission would constitute a quorum. Representative Murphy, the trusted lieutenant of Speaker

McGee, often sided with the Senate in demanding these various weakening changes. Client disclosure was also eliminated, with even Common Cause agreeing this would go too far in the direction of violating public officials' privacy.

Despite these changes that watered down the initial financial House— Common Cause disclosure requirements, the conferees actually *strengthened* the disclosure requirements in four other ways. They did so by requiring the reporting of (1) honoraria from lobbyists, (2) creditors who had forgiven debts, (3) businesses from which a leave of absence had been taken, and (4) equity in businesses recently transferred to a family member. The Senate conferees also conceded on their opposition to the House–Common Cause provisions prohibiting lawyer-legislators from appearing before most state agencies for compensation. They also concurred "with strong protest" in the House proposal for a $100 cap on gifts from lobbyists, in exchange for the House accepting the Senate's disclosure cap; the Senate bill required income over $100,000 to be reported, whereas the House had capped disclosure at $50,000 in income.[70]

These various changes in the original Common Cause petition were what a *Boston Globe* reporter called a "legislatively choreographed effort" designed to achieve compromise with Common Cause. A *Boston Globe* article on May 16, shortly before the conference committee met, stated, "The goal of the strategy is to have the Legislature produce an ethics bill that meets Common Cause standards. If that happens, Common Cause would drop its plans to put its original version of the ethics bill on the November ballot."[71] The strategy worked. An interesting question is why the public interest group was willing to compromise with the Legislature, when it had already gathered enough signatures to put its own proposal on the ballot in November. Perhaps the major reason was growing media criticism of the public interest group's petition. Even the *Boston Globe*, a strong supporter of the principle of ethics legislation, editorialized against the "flawed" provisions of the petition and urged Common Cause to accept a "reasonable compromise" with the Senate, to spare the public from "the absurd choice between flawed reform and no reform at all."[72] Recognizing the need for the media as an ally in future clean government efforts, state Common Cause executive director Jay Hedlund indeed compromised and withdrew from the goal of placing the group's preferred version of reform on the ballot.

Although ethics reform never went before the voters in Massachusetts, the impact of a direct democracy option on the ultimate success of reform should not be underestimated. Common Cause's use of the initiative process to play hardball with the state Legislature was an important factor in the ultimate success of reform. Although the group compromised with the Senate and the House on some provisions, in the end the public interest group got the main things it wanted: statutory financial disclosure requirements and an independent ethics commission. The commission would have three members appointed by the governor, one by the secretary of state, and one by the attorney general. Common Cause also succeeded in having the rules changes of the previous year regarding limits on gifts and on lawyer-legislators included in the new law. In addition, a one-year postemployment lobbying prohibition for former state elected officials, including legislators, was included, although a concession was made at the request of the House leadership that the ban would not take effect until February 1, 1979.[73] Overall, then, this was a comprehensive and detailed ethics law that gave Common Cause a decisive victory. Without the threat of the initiative process to prod legislators, the group might not have been so successful.

To summarize, in Massachusetts as in California, reform success was preceded by a major legislative scandal—in this case, one involving two powerful legislators, one from each chamber—whereas there were no major reported scandals in the period of failure. There was an increase in compensation between the period of reform failure and success, but it was significantly smaller than the pay hike in California, and secondary-source accounts of reform success make no mention of the raise as a factor contributing to reform success. Party competition was not associated with success versus failure. In fact, success followed a *decline* rather than an increase in party competition. Finally, some legislative power-holders attempted to block and to weaken reform, while the governor stayed largely neutral in the reform process.

New York, 1985–87: Another Scandal and a Gubernatorial Advocate

On June 31, 1987, the New York Legislature and Democratic governor Mario Cuomo announced that they had reached an agreement on an ethics bill that had been a source of considerable conflict. The bill, passed unanimously by the Assembly and Senate two days later and then signed by the governor, was described by the *New York Times* as "perhaps the biggest victory of Cuomo's term in office."[74] Just three months earlier, Cuomo had vetoed an ethics bill drafted by the Legislature without his input, calling it unacceptably weak and demanding that legislators go back to the table and address some of his concerns. His victory represented the coming to fruition of a year of effort on his part and an even longer-term effort on the part of some reformist legislators.[75]

The bill enacted in June strengthened New York's existing ethics-in-government statute, first passed in 1954 and amended in 1964 and 1965, in several regards. It added to the existing requirements for financial disclosure, bolstered limits on representation of clients before state agencies by lawyer-legislators, and strengthened ethics enforcement, although not as much as advocates would have liked. The existing law had required financial disclosure only where the entity in which an official had an interest was "subject to the jurisdiction of a regulatory agency" or if an official himself determined "in his discretion" that the interest "might reasonably be expected to be particularly affected by legislative action." The new law moved far beyond leaving disclosure to legislators' discretion and required them to file extensive mandatory disclosure forms. For example, they would now have to disclose offices, directorships, business and professional positions, sources of gifts and reimbursements, interest in trusts, postemployment agreements, real property and securities, and sources of income over $1,000. However, the *amount* of income would be kept confidential and shielded from public view.[76]

In addition to expanding disclosure, the new law also eliminated exemptions in the existing statute regarding lawyer-legislators' appearances before state agencies. Importantly, quasi-judicial appearances, such as applications for a liquor license, were no longer allowed. The final version of the ethics act banned legislators from representing clients for pay on a wide range of issues: purchase, sale, rental, or lease of property; rate making; adoption or repeal of regulations; obtaining of grants and loans; licensing; and franchising. Members of legislators' law firms were still allowed to appear before state agencies for compensation, however.[77]

The 1987 law also introduced a new enforcement mechanism to replace the weak existing system based on an Advisory Committee on Ethical Standards in the attorney general's office, whose purpose and power extended only to issuing advisory opinions on the application of the ethics code. The 1987 law substituted an independent Ethics Commission to monitor executive branch officers and employees. However, jurisdiction over legislators was placed in the hands of a new eight-member Joint Legislative Ethics Committee (to replace existing committees in each house), consisting of four legislators from each party. The governor had wanted legislators to be under the jurisdiction of the independent commission, but he lost out on this point. Both oversight bodies were given the power to impose civil penalties up to $10,000 for violation of the conflict-of-interest rules as well as for failure to file or false filing of the disclosure form.

The 1987 Ethics Act had its genesis in bills championed previously by Democratic Assembly members Oliver Koppell and Alexander Grannis, and by Democratic senator Franz Leichter. As far back as 1978, Grannis had been introducing financial disclosure bills in the House that never made it out of the Committee on Governmental Operations. The focus here is on the efforts that began in 1985, because the bills that failed that year were most similar to the successful bill of 1987. On January 9, 1985, Leichter and Grannis, both liberal Democrats from Manhattan, respectively introduced bills in the Senate and Assembly. Leichter was a member of the Senate minority party, whereas Grannis was a member of the Assembly majority party. Their virtually identical bills called for annual financial disclosure, including requirements that legislators report the sources of income in categories of value above $1,000 and that they report honoraria over $100. The reports for legislators would be filed with the clerk of the assembly and secretary of the senate, whereas those for executive branch officials would be filed with the secretary of state. Violation of the law would constitute a misdemeanor. The bills languished in the Democratic-controlled Committee on Governmental Operations and the Republican-controlled Senate Committee on Governmental Operations without coming to a vote.[78]

In 1986, Grannis reintroduced his bill in the Assembly. Three other financial disclosure bills were also introduced later that year in the Assembly. One of these was a leadership bill sponsored by Assembly Member Koppell (D-Bronx), a liberal chair of the judiciary committee and a member of Ways and Means. The Koppell bill was very similar to Grannis's original financial disclosure proposal; it required reporting sources of income above $1,000, as well as reporting gifts totaling $250 from a single source (with important exceptions for transportation, lodging, food, and entertainment).[79] Koppell's bill was weaker, however, than the non-leadership bill with regard to the disclosure of gifts and certain financial information. The Koppell bill received a favorable report from the Committee on Governmental Operations, was passed by the Ways and Means and the Rules Committee, and then was passed by the Assembly on June 26 by a vote of 144–1.

In the Senate, however, Leichter's reintroduction of his 1986 financial disclosure bill met with less success. It was not reported out of the Committee on Governmental Operations. An even bigger blow to the cause of ethics reform occurred when the Assembly sent the Koppell bill to the

Senate for concurrence on June 25. The bill was referred by Senate president Warren Anderson to the Committee on Finance—an unusual move given that it was not a financial bill—and no further action was taken on it. President Anderson, an attorney, had already expressed his opposition to the bill, in particular to its representation limit. Governor Cuomo, in a public address later that day, said, "I regret the refusal of the Republican majority in the Senate even to allow public debate of my recommendations. . . . I will continue to urge Senator Anderson to reconsider this position."[80]

Why did ethics reform fail to come to a vote in either house of the Legislature in 1985 but pass both houses two years later? The first factor to consider is scandal. In 1983 and 1984, the *New York Times* reported no major conflict-of-interest scandals involving legislators, the governor, or other statewide officials.[81] In May 1985, the *Times* reported that the state investigative committee was holding hearings on evidence that state employees had received money for helping landlords negotiate leases on office space for state agencies, a violation of the basic principle of the state's ethics law that government officials should not profit from their public positions. However, the investigation did not lead to any indictments or convictions and received no further coverage.

Beginning in January 1986, news broke of a federal investigation into a bribery scandal involving the New York City Parking Violations Bureau and the leasing of contracts to collect fines from parking scofflaws. Federal prosecutors said in January that up to $2 million in bribes had been paid by bureau contractors over the previous five years; that figure was later increased to almost $4 million paid or promised to city and Democratic Party officials. As the scandal—described as the city's "worst corruption scandal in decades"—played out that year, the Queens Borough president of the Democratic Party was implicated and later committed suicide.[82] The Bronx Democratic Party chair was also indicted in 1986 on related bribery and racketeering charges. The parking bureau scandal received considerable attention from the *New York Times*, and it also led to comments by both New York City mayor Ed Koch and Governor Cuomo about the need to eliminate corruption in city contracting. In December, Cuomo called for a commission to investigate city corruption. However, it is important to note that this was a scandal involving *city*, not state, officials.

Late in 1986, after the Legislature had already convened for the year with the Senate failing to support ethics reform, a big scandal broke that centered on state legislators rather than city officials. The *New York Times* reported in October that a federal grand jury was investigating two Democratic members of the state Assembly on charges of placing no-show employees on the office payroll. The employees were secretaries from the law firm of the special counsel to the Assembly speaker. In the following months, more state legislators were implicated in the scandal. The records of all eighteen representatives from Manhattan were subpoenaed in March 1987, and one resigned after the Assembly Ethics Committee recommended that she be censured. The scandal widened over the course of the year to include the Senate minority leader (Manfred Ohrenstein, a Democrat), and five other Democratic senators. In total, eight state legislators were charged with payroll abuses, including charges of using legislative aides to perform campaign work.

The legislative payroll scandal, centering on the misuse of public power by members of both houses of the Legislature, seems to have helped push the cause of legislative ethics reform to a more central position on the legislative agenda. Just a month after the scandal broke, both Republican and Democratic leaders of the Legislature announced that they would support a broad ethics measure to curb official abuses, including a provision for detailed financial disclosure. On April 7, both houses of the Legislature—including the previously recalcitrant Senate—voted overwhelmingly for stricter ethics rules governing themselves and others. The vote was 57–0 in the Senate and 142–1 in the House. Governor Cuomo, however, said the legislation was unacceptably weak and vetoed it. As I describe in more detail below, the Legislature would rewrite much of the bill to meet his demands. The *Times* reported in July that Cuomo was able to "rally public sentiment in favor of the ethics code and against the Legislature in large part because of the investigations by half a dozen different prosecutors into legislative payroll abuses."[83]

In this changed political environment, with negative media attention focused directly on the Legislature, it became more of a political liability for legislators to continue balking at ethics reform. Under these circumstances, Cuomo was finally able to get the support of Senate President Anderson and the other legislative leaders who had wanted to water down his earlier proposals.

What about the potential role of increased compensation in facilitating ethics reform success in 1987? In 1985 and 1986, the period of reform failure, annual compensation was $43,999.[84] The only state that paid its legislators more was Michigan. However, legislators wanted a raise, and on July 11, ten days after the ethics bill was signed, they voted themselves a 33.7 percent salary increase, bringing the annual salary to $57,500. A *New York Times* article on July 2, two days after Cuomo and the Legislature announced their agreement on the ethics bill, suggested that a deal regarding the salary increase had been "struck with Senate Republicans to win passage of the ethics code."[85] Cuomo's aides told the *Times* that the governor had played "hardball," threatening to hold up the pay raise unless the Senate majority leader agreed to support the ethics bill Cuomo wanted (with some important concessions, as noted above). To get the raise, Anderson agreed to give Cuomo enough of what he wanted to assure that the governor did not veto this bill as he had vetoed the bill passed by the Legislature three months earlier.

Party competition did not seem to play an important role in the success of ethics reform. In 1985 and 1986, the years when reform languished, there were a Democratic governor (Cuomo, first elected in 1982) and a Democratic Assembly (97–52). As during the past fifty years, the Senate was controlled by the Republicans. That year, they had a nine-seat margin, with thirty-five seats to the Democrats' twenty-six. In the 1986 elections, Cuomo was reelected and the Senate stayed in Republican hands with no net change in the balance of seats between the two parties. The Democrats did lose three seats in the House, but this was not really significant, given that they still had a thirty-eight-seat lead, controlling 62.6 percent of the seats, as opposed to 65.1 percent before. The 1986 electoral change was not big enough to be considered a serious increase in interparty competition, because control of the Assembly, Senate, and executive branch remained in the same hands, with no change in the numbers in the Senate and only a small change in the Assembly.[86]

As the above account suggests, the legislative leadership, particularly in the Senate, did not show enthusiastic support for strong conflict-of-interest regulation in the period either of reform failure or of reform success. In 1985, there was no push by legislative leaders in either house to bring the Leichter and Grannis bills out of committee. In 1986, a leadership-sponsored bill did make it to a vote in the assembly, but as described above, this bill was weaker than the nonleadership bill with regard to disclosure, gifts, and representation limits. The *New York Times* suggested that top leaders in the Assembly and Senate "demonstrated considerable discomfort" during informal discussions about stronger proposals floated by the governor and by legislative supporters of strong ethics reform such as Grannis and Leichter. On the day Cuomo formally introduced his proposal, April 27, both Democratic Assembly speaker Stanley Fink and Republican Senate Majority Leader Anderson refused comment. As the legislative session went on, Anderson's opposition became even more evident. As discussed above, he refused to let Cuomo's plan, which was approved with modifications by the Assembly, come to a vote in the Senate. Regarding the provision to limit lawyer-legislators' appearances before state agencies, he said publicly, "I just don't see the need for it," a statement echoing that of California state senator George Miller.[87]

In March and April 1987, the top four legislative leaders—the new Democratic Assembly speaker Mel Miller, Assembly minority leader Clarence Rapplyea, Republican Senate majority leader Anderson, and Senate minority leader Ohrenstein—met to discuss the Cuomo plan. During these negotiations, Anderson again played a key role in weakening Cuomo's proposed legislation. Miller said that he went along with the weaker Senate version "to win Senate support of some kind of ethics bill when the Legislature was being criticized on ethics issues." He also asserted that the Assembly had "given in" to a weaker ethics bill only as a "last resort" to get some legislation rather than none at all.[88]

The Senate version was weaker in several respects. First, it exempted from the ban on appearances before state agencies all "quasi-judicial" proceedings, such as appearances before the Workers' Compensation Board or Department of Social Services. It also allowed members of legislators' law firms to appear before all state agencies; Cuomo had wanted these attorneys to be covered in the ban. Political party officials were also allowed to appear before government agencies on behalf of clients. Perhaps the most significant difference, however, between the Cuomo plan and that of the legislative leadership pertained to the enforcement and oversight of the financial disclosure provisions. The attorney general noted that the disclosure enforcement provisions of the leadership bill were actually weaker than those required by current law.[89]

Moreover, the provision for a legislatively controlled Ethics Committee rather than an independent commission to enforce the substantive conflict-of-interest provisions represented a significant watering down of Cuomo's original plan. Whereas the weakened financial disclosure and watered-down lawyer-legislator provisions were primarily the work of the Senate leadership, Assembly leaders were equally adamant in insisting on legislators' autonomy to monitor their own ethics.[90]

It appears that the most potent opposition to strong ethics reform—the proposals of Cuomo and the initial legislative sponsors—came from Senate Republican majority leader Anderson. This was probably due in part to the condition of divided government, in which the Republicans were the opposition party to the Democratic-controlled executive branch and Assembly. But recall that Senate leaders in California and Massachusetts, despite belonging to the same party as the governor and the lower house, also exhibited stronger resistance to ethics reform than leaders in the lower house. More than raw partisanship was obviously at work in the dynamic of stronger Senate opposition relative to lower house opposition. A possible explanation is the difference in the perceived threat of ethics reform by members of the two bodies. Perhaps because upper houses have fewer members than lower houses, power is worth more in the Senate, and hence Senate leaders, chairs, and other power-holders perceive a greater threat from ethics reform than their counter-parts in the lower house. For example, if honoraria are spread among fewer members, this perk is worth more to individual senators; hence, limits on acceptance of honoraria would be perceived as more unpleasant by senators than by lower house members. Thus the stronger opposition of Senate leaders compared with lower house leaders in California, Massachusetts, and New York could have resulted from the fact that the perks that are targeted by ethics reform were seen as more valuable by senators.

Such an explanation seems more plausible than party differences across the chambers or across the branches of government, because in California and Massachusetts the same party controlled both the upper and lower houses and the entire state government. It is also worth noting that in the U.S. Congress, opposition to honoraria reform was always stronger in the Senate than in the House throughout the history of honoraria reform from the 1970s up to the Senate ban in 1991. Senate opposition in the U.S. Congress coincided with both Democratic and Republican control of the upper house and with conditions of both unified and divided government.

The gamble made by Senate Majority Leader Anderson and the Assembly leaders who went along with him—that the bill would be acceptable to the governor—failed. After Cuomo vetoed the leadership bill, the leaders went back to the table and restored several key provisions that Cuomo had wanted: (1) limits on quasi-judicial appearances, (2) limits on written communication with state agencies by lawyer-legislators on behalf of clients, and (3) limits on county-level political party chairs appearing before state agencies. They also restored the provision mandating jail terms for violating financial disclosure requirements and agreed to an independent audit of the Legislature. However, the leadership held firm on the matter of separate ethics enforcement bodies for the executive and legislative branches, and it also won on the matter of lawyer-legislators not having to disclose the identities of their clients.

The preceding account of reform success in 1987 suggests that the governor was a strong supporter of legislative ethics regulation. What was the governor's role in the process more specifically, not only during the period of reform success but also in the period when reform efforts were stagnating?

Mario Cuomo first ran for governor in 1982 on an anti-Reagan platform. Corruption, conflicts of interest, and legislative ethics did not feature prominently, or even in a minor way, in his campaign. In his first annual address on January 5, 1983, he emphasized the need to increase state funding of programs for the poor. He did not mention legislative ethics. In 1984, his annual address emphasized job training programs, education, housing, and aid to the homeless.

The next year, Cuomo's priorities changed somewhat. In his 1985 State of the State address, he called for tax cuts and a decrease in the state debt. Within this framework of budget adjustment, he argued for additional money for public housing, teacher salaries, and the environment. Again, there was no mention of legislative ethics or political ethics more generally. In December 1985, he called a special session of the Legislature to address proposals for malpractice insurance, environmental cleanup, and housing that been blocked by the Republican Senate. Although ethics bills had been introduced in the House and Senate that year, including one by a liberal Democrat, Cuomo did not push for any sort of ethics legislation in 1985. He made no mention of ethics reform in his public addresses that entire year.[91]

In January 1986, Cuomo's State of the State address again emphasized the environment and housing for the homeless, as well as jobs for welfare applicants and economic development. Again, there was no mention of ethics legislation.[92] After the New York City parking bureau scandal broke later that month, however, Cuomo, along with mayor Ed Koch, became interested in anticorruption regulation pertaining to the state legislature. Cuomo had issued an executive order shortly after taking office that required his appointees who were serving in policymaking positions to file more detailed annual financial disclosure than that required by statute. Though this order was designed to set a high standard for the executive branch, Cuomo did not propose any new ethical standards for legislators until the 1986 city scandal apparently sparked his interest.

On April 27, 1986, Cuomo introduced his own ethics proposal, discussed above, which covered legislators as well as executive branch officials and included expanded financial disclosure, representation limits, and an independent ethics commission. In a public address to the Citizens Crime Commission and in public comments from the executive chamber in May and June 1986, Cuomo attacked the Senate majority leader for his refusal to allow public debate on the proposal. He also announced that he would make legislative ethics reform a campaign issue when he ran for a second term in November. His Republican challenger in the election, Andrew O'Rourke, also made corruption one of his top campaign issues.[93] During the campaign, both candidates frequently discussed political corruption and the need for politicians to hold higher ethical standards. It is plausible that the attention of both men to the issue of political ethics helped move legislative ethics reform to a more central place on the agenda. It had moved out of the periphery earlier that year with Cuomo's late-in-the-legislative-session ethics proposal, but it appeared to gain additional fuel from the attention by both candidates during the campaign season.

In January 1987, Cuomo began the year by renewing his call for ethics legislation, saying he would make it a priority for the legislative session. He vowed to press for enactment of the proposal that had failed the previous year.[94] This was the first year that Cuomo started off by making legislative ethics a priority. We have seen in the above discussion how he kept the pressure on the Legislature as the year went on, vetoing the weaker version of reform that the legislative leadership drafted without his input. With the strike of his veto pen, Cuomo turned the issue into a high-stakes battle between himself and the Legislature. As the discussion of legislative compensation suggested, he was not averse to playing hardball by threatening to block a legislative pay raise. In the end, he succeeded in getting much of what he wanted, with the important exception of an independent commission to monitor legislators' ethics.

This evidence suggests, then, that the governor was a strong advocate of ethics reform and that he played a leadership role in the process. Indeed, it was his proposal that provided the starting point for debate in 1986 and 1987, rather than the Leichter or Grannis bills. In the end, the legislative leaders acquiesced on many points of contention with the governor. It is important to note that their position was precisely that—acquiescence—while the driving force behind stronger ethics laws was Cuomo. If the chief executive had been less committed to ethics reform, legislative leaders would most likely have succeeded in passing their weaker, preferred version of reform.

It appears, then, that legislative ethics reform in New York was facilitated by several factors. The first was a major scandal that implicated members of both the state Senate and state Assembly, including one member of the Senate leadership. This scandal cast a negative media spotlight on the Legislature and brought legislative ethics to the forefront of the political agenda. Second, a substantial legislative pay raise in the year of ethics reform success seems to have increased legislators' willingness to give Cuomo the stronger reform package he wanted. Finally, beginning in the summer of 1986, the governor made the regulation of legislative ethics a top priority. The fact that ethics reform received the endorsement and attention of both candidates in the gubernatorial election that year helped focus media attention on the issue. In April 1987, Cuomo risked a veto override to win concessions from the Legislature. Finally, as suggested above, he used the "stick" of refusing to sign off on a pay raise as an additional weapon. All these factors likely contributed to the ultimate success of the bill at the close of the legislative session.

Vermont, 1990–96: A Cursory Exploration of Continued Inaction

None of the three cases studies presented above offers an example of continued reform failure within a single state. Here I consider, albeit briefly, the case of Vermont, an example of continued failure. The discussion that follows is only suggestive, for it is not based on a complete case study.

Vermont in 1996 was one of three states with no legislative ethics laws or legislative rules pertaining to ethics or conflict of interest.[95] From 1990 to 1996, Vermont Common Cause and supportive legislators introduced a comprehensive ethics bill based on Common Cause's model state ethics law, which would cover legislators and other government employees. The bill contained a financial disclosure provision, a ban on representation before state agencies, and a one-year revolving door limit. None of these provisions were enacted, however.[96]

Why did Vermont fail to enact any substantive ethics restrictions for legislators during this time? Consider the two variables that have been identified as important by the main case studies: scandal and compensation. During this period, there were no major reported conflict-of-interest scandals involving legislators, the governor, or statewide officials.[97] Also, annual legislative compensation in Vermont remained quite low during this time. In 1990 it was $6,750 per year; it rose to $7,680 in 1996. Though this represents a 13.77 percent raise, the overall level was still very low relative to other states. Only thirteen states had lower salaries in 1996.[98]

Low compensation and an overall absence of scandal, then, may help explain Vermont's continued failure to enact a legislative ethics law in this period. Besides Vermont, the states with the weakest legislative ethics laws in 1996 were Idaho, New Hampshire, South Dakota, and Wyoming. All these states had relatively low compensation as of 1996 and also relatively few conflict-of-interest scandals for the entire period in which ethics laws could have been enacted, 1954–96.[99] Just as scandals and increases in legislative compensation were associated with the success of ethics reform in the three cases of this chapter, states with few or no scandals and low compensation over a period of many years seem to have a continued failure to enact legislative ethics laws. The following chapters examine whether this relationship holds for a larger number of states over a forty-three-year time frame, beginning in 1954 and ending in 1996.

The Driving Factors

In the three main cases examined, political scandals involving legislators appeared to play an important role in the success of legislative ethics reform. There is also evidence that an increase in legislative compensation made legislators more willing to accept regulation of their professional activities and outside income. The evidence for the compensation–ethics reform link is strongest for the California case, strong for the New York case, and less compelling for Massachusetts.

In none of the cases did successful ethics reform appear to be facilitated by an increase in party competition. In the Massachusetts case, the evidence even points in the opposite direction. In two of the cases, California and New York, governors played a strong role in leading the drive for ethics reform. However, in Massachusetts, the governor did not take a strong stand in favor of reform. He mostly stayed out of the fray and even came down at one point on the side of less extensive regulation.

In two of the three cases, Massachusetts and New York, legislative power-holders opposed strong proposals for ethics reform. Interestingly, the strongest opposition in all the cases seemed to come from Senate rather than House leaders. In New York, this may have been due partly to partisan competition between a Republican Senate and Democratic governor, but in Massachusetts and California, both houses of the Legislature were Democratic and so was the executive branch. As suggested above, the reason for greater Senate opposition may be that power and perks are greater in the upper house because they are dispersed among fewer members, and hence reforms are perceived as more threatening.

Although speakers, Senate presidents, majority leaders, and chairs of the committees overseeing the ethics bills generally worked to block or water down reform, this was not universally true. In California, the Assembly speaker championed the cause of reform. I have argued that his interest in an ethics code was tied to a broader interest in legislative modernization, with an eye to strengthening the branch relative to the executive. In the other two states, legislative leaders only accepted reform under the pressure of external events and outside actors. Scandals and negative media publicity about the Legislature—combined with a highly public effort by the governor of New York and the threat of a ballot initiative by Common Cause in Massachusetts—created a political environment in which leaders felt compelled to enact some version of reform.

Thus outside forces played a central role in the success of ethics reform. Legislative leaders in Massachusetts and New York wrested key concessions from these outside forces, however, refusing to allow Common Cause or Cuomo to fully determine the form that ethics laws and their enforcement would take. Thus, for example, New York legislators held out against Cuomo and the media and refused to authorize an independent commission, insisting on retaining jurisdiction over the policing of legislative ethics. Though penalties for violating the laws were increased, legislators did not acquiesce in demands for an independent commission.

Another factor that appeared to have been important in facilitating reform success in the Massachusetts case was the initiative process, as utilized by an important outside interest group, Common Cause. Without this group's threat to bring the matter directly before the voters, it is unlikely that the Legislature would have supported such a strong version of reform. Though California's ethics law was ultimately enacted through a constitutional referendum, this form of direct democracy is distinct from the initiative process. Constitutional amendment questions must first be approved by the legislature in California and other states. Thus the constitutional referendum process does not provide a method of bypassing legislators, as does the initiative. The next three chapters consider whether, in general, states with an initiative option are more likely to have strong ethics laws and strong enforcement mechanisms.

The rest of the book also pays attention to an issue raised by the research design of these case studies—namely, whether and how policy efforts are conditioned by past success and failure. Numerous scholars argue that policy legacies can exert a powerful influence on future policy decisions.[100] Past successes can shape the parameters of future legislation. In the case of ethics regulation, recent success may hinder the passage of additional ethics regulations, because legislators may feel they have done enough in addressing the problem of legislative ethics. Conversely, where reform legislation has been proposed and failed over a period of years, that very failure may increase the likelihood of legislation being passed at a later date. Continued failure can help generate support for reform by making the need for reform seem even more pressing. Perhaps most important, the fact of continued failure can be used by reform advocates to justify the need for reform legislation.

The following chapters show that legislative ethics reform appears to come in waves, both within and across states. The issue of legislative conflicts of interest has been addressed and revisited by the states collectively at punctuated time periods between the 1950s and 1990s, with differing emphases in different decades. For example, financial disclosure was a central emphasis in the middle to late 1970s, whereas honoraria and gift limits were important in the 1990s. Very few states enact reform in one year and then additional reform in the next few years (see appendix A). A decade or more often elapses within a given state between enactments of major new legislation. Thus it appears that recent success reduces the likelihood of policy action in the near future, just as continued failure may fuel the movement for new laws and increase the likelihood of reform success.

In summary, the case studies provide initial findings regarding the contribution of scandal, legislative compensation, direct democracy institutions, governors, and legislative leaders to the reform process. The two strongest results are that scandal and legislative compensation were found to influence reform success. When scandals were present and compensation increased, ethics legislation succeeded. Chapters 3, 4, and 5 extend the examination of these key factors across a broader range of states and years. In addition, other potentially important influences on ethics reform failure and success are considered, along with the specific content of ethics laws and enforcement mechanisms.

three

Ethics Laws in the Pre-Watergate Period, 1954–72: Early Innovation in Regulating Legislative Conflicts of Interest

A 1949 book on state legislatures declared them to be "the bawdy houses of state government. Without exception [they] . . . are a shambles of mediocrity, incompetence, hooliganism, and venality. . . . Their annals are filled with the blackest pages of corruption." Twelve chapters, each written by a veteran newspaper reporter intimate with the operations of a particular state legislature, documented the ways that lawmakers did the bidding of lobbyists and frequently pursued their own private financial interests at the cost of making good public policy. The chapter on New York, for example, castigated legislators for allowing the insurance and legal firms they worked at to be retained by lobbyists. The author likened the practice to "taking a bribe and calling it a fee."[1]

In Pennsylvania, Herman Lowe wrote,

> the Legislature is lobby-run, lobby-ridden, and lobby-captive. There is nothing . . . to prevent a member of the Legislature from accepting a retainer from one or more special interests. In some recent sessions, as many as 40 of the 50 Senators were reportedly on the payrolls—legally— of organizations having a direct dollar-and-cents interests in bills under consideration. To a lesser extent the same situation prevails in the House. Smartest trick is to engage a committee chairman as a "legal consultant." That ensures that an undesired bill will not see the light of day. . . . Aside from "retaining" legislators . . . there are other safe ways to operate. . . .

One is poker and other forms of entertainment. . . . What the lobby spends during a session is wholly a guess. It has been estimated at anywhere from $100,000 up. Old-timers around the Capitol laughingly stress the "up."[2]

The author of the chapter on Texas reported, "During the heat of a session, the lawmakers are pampered like prize cattle, and *with* prize beef. On their lean ten dollars a day, which drops to five dollars late in every session, they can eat juicy steaks, at the expense of lobbyists."[3] The book's revelations suggested that such practices, though not illegal, were common, unsavory, and damaging to the democratic process. It would be another five years, however, before any state responded to the charges leveled by the book. New York was at the forefront of the movement to set standards for its legislators and their interaction with lobbyists, acting—as it often had in other policy areas—as a policy innovator and example for other states to follow. The 1954 enactment of an ethics law by and for legislators in New York is a puzzle, given that lawmakers generally oppose ethics laws for economic and political reasons and because many are offended by the perceived insult to their integrity that they believe such laws imply.

Chapter 2 highlighted some ways that this reluctance to enact ethics laws was overcome in selected states, for example, through the catalyzing influence of scandal, by increasing official salaries, and by the pressure of direct democracy. This chapter considers the passage of ethics reform across a larger group of states, focusing on the early years when states began to enact general conflict-of-interest laws for legislators. In particular, it zeroes in on the two decades prior to Watergate. Why did slightly over half the states enact ethics laws during this time, while the other half did not? Did the contributing factors identified by the cases of chapter 2 apply to a larger group of states during this specific time period? What kinds of concrete restrictions did the new laws place on legislators' activities, and how did these vary across states?

The years from 1954 to 1972 represent an era that has received little attention from scholars of political reform. Most political scientists and historians with an interest in anticorruption legislation have focused on the late nineteenth and early twentieth centuries.[4] However, the good-government laws enacted during the Progressive era—the period from roughly 1880 to 1920—were not *generalized* ethics laws. The emphasis of reformers during this era was more on the corruption posed by the electoral system and by the widespread practice of party patronage. Thus Progressive reformers focused on passing civil service laws such as the federal Pendleton Act of 1883 and merit requirements for state and local jobs; on restricting campaign spending, contributions, and disclosure; on changing the way citizens cast their votes at the ballot box; and on establishing mechanisms of direct democracy.[5]

Although many political scientists interested in political ethics in general—and in legislative ethics in particular—have focused on the Progressive era, others have concentrated on the post-Watergate period as a particularly fruitful time for the passage of ethics and campaign finance laws aimed at curbing the power of special interests.[6] But whereas Watergate was indeed a critical catalyst to the enactment of both general ethics laws and campaign finance laws, many states did not need that impetus to enact general standards of ethical conduct for legislators. The question is *why* they took such action even before this landmark national event. Multivariate regression analysis is used here to examine states' action on legislative ethics by focusing on (1) the enactment of basic ethics codes that laid out general principles to guide legislators, and (2) variation in the specific *content* of those codes.

Before turning to the quantitative analysis, a brief discussion of the history of anticorruption laws prior to this period is in order. I also describe the first general ethics law for legislators, enacted by New York at the start of this period, which served as a model for other states. The quantitative analysis follows this narrative.

Regulating Legislative Corruption before 1954

Prior to 1954, virtually all states had an antibribery statute on their books. Some states had also taken steps to address less clear-cut forms of corruption than those covered by bribery laws. But these latter efforts did not take the form of broad, general ethics codes. Thus states' actions to fight legislative and other political corruption prior to 1954 involved measures that were qualitatively different from the efforts after that point to create *generalized* standards of conduct.

Some early state constitutions barred legislators from voting on bills where they had a financial interest at stake. Most early state constitutions also prohibited bribery. The initial prohibitions on bribery in many states, however, covered only judicial and/or executive branch officers; legislators were added later on. In the second half of the nineteenth century, with newspapers reporting on the myriad ways that lobbyists aimed to exert influence over state and national legislators—for example, by offering them stock options and retainers—many states began to conduct hearings on lobbyist influence. The additional revelations that resulted led to the removal of the exemption for legislators from most state bribery statutes.

For example, Massachusetts in 1875 added legislators to their list of covered officials, a list that already included state and municipal purchasing officers and municipal officials.[7]

Additional, sporadic laws aimed at legislative conflicts of interest were enacted well before the onset of the Progressive era. For example, in the first half of the nineteenth century, it was common for members of Congress to earn large fees for appearing as lawyers before the federal claims commission and other executive branch agencies. But in 1853 Congress prohibited its own members and other federal employees from receiving such compensation, after highly publicized scandals involving the secretary of war and secretary of the treasury. Unethical behavior prior to 1900 was also addressed through action by congressional ethics committees, which issued verbal rebukes such as reprimands and censures to members on occasion. For example, the Credit Mobilier scandal that broke during the Ulysses Grant administration (1868–76) resulted in the censure of two House members for reaping questionable profits from construction of the railroads.[8]

During the Progressive era, many states put in place additional anti-corruption laws targeted at lawmakers. The goal was to address the corruption that was seen as infiltrating the legislative process. As suggested above, this was done partly through civil service laws that eliminated patronage opportunities for lawmakers and partly by creating direct democracy mechanisms that the public could use to bypass state legislators. In addition, some states passed laws that regulated the relationship between legislators and railroad executives, because the railroad industry was widely viewed as exerting a major corrupting influence on both state legislators and members of the U.S. Congress. Investigations initiated by legislatures themselves led to revelations about the bribery of political bosses by railroad, insurance, and utility company executives. The result was new laws that regulated lobbying, mandated direct primaries, and "in the unkindest cut of all, forbade railroads to issue passes (and give jobs) to legislators and other state officials."[9] Corrupt practices laws were also passed to regulate the flow of campaign dollars from corporations to legislators at the state and national levels, although enforcement of these early campaign finance laws was sorely lacking.

New York's Pioneering Conflict-of-Interest Law

The New York conflict-of-interest law of 1954 was a response to a series of scandals. In the first half of 1953, a state Crime Commission appointed by the governor issued several reports describing a web of corrupt relationships between local and state politicians and organized crime figures. The commission's investigations uncovered evidence of the bribery of public officials by racketeers. Throughout the rest of the year, a stream of articles in the *New York Times* pointed to questionable behavior by public officials, centering on their close relationships with labor leaders who had been charged with extortion and to instances where officials had reaped financial gain through dubious business ventures with such individuals. The horse-racing industry was at the center of these official investigations and news reports. Though horse racing and other forms of gambling were legal in New York, the practices of extortion and racketeering—using threats or intimidation to obtain profits—by some of the labor unions that employed workers at these raceways were not. Hence racetracks, labor unions, and those associated with them came under the scrutiny of two commissions, the state Crime Commission and the Moreland Commission, and drew substantial attention from the media.

Numerous stories in the second half of 1953—at least five over a twelve-day period in October, for example—linked legislators and other state officials to unsavory activities at different race tracks, and put pressure on the legislature and governor to take action. One story pointed out that several Republican politicians, including lawmakers, owned shares in a raceway association, and suggested that this financial interest had led them to route a state superhighway along the Yonkers racetrack. Other stories pointed to shareholding by legislators in additional raceways throughout the state. Yet another article described a joint business venture between a Republican state judge and a labor leader who had been indicted on extortion charges. The business was ostensibly set up to produce programs for the Roosevelt Raceway, but it never printed a single program. Still, it made money by selling its assets to the company that was already printing the programs and by getting a cut of future profits through the use of threats and intimidation. The judge was also revealed to have owned shares in a catering company based at the same raceway, a company that had allegedly been forced to give $16,000 in profits to the same labor leader involved in the fake printing venture.[10]

An October 18 story in the *Times*, "Dewey Political Future Tied to State Scandals," suggested that the accumulation of revelations posed a threat to the governor's political career, because he was from the same party as many of the Republican politicians charged with having "reaped huge profits and consorted with labor extortionists in the operation of harness racing tracks." The potential political damage to the governor became even more acute when the *Times* reported that the state Republican Senate majority leader Arthur Wicks—who was also president pro tem of the Senate and acting lieutenant governor—had visited a convicted labor extortionist, Joseph Fay, at Sing Sing prison. Because Fay and other labor leaders had been linked in recent years to crimes including extortion and murder, Wicks's attempt to defend his visits was a tough sell to the journalists who set themselves up as judges in the case. The majority leader claimed that he had gone to see Fay to gain his intercession and assistance in preventing a "costly strike" that was likely to occur due to a dispute between two unions regarding jurisdiction over a construction job at a power station. Wicks insisted that he did not do any "personal favors" for the labor leader, and that he had not been "motivated by any desire for personal financial gain."

Although the *Times* did not challenge these claims, the paper still urged that the majority leader resign, arguing in a November 16 editorial, "The people expect their public officers to fight the power of this type of labor leader, not yield to it and help perpetuate it. By treating with such a man as Fay, Mr. Wicks . . . undermined public confidence . . . (and) acted in a fashion detrimental to the decent labor movement and to the interests of the people." The paper added, "It is incredible that our State Senate . . . entrusted with this decision, should continue Mr. Wicks in the leadership posts that put him next in line to the Governor's seat in the event of emergency." Two days later, Wicks resigned as majority leader. The paper commended Dewey for pressing Wicks to resign but took a swipe at "the Senate Republican membership (that) could not bring itself to take an open, forthright stand on the issue, to declare publicly a conviction that the moral standards of public office must be lifted." With the last phrase about raising the ethical standards for public officials, the *Times* stood clearly on the side of ethics reform; it would quickly be joined by the governor.[11]

In response to the assorted revelations about questionable behavior by public officials, Governor Dewey used his annual message in January 1954 to urge the creation of a new commission that would be authorized to "define business and professional activities which are improper for government and party officers (and) to promulgate an ethics code to deal with conflicts of interest of public and party officers between business and professional interests and public duties." The law that was enacted later that year was therefore passed in response a series of state-specific scandals. But it also occurred in a broader historical context, namely the investigatory activities of the U.S. Senate Judiciary Committee in the early 1950s. Under the leadership of Democratic senator Estes Kefauver of Tennessee, the committee held the famous "Kefauver hearings," which exposed the

links between organized crime figures and state and local government officials across the nation. Senator Kefauver interpreted the mandate of this
committee as a "directive to survey the total structure of organized crime
operating in interstate commerce and the corrupting influences that such
activities had created in American politics."[12] New York City was a primary target.

The Kefauver Committee also shone a spotlight on the power that
organized crime figures exerted over local and state politicians in states
such as Massachusetts and New Jersey. The revelations of the committee
created an impetus for policymakers in these and other states to conduct
their own follow-up investigations. These investigations, it is suggested
below, helped catalyze the passage of state legislative ethics laws.

In the case of New York, it appears that Governor Dewey played an
important leadership role, much as chapter 2 argued that California's governor Edmund Brown in the 1960s and New York's governor Mario
Cuomo did in the 1980s. Like Brown, Dewey was an ambitious politician,
who had run unsuccessfully for president against Truman in 1948. Like
Cuomo, he felt compelled to respond to state scandals by pressing for an
ethics code that would force public officials to adhere to higher standards
of conduct. Dewey's annual message of January 6, 1954, noted the prece-
dent for such a code in the existing codes of the bar and judiciary. The
heart of this new code would be a focus on the problem of conflicts of
interest that lay beyond the neat parameters of outright bribery:

> The problem of ethical standards is not the simple issue of bribery or
> corruption, on which there is no difference of opinion. It involves a
> whole range of border-line behavior. . . . The public is entitled to expect
> from its servants a set of standards far above the morals of the market
> place. . . . Many members of (licensed occupations) are in the Legisla-
> ture . . . and are frequently called upon to vote on matters affecting their
> own occupations. . . . The problem is to separate the unavoidable con-
> flicts of interest from the venal and the doubtful; to chart the shadow-
> lands of conduct where men of goodwill may have difficulty in deciding
> whether a course is proper or improper.[13]

The New York law set out guidelines for legislators and other officials
concerning "possible conflict between private interests and official
duties." Among the somewhat vague and general standards framed in
terms of "shoulds" were the following: "No officer of employee of a state
agency, member of the legislature or legislative employee should accept
other employment which would impair his independence of judgment in

the exercise of his official duties." He should not "engage in any business or professional activity [which requires] the disclosure of confidential information gained through his official position." Nor should he use or attempt to use his official position to secure unwarranted privileges or exemptions for himself or others. Two standards were even more general: (1) No covered official should "by his conduct give reasonable basis for the impression that any person can improperly influence him or unduly enjoy his favor in the performance of his official duties," and (2) each covered official should "endeavor to pursue a course of conduct which will not raise suspicion among the public that he is likely to be engaged in acts that are in violation of his trust."[14]

Other provisions of the law were more specific. For example, the law barred elected officials and public employees from representing clients before state agencies on a contingent basis, meaning contingent on a particular outcome. Some members of the commission that proposed the regulations, and a few legislators, had wanted the law to go further by banning appearances for compensation—not just contingent ones but *any* appearances. Still, the limit on contingent compensation represented the first step toward more extensive regulation of representation; in 1964 (and then again in 1965 and 1987), the state would ban representation for a fee before various state agencies. Certain regulatory agencies were also required to keep a public record of appearances by public officials.

The last provision had special significance for legislators, many of whom were attorneys with substantial practices before state agencies. The law also barred legislators and other officials from selling over $2,500 worth of goods or services to the state unless they did so by a competitive bidding process. Finally, the law took a first step toward public financial disclosure by requiring that officials with an interest of $10,000 or more in any activity regulated by various state departments would have to file a statement with the secretary of state. Covered agencies included the Departments of Banking, Insurance, Public Service, and Labor.

No new enforcement agency was established to address alleged violations of the law's provisions. The law did, however, state that violators of code provisions could be "fined, suspended, or removed from office or employment," although no specific range of fines was enumerated. The attorney general could step in to enforce the law, or, in the case of the legislature, members could police themselves through legislative ethics committees. The law authorized the attorney general to set up an advisory committee to which he could submit requests for opinions, but only regarding executive branch officers and employees.[15]

Following New York's Lead: Other States and the Enactment of Ethics Codes Prior to Watergate

From 1955 to 1972, 26 other states followed New York's example and enacted ethics codes for legislators. Sidebar 3.1 shows the states that enacted legislative ethics codes during the two decades prior to Watergate. In most cases these codes were enacted as statutes, but in a small number of cases they were put in place through changes in the legislative rules, meaning the rules passed by each house of the legislature at the beginning of the legislative session without input from the governor. Some states, such as Maine, enacted sparse, vague codes of two paragraphs or less. Others such as California, New Jersey, and Illinois went further and placed substantive restrictions on legislators' activities, including limits on lawyer-legislators' appearances before state agencies, limits on gifts, limits on legislators becoming lobbyists after leaving office, and mandatory financial disclosure.

Even though the pre-Watergate state ethics laws, like the federal ethics laws of the days, lacked strong enforcement mechanisms, the restrictions they placed on legislative behavior in some respects went further than federal law. The main effort at the federal level during this pre-Watergate time frame occurred in the 1960s, when first the Senate and then the House put in place ethics codes for their members and set up permanent ethics committees.[16] An even earlier effort is also instructive: the 1958 code of ethics for federal employees passed by resolution of the U.S. House and Senate. Unlike some of the state laws that existed at the time, the 1958 federal code did not specify any penalties for violation. It was replete with even vaguer statements than most state codes of the day. It reads almost like a Ten Commandments of government ethics, urging public officials to "put loyalty to the highest moral principles and to country above loyalty to persons, party, or Government department . . . uphold the Constitution . . . give a full day's labor for a full day's pay . . . never discriminate unfairly by the dispensation of special favors to anyone [and] expose corruption wherever discovered."

Like some state codes of the day, it banned the use of confidential information in the pursuit of private profit. By 1958, however, certain states had already gone beyond the provisions of the federal code. For example, New York's 1954 law, Texas' 1957 law, and Massachusetts' 1961 code required legislators to disclose certain business interests, such as contracts with regulated state agencies, and barred them from entering into contracts with the state except under conditions of competitive bidding.

Sidebar 3.1   The Passage of State Legislative Ethics Codes, 1954–72

States That Enacted a Code during This Period

Arizona, Arkansas, California, Colorado, Connecticut, Florida, Georgia, Illinois, Iowa, Kansas, Kentucky, Louisiana, Maine, Maryland, Massachusetts, Minnesota (not in the data set), Michigan, New Jersey, New Mexico, New York, Oklahoma, Pennsylvania, Texas, Utah, West Virginia, Washington, Wisconsin

States That Did Not Enact a Code during This Period

Alabama, Delaware, Idaho, Indiana, Mississippi, Missouri, Montana, Nevada, New Hampshire, North Carolina, North Dakota, Ohio, Oregon, Rhode Island, South Carolina, South Dakota, Tennessee, Vermont, Virginia, Wyoming

Year of Enactment

1954	New York
1957	Texas
1958	New Jersey
1961	Maine, Maryland, Massachusetts, Minnesota (not in the data set)
1964	Louisiana
1965	Washington
1966	California
1967	Arizona, Florida, Illinois, Iowa, New Mexico, Pennsylvania, West Virginia, Wisconsin
1968	Georgia, Michigan, Oklahoma
1969	Utah
1970	Kansas
1971	Arkansas, Colorado, Connecticut
1972	Kentucky

Sources: State conflict-of-interest statutes, legislative rule books, and Committee on Legislative Rules of the National Legislative Conference, Council of State Governments, Conflict of Interest and Related Regulations for State Legislatures (Lexington, Ky.: Council of State Governments, 1972).

In addition, New York and New Jersey established permanent bipartisan legislative ethics committees in the 1950s, a decade before the U.S. House and Senate.

One main area where the federal government was ahead of the states in legislative conflict-of-interest regulation was mentioned above: Members of Congress had been banned from compensated representation before federal agencies since 1853. But with regard to public financial disclosure for legislators, the states prior to 1968 also led both the U.S. House and Senate. In 1964, the Senate passed a rule requiring disclosure with the U.S. comptroller general, but voted 44–40 to keep the disclosure forms confidential.[17] In 1968, the House voted for a rule to require public disclosure, and it strengthened the provision in 1970. But it was not until the enactment of the House and Senate ethics codes of 1977 that the Senate required *public* financial disclosure, and not until 1978 that disclosure became a matter of statute rather than part of the legislative rules. As chapter 2 noted, ethics advocates prefer statutes to legislative rules because they tend to be more durable. By 1978, the majority of states already had statutes that mandated public financial disclosure for legislators.

Balancing Act: Incentives to Ethical Behavior and Disincentives to Recruitment and Retention

These pre-Watergate state laws generally contained declarations of intent (preambles) filled with lofty statements about democracy and public trust. An example comes from New Jersey's 1971 ethics code: "In our representative form of government, it is essential that the conduct of public officials and employees shall hold the respect and confidence of the people. Public officials must, therefore, avoid conduct which is in violation of their public trust or which creates a justifiable impression among the public that such trust is being violated."

Many preambles also pointed to the delicate balancing act involved in regulating legislative ethics. The Maine code of 1971 noted, "The public interest will suffer if unduly stringent requirements deprive government of the 'services of all but princes and paupers.'" The 1964 Louisiana code was similar: "Legal safeguards against conflicts of interest must be so designed as not unnecessarily or unreasonably to impede the recruitment and retention by the government of those men and women who are best qualified to serve it . . . elected officials and employees should not be denied the opportunity, available to all citizens, to acquire and retain private economic and other interests, except where conflicts with the responsibility of such elected officials and employees to the public cannot be avoided."

Utah's 1969 Public Officers and Employees Ethics Act exhibited a similar sensitivity. The preamble stated that the law "does not intend to deny any public officer or employee the opportunities available to all other citizens . . . to acquire private economic or other interests so long as this does not interfere with the full and faithful discharge of his public duties." The caution being expressed is that legislators and other public officials need to maintain economic opportunities outside the public sector, given their likely return there and the inadequacy of their official salaries. Similarly, the 1971 code of Maine states, "Most legislators must look to income from private sources . . . for their sustenance and support for their families; moreover, they must plan for the day when they must return to private employment, business or their professions."[18] Concern over the potential negative effects of limiting outside income opportunities clearly weighed heavily on the minds of those writing the early codes, and it still influences those writing ethics laws today.

The salience of this issue was clear in the debates over state legislative ethics laws during the pre-Watergate period. For example, Senator John Hughes, who had served eight years in the New York state legislature, commented during the debate over the proposed 1954 law in his state, "I am against making it more difficult to get people to participate in public office. If you have too many restrictions on business men and lawyers, you end up with rich men (or their) sons in office or people who can't support themselves." Drafters of the early state ethics laws thus sought a balance between clear standards of conduct and making sure the ethics bar was not raised so high that nobody would want to serve. It was not only legislators who expressed these concerns. Consider the words of a law professor speaking before the governor's commission charged with recommending a code of ethics for public officials. Finla Crawford of Syracuse University urged that any such code should avoid "such detail as to make public service anathema to every honest man." Judge William Bray, the former lieutenant governor of New York who testified before the commission, went even further in expressing this concern: "Morality cannot be legislated. It comes from the heart and can't be taken from the statute books. We cannot put restrictions or inhibitions on the men and women whom we select to make our laws and make it undesirable for them to serve us."[19]

In the face of such widespread sentiments among nonlegislators and legislators, the writers of the early legislative ethics codes had to tread carefully. This balancing act and how it was typically resolved can be seen in the passage of the first general ethics code in Massachusetts in 1961. In his public comments on the code, Republican governor John Volpe noted that the goal of "protect[ing] government integrity . . . must be balanced with facilitating the recruitment and retention of personnel needed by government." With this in mind, Volpe accepted the watering down of his initial proposal by legislators. The bill he ultimately signed removed his proposed restriction on gifts and also contained a very weak enforcement provision. Only one section of the code provided a penalty; state officials who failed to submit a statement of financial interest in contracts with the state worth over $10,000 could be fined up to $1,000. And the following year, legislators repealed the limited financial disclosure provisions of the 1961 code.[20]

When crafting ethics laws in this period—and afterward—lawmakers therefore sought to maintain substantial latitude for the pursuit of economic activities outside the legislature and to assure relative freedom from what many legislators see as invasive requirements for public disclosure of their financial interests. As the second half of this chapter makes clear, few states enacted laws of great breadth and depth during the pre-Watergate years. There were numerous gaps in coverage and loopholes in even the ostensibly strongest substantive limits.

Explaining the Passage of Legislative Ethics Codes Prior to Watergate

Why did some states, but not others, enact ethics codes regulating legislators in the period 1954–72? And why did some states enact codes with significant substantive restrictions while others enacted relatively weak, vague codes or no codes at all? Multiple regression analysis is used to examine the influence of various factors on the likelihood of states enacting an ethics code in this period.[21] Details on the model used are provided in appendix B. In defining "ethics code," the focus is on regulations that fall into the category of conflict-of-interest legislation, statutorily speaking (they are typically found in the civil statutes under "conflict-of-interest" or "ethics laws" rather than in the criminal statutes). Excluded are regulations enacted to deal specifically with campaign financing, which are part of state election statutes. This is not to say that campaign finance practices pose no conflicts of interest for legislators. Indeed, some scholars argue that some of the most serious conflicts of interest in American politics relate to campaign financing.[22] For this study, however, the focus was narrowed to non-campaign-related regulations, because a broader focus would confound explanation of the variation in states' regulatory efforts.[23]

The result we want to explain—the dependent variable—is passage of an ethics code. The explanatory factors—factors which help explain passage of a code or independent variables—fall into seven categories: (1) party competition, (2) ideology / political culture, (3) policy diffusion, (4) scandal/corruption, (5) economic self-interest, (6) direct democracy, and (7) policy legacies.[24] These categories are explained in more depth below.

Some of the theories about why states enacted or did not enact ethics codes during this time represent familiar explanations in studies of cross-state policy variation. However, as was suggested in chapter 1, ethics policy may differ in important ways from policymaking in other areas. Thus the potential explanations draw both on familiar theories regarding state policymaking and also on less familiar theories that apply specifically to the enactment of political reform. Appendix B provides details on the measurement of the explanatory factors or independent variables. Below the different theories are fleshed out.

Party Competition

Policy studies and median voter theories posit that party competition affects the passage of legislation. Greater party competition may spur the enactment of laws that are popular with the public and hinder the enactment of unpopular laws. Ethics laws are a classically popular policy. The public generally supports legislation that is seen as reducing corruption and making politicians less responsive to "special interests."[25] Along these lines, intense interparty competition is claimed to have facilitated the passage of federal civil service reform in 1883 and Progressive era electoral reform in the states.[26]

Applying this claim to the modern ethics reform movement, we would expect states with greater party competition to be more likely to enact ethics codes. Party competition is measured in two ways: first, by whether the government is unified or divided; and second, by the extent to which one party controls the legislature.[27] This leads to two hypotheses:

H1. Unified governments will be less likely to enact ethics codes.

H2. The greater the level of majority party control of the state legislature, the less likely a state will be to enact an ethics code.

Beliefs: Ideology and Political Culture

Ideology is likely to have a significant influence on ethics policy making. Liberal ideology of a state's citizenry has been shown to facilitate the enactment of more generous or expansive policies, for example, with regard to welfare, health care, and taxation.[28] Ethics laws bear an important similarity to taxing and spending policies. Whereas the latter regulate the economic activities of citizens and businesses, ethics laws similarly regulate the economic activities of legislators. Thus states with more liberal ideologies should be more likely to enact ethics laws, just as they are more likely to enact other regulatory laws. At the level of the individual legislator, there is evidence of a positive connection between liberal ideology and support for ethics reform. Two other works suggest that liberal ideology facilitated the passage of legislative ethics laws in Wisconsin and Massachusetts during the 1970s (Bradbury 1996; Loftus 1994). Further, studies of modern public interest groups such as Common Cause have also emphasized the relationship between liberal ideology and ethics reform advocacy.[29] This leads to a third hypothesis:

H3. The more liberal a state's ideology, the more likely the state will be to enact an ethics code.

Political culture is another factor that is sometimes used to explain variation in state policymaking. It is arguably of particular relevance to understanding the passage of ethics laws. Elazar's discussion of the three cultures that characterize the United States—traditionalist, individualist, and moralist—specifically encompasses ideas about political corruption. In states with a moralistic culture, politics is seen as a means for establishing a good and just society. Public service "is viewed as a responsibility to be carried out honestly, conscientiously, and even selflessly for the sake of public rather than private interests." By contrast, the individualistic culture tends to view politics as a marketplace where private interests play a key role. The traditionalist culture is dominated by established elites. As in the individualistic culture, those "active in politics are expected to benefit personally" from public service, which includes financial gain that may or may not be legitimate. On the basis of this discussion, we might expect moralistic states to be more likely to enact legislative ethics codes than individualistic or traditionalistic states. Elazar's typology is used to measure political culture.[30] This leads to a fourth hypothesis:

H4. States with "moralistic" political cultures will be more likely than other states to enact ethics codes.

Policy Diffusion

Policies concerned with questions like state lotteries, education and taxes, and moral issues such as gay rights and the death penalty have been shown to diffuse among the states as policymakers in one state copy the

innovations of other states.[31] Policy diffusion studies do not always specify the precise process by which diffusion occurs. It is plausible to sup-
pose, however, that states learn from their neighbors and are more willing
to adopt laws that have already been tried in other states. Berry and Berry
suggest that previous policy adoptions by nearby states provide a key
resource to policymakers, namely information, which helps alleviate
uncertainty about the potential impact of new laws. Similarly, Elazar
maintains that state policymakers tend to view nearby states as "experimental laboratories" for policies.[32] I therefore look to see if a pattern of
regional diffusion exists. This leads to a fifth hypothesis:

H5. Ethics codes will diffuse among neighboring states.

Scandals and Corruption

Despite these expected similarities between ethics policy and other policy areas, the enactment of ethics codes may differ from that of other policies in important ways. Several scholars argue that scandal and the media
play an unusually prominent role in the process of ethics reform compared with other policy areas.[33] Chapter 2 suggested that scandals were
influential in explaining the success of ethics reform success in three states.
One recent work makes a similar argument for the role of scandals and
corruption in explaining variation in states' lobby laws in the 1990s.[34]

Other scholars have emphasized the role of scandal in catalyzing earlier political reforms. As noted above, scandal was argued to have catalyzed changes in legal representation by federal employees in the 1850s.
A scandal uncovered during the Grant administration was critical to the
passage of legislation in 1874 that ended the federal "moiety" system,
whereby officials who were collecting delinquent taxes or confiscating
smuggled goods got to keep part of the money or goods. Scholars of the
Progressive era also argue that scandals were a critical catalyst to anticorruption efforts during that period.[35] Link and McCormick, making a
common argument, suggest that although "people had talked about . . .
reforms for many years . . . the disclosure of corruption in 1905 and 1906
catalyzed their enactment and set off a fundamental transformation of the
functions of state governments," one that included the institution of election reforms and direct democracy mechanisms designed to weaken the
power of corrupt parties, legislators, and lobbyists.[36]

The main theory that applies here is that of agenda setting.[37] The issue
of legislative ethics should be more likely to reach the forefront of a
crowded legislative agenda if there has been a recent scandal that has

received significant media coverage. As suggested by chapter 2, scandals are focusing events that fix media attention on the problem of legislative ethics and generate pressure on public officials to adopt new policies in this area.

States in which scandals involving official misuse of power and resources for personal gain are infrequent or nonexistent will lack such a catalyzing stimulus to reform. Because space on the legislative agenda is limited, it is less likely that the issue of legislative ethics will become a priority in such states. Conversely, in states with frequent scandals, legislators are forced to confront the issue of conflict of interest by the media, by public interest groups, and by other political actors such as governors and concerned constituents. Constituents do not have to be organized or attentive on the matter as a requirement for legislative action; the possibility that they could later be roused to electoral retaliation if legislators fail to act is sufficient.

Thus scandals make it more likely that legislators will respond by enacting an ethics code. Though not all states will respond to every stimulus, they will be *more* likely to take action in the presence of a stimulus such as scandal. The stimulus of scandal will affect outcomes by affecting what one scholar calls the motivation to innovate, in this case by enacting new regulations to reduce the likelihood of future corruption.[38]

Not only the impetus of a particular and recent scandal, but also a more enduring history of corruption, should make states more likely to enact ethics codes. Two measures are therefore used to test the scandal/corruption hypothesis. The explanation of these measures is detailed in appendix B. I note here simply that one measure reflects the short-term effects of specific scandals. A second measure is used to gauge the effects of a state's underlying or long-term history corruption. This leads to a sixth and a seventh hypothesis:

H6. The occurrence of scandals involving state legislators or other state officials will increase the likelihood of states enacting an ethics code.

H7. A long-term history of corruption will make a state more likely to enact an ethics code.

Economic Self-Interest

Economic calculations by legislators about the likely impact of ethics laws on their financial well-being may influence their willingness to enact ethics codes aimed at restricting their own income-generating activities outside the legislature.[39] Several studies have suggested that economic self-interest influenced legislators' votes on industrial regulation and on ratification of the U.S. Constitution.[40] Chapter 2 suggested that economic calculations also affected legislators' decisions about whether to support or oppose ethics laws in California and New York.

As in chapter 2, the expectation is that where official compensation for legislators is higher, lawmakers will be less resistant to enacting outside income limits. Compensation has been shown to be an important factor motivating legislative decisions, for example, with regard to recruitment and turnover.[41] Several scholars have argued that there is a link between higher legislative salaries and legislators' willingness to support ethics reform, both here and in the United Kingdom. For example, it has been suggested that pay raises were a critical element of ethics reform legislation passed by the U.S. Congress in 1853, 1977, 1983, and 1989.[42]

With regard to the pre-Watergate period, Sacks and Pound posit a link between the state legislative professionalization that began in the 1960s and the passage of the early ethics codes under study here. Increasing compensation was a critical, though not the only, component, of the modernization and professionalization movement that began to occur in state legislatures as early as the mid-1960s.[43] This movement aimed at making state legislatures more effective bodies, which meant not only increasing salaries but also lengthening sessions and increasing legislative staff. The movement was more pronounced in some states, such as California, than in others, such as Kentucky and North Dakota. The hypothesis here is that states that modernized their legislatures more during this time, specifically by raising official salaries, were more likely to enact ethics codes. This should be the case both because higher salaries decreased legislators' resistance to limiting outside income, and because the development of ethical standards was part and parcel of the movement toward creating more capable, professional institutions. This leads to an eighth hypothesis:

H8. The higher the level of legislative compensation, the more likely a state will be to enact an ethics code aimed at regulating outside income.

Further, ethics codes often place special restrictions on lawyer-legislators and their ability to represent clients before government agencies. Indeed, this was an important feature of the pre-Watergate codes enacted by California, Illinois, New York, and other states. I show that lawyer-legislators are more likely to oppose such restrictions than other legislators.[44] The more lawyers there are in a given legislature, then, the less likely a state may be to enact an ethics code. This leads to a ninth hypothesis:

H9. The higher the proportion of attorneys in the legislature, the less likely that state will be to enact an ethics code.

Direct Democracy

The initiative process may play an important role in the passage of legislative ethics laws, more so than for other laws. The initiative can be a powerful method of bypassing legislative opposition to policies that legislators dislike, especially political and electoral reforms. In recent years, it has been used by public interest groups such as Common Cause to enact laws that legislators have been unwilling to enact themselves, such as public financing for electoral campaigns. Even where the initiative is not used directly, it can serve as an indirect tool to prod legislators to act as a preemptive strike against voters writing their own laws.[45] This is what happened in the Massachusetts case study of chapter 2. Tolbert has shown that the initiative process contributed to the adoption of certain "governance" policies that legislators may be unenthusiastic about enacting themselves—such as term limits.[46] The question here is whether the availability of an initiative option similarly increased the likelihood of ethics code enactment. This leads to a tenth hypothesis:

H10. States with an initiative option should be more likely to enact a code.

Policy Legacies

Finally, policy legacies can exert a powerful influence on future policy decisions. Past choices may preclude or limit future options. Existing laws that regulate legislative conflicts of interest may affect the likelihood of a state enacting additional laws. In other words, states that have already taken steps to control legislative conflicts of interest through other means such as campaign finance laws may be less likely to adopt ethics laws. Preexisting laws may substitute for ethics laws, or prevent them from being adopted, much as Gottschalk argues that existing health care policies made proposals for dramatic change in the nation's health care system less likely to succeed in the 1990s.[47] This leads to an eleventh hypothesis:

H11. States with strong campaign finance laws will be less likely to adopt a code.

Internal and External Determinants of Ethics Code Adoption

The results suggest that five factors shaped the likelihood of states' enacting ethics codes in the pre-Watergate period: scandals, legislative compensation, state ideology, other states' actions, and political culture. A basic summary of the regression results is presented in sidebar 3.2. The factors listed are those that are statistically significant, when controlling for other explanations. The full regression results are presented in table C.1 of appendix C.[48] Because it is difficult to interpret the coefficients in logistic regression—the type of analysis used here—table C.2 in appendix C provides a way of understanding the quantitative impact of key explanatory factors, known as "mean effects."

State-level scandals, as expected, were an important stimulus to the enactment of early ethics codes. Very few states enacted ethics codes in the absence of a specific scandal or investigation. Maine and Utah were two rare exceptions. The scandals that catalyzed code enactment included bribery cases involving legislators and also investigations into possible linkages between organized crime operations and state politicians. As suggested earlier in the chapter, some of these investigations were conducted as a follow-up to the work of the U.S. Senate committee chaired by Tennessee Democrat Estes Kefauver. This committee held hearings in 1950–51 and uncovered ties between organized crime figures and elected officials in cities including Chicago, Kansas City, Miami, and New Orleans.[49]

The Kefauver Committee's investigations implicated not only local police chiefs and other local officials but also state legislators and governors in certain states. The revelations put the issue of political corruption on the agenda, broadly speaking, and stimulated states to conduct their own investigations over the next decade and a half. In the 1950s and 1960s, for example, ambitious politicians in Florida, New Jersey, and New York followed the committee's lead and initiated their own investigations into the ties between organized crime and state and local officials. The

---

Sidebar 3.2   Key Influences on the Enactment of Ethics Codes, 1954–72

Scandal
Compensation
Ideology
Actions by other states
Political culture

Source: Regression results of table C.1 in appendix C. Factors listed are those that are statistically significant, controlling for other factors.

timing of these investigations preceded the enactment of ethics codes by a year or two, consistent with the scandal hypothesis.

A state with the maximum scandal score in a given year was 16.41 percentage points more likely to enact an ethics code than one that had no scandals, all else being equal (see table C.2). The next greatest effect was for legislative compensation. A state with the highest level of compensation was 12.52 percentage points more likely to enact an ethics code than a state with the lowest level of compensation. As hypothesized, legislators were more likely to enact ethics codes in states where they were paid more.

Ethics codes also diffused between neighboring states, consistent with the theory of regional policy diffusion. The mean effect was small, however. A state with the maximum number of neighbors that had already enacted a code—five—was 1.05 percentage points more likely to enact a code than a state with no neighbors that had already enacted a code. An example of this neighbor-to-neighbor diffusion was California, where passage of a code in 1966 was followed by code passage in Arizona in 1967. Similarly, Florida's 1967 code was followed the next year by code enactment in Georgia.

Closer examination of the data, however, shows that there was also diffusion of ethics codes among *non*-neighbors. This suggests that the pattern of diffusion was more complex than that measured by the neighbor variable, something that has been suggested by recent work.[50] For example, after California restricted representation by lawyer-legislators before state agencies in 1966, a number of states followed suit the next year. The text of the laws in some of these states, such as Illinois and New Jersey, was remarkably similar to the California law. Many states that enacted codes after 1966, drawing upon the language of the California code, were not neighbors of California. An alternative model was tried to determine whether states followed national and regional "leader" states, rather than just neighboring states, but this measure of diffusion proved insignificant. The statistical evidence suggests that states do follow their neighbors, but they also seem to follow other non-neighboring states in a manner that is difficult to model or at least that is beyond the scope of the analysis here.

One likely source of policy diffusion among non-neighboring states during this early period was the national governors' conference. Proceedings from the conference in the 1960s show that the issue of ethics regulation was raised there. Another national organization, the nonprofit Council on State Governments (CSG), may have served to foster diffusion of legislative ethics regulation among the states. In 1972, the CSG issued a staff report, "Conflict of Interest and Related Regulations for State Legislators," which summarized ethics restrictions in the fifty states. It is also possible that states interested in addressing the problem of legislative ethics *prior* to 1972 consulted the CSG, as a clearinghouse for information on state laws. There were also three nonprofit organizations dealing with state legislatures in operation at this time, which served as a conduit for the sharing of ideas and are likely to have contributed to the diffusion of ethics codes. These were the National Conference of State Legislative Leaders, National Legislative Conference, and Society of State Legislatures, which merged into the National Conference of State Legislatures in the late 1970s. All three were part of the reform and modernization movement that focused on increasing the capacities and professionalism of state legislatures, including the development of clearer ethical standards for legislators.[51]

Ideology and political culture also influenced the passage of ethics codes. These two factors appear to have provided important background conditions that affected the likelihood of code enactment. The positive impact of liberal ideology on support for ethics reform noted at the level of the individual legislator thus appears to hold at the aggregate, cross-state level, at least for this early period. The most liberal state was 1.6 percentage points more likely to enact a code than the least liberal state. The two culture variables were also marginally significant. As expected, states with individualistic cultures were significantly less likely to enact codes than moralistic states. However, states with traditionalist cultures were actually *more* likely to enact codes than moralistic states. Thus culture did not influence the passage of codes in exactly the way predicted. It may be that traditionalist states, with their greater tolerance of political corruption and politics dominated by a narrow elite, have a certain amount of long-term corruption that is not picked up by the traditional party organization measure, and that this corruption contributes to the perceived need to enact ethics codes for legislators.

Although the quantitative impact of the key explanatory factors was not large when each was considered in isolation, their impact in combination with each other was more substantial.[52] For example, a state with the maximum value for the scandal and diffusion variables was 62.41 percentage points more likely to enact a code than one with minimal levels of these two variables. The mean effect for scandal and ideology combined was 69.92 percent, meaning that a state with the maximum number of scandals in a given year and the most liberal ideology was 69.92 percentage points more likely than a state with minimal values of these two variables to enact a code. The mean effect for scandal and compensation combined was 95.25 percent, meaning that a state with the maximum number of scandals in a given year and the maximum level of compensation was 95.25 percentage points more likely than a state with minimal values of these two variables to enact a code.

A final factor that is not measured by the model is the role of governors in the process of ethics code enactment. Newspaper coverage of ethics reform efforts in California, Massachusetts, and New York during this period suggests that Governors Dewey, Volpe, and Brown—two Republicans and a Democrat—all pressed for the enactment of ethics codes, often fighting the resistance of legislators in their states.[53] The amount of time it would take to measure whether governors took a public stand in favor of reform in all the states for all the years considered here was prohibitive. Still, it remains plausible that this leadership role of governors was also important in other states.

An examination of the passage of legislative ethics codes in the pre-Watergate period thus shows that legislators were more likely to engage in self-regulation under certain conditions. Recent scandals, relatively high legislative compensation, liberal citizen ideology, and a nonindividualistic political culture all increased the likelihood of code enactment, as did action by neighboring states. What is notable is that all but one of these key factors is *external* to the legislative institution. Only compensation is an institutional feature of the legislature itself. Thus the likelihood of code enactment was shaped primarily by factors *outside* the legislature. Ethics regulation appears to be mainly an externally motivated and externally shaped process.

Overall, the findings indicate that external pressures are key to getting legislators to overcome their innate loathing of self-regulation. However, as chapter 2 suggested, and the rest of the book highlights, when it comes to determining the specific content of ethics laws and how they are enforced, legislators do not allow outside actors to determine all the critical details.

The Content of the Codes: Types of Ethics Restrictions

Beyond the simple dichotomy of passage versus nonpassage of a basic ethics code, there was also variation in the overall *content* of the early codes. The focus of the rest of this chapter is on why some states enacted more extensive codes than others over this nineteen-year period. Some states enacted laws at more than one point during this period, which virtually always meant that they strengthened their original laws, placing new restrictions on legislators.[54] For example, New York enacted legislative ethics laws in 1954, 1964, and 1965. Massachusetts enacted ethics regulations in 1961 and then again the next year. New Jersey first enacted an ethics law in 1967 and then strengthened it in 1971. Illinois also enacted its first ethics law in 1967 and strengthened it five years later.

During this period, the states began to enact limits in four different areas: representation, disclosure, gifts, and postgovernment employment. State honoraria limits would not appear until after Watergate. As suggested above, the page length of the new laws in California, Massachusetts, and New York numbered in the double digits and contained various substantive restrictions on legislators. Conversely, some states opted for very brief codes, often less than one page long and written at a very high level of generality. Such weaker codes, such as that of Maine, were often adopted through legislative resolution rather than by statute.[55]

Representation Limits

California's 1966 statute was path breaking in the comprehensiveness of the limits it placed on representation by lawyer-legislators before state agencies. The only exception the law made was for appearances before the Workers' Compensation Appeals Board. The restriction on legislators' *partners'* appearing for compensation was a significant limit that few states have even today, nearly forty years later. States that restrict lawyer-legislators generally leave a loophole for other members of their law firms. Other states followed similar, if less extensive paths, to that of California with regard to lawyer-legislators. In 1971, New Jersey limited legislators and other state officers from appearing before most state agencies, with a number of exceptions. Also in 1971, Connecticut simply listed a group of thirteen agencies before which legislators could not appear for compensation.[56]

These representation limits were aimed at the concern that agencies "might feel intimidated if a legislator . . . appeared as an advocate" and that such an appearance might "create an aura of a threat of political repercussions if the result is unfavorable." Indeed, John Quincy Adams had criticized the practice of legislators representing clients over 100 years earlier. In the 1840s, when he was serving in Congress, the former president wrote in his diary, "It occurs to me that this double capacity of a counselor in courts of law and a member of a legislative body affords opportunity and temptation for contingent fees of a very questionable moral purity."[57]

In the pre-Watergate period, only nine states chose to restrict such appearances or require disclosure of such appearances. However, this limited early action would be followed by many other states in the post-Watergate period. By 1996, seventeen of the fifty states would restrict appearances, and another sixteen would require legislators to publicly disclose these appearances.

Gift and Financial Disclosure Limits

With regard to limits on legislators receiving gifts from lobbyists and other "interested" parties, there was again wide variation among states prior to 1972. Wisconsin was the earliest innovator and the toughest regulator in this regard. In 1957, Wisconsin enacted the first "no cup of coffee" law, which banned legislators from taking anything of value from lobbyists and principals. This extremely restrictive statute defined "anything" to include "food, meals, lodging, beverage, transportation, money, campaign contributions or any other thing of pecuniary value." New York's 1964 law, though not as severe as Wisconsin's, was still relatively stringent for the time. It placed a $25 limit on any gift that a legislator could solicit or receive. Kentucky's 1972 law placed a $100 limit on gifts (this would be increased to $200 in 1976). Other states did not set a numerical limit but simply, and less specifically, barred those of "substantial value."[58]

With regard to financial disclosure, New York was again a leader among the states. Though most states did not enact disclosure laws until after Watergate, New York by 1965 required that legislators and legislative employees file with the clerk of their house a written statement including (1) any offices and directorships they held in a corporation, firm, or enterprise subject to the jurisdiction of a regulatory agency; and (2) any financial interests subject to the jurisdiction of a regulatory agency. The specific value of the interests did not need to be disclosed. Arizona also required disclosure of directorships and certain business interests in its 1967 law. Arkansas in 1971 required legislators to disclose the names of any businesses regulated by a state agency and directorships in corporations or firms. The 1971 Arkansas law also required legislators to disclose any business activities from which they received compensation over $1,500. Other states required disclosure in connection with a vote on a matter in which the legislator had a related financial interest, but did not require general, regular disclosure prior to Watergate.[59]

Explaining Variation in the Content of the Codes: The Influence of Scandal, a History of Corruption, Compensation, and Political Culture

The preceding section suggested that there was substantial variation in the extensiveness of the restrictions contained in the early legislative ethics codes. Table 3.1 shows more precisely the range in the breadth and depth of states' early efforts to regulate legislators. States' scores range from 0 to 7.5. The index to calculate change in a state's ethics laws between 1954

Table 3.1   Change in State Legislative Ethics Laws, 1954–72

State	Change	State	Change
New York	7.5	Maine	1.0
Illinois	6.5	Michigan	1.0
New Jersey	5.5	New Mexico	1.0
California	4.5	Tennessee	1.0
Louisiana	4.0	Ohio	0.0
Maryland	4.0	Nevada	0.0
Florida	3.5	North Carolina	0.0
Pennsylvania	3.5	South Carolina	0.0
Washington	3.5	Indiana	0.0
Arkansas	3.0	North Dakota	0.0
Connecticut	3.0	Rhode Island	0.0
Wisconsin	3.0	Mississippi	0.0
Colorado	2.5	Delaware	0.0
Georgia	2.5	Virginia	0.0
Iowa	2.5	Alabama	0.0
Kentucky	2.5	Oregon	0.0
Texas	2.5	South Dakota	0.0
Utah	2.5	Montana	0.0
Arizona	2.0	Vermont	0.0
Massachusetts	2.0	New Hampshire	0.0
Oklahoma	2.0	Idaho	0.0
West Virginia	2.0	Missouri	0.0
Kansas	1.0	Wyoming	0.0

Note: Minimum, 0; maximum, 7.5; mean score, 1.72; standard deviation, 1.92. Scores represent an additive index that consists of five categories of ethics restrictions for legislators: (1) basic ethics code, (2) gift limits, (3) limits on representation of clients before state agencies, (4) postgovernment employment limits, and (5) financial disclosure requirements.

Sources: State conflict-of-interest statutes and state legislative rule books. See appendix A for details on the index and scoring.

and 1972 is an additive measure based on five different categories of ethics restrictions: a basic ethics code, gift limits, postgovernment employment limits, representation limits, and financial disclosure requirements.[60] A score of 0 represents no change, or no new laws enacted. A state that enacted, for example, a basic code, a two-year postemployment limit, and a requirement for disclosure of gifts would receive a score of 4.

Multiple regression analysis was used to probe beyond the simple difference between code enactors and nonenactors and address the causes of variation in the *content* of state codes during this time. The outcome we want to explain—the dependent variable—measures the total amount of change in states' ethics laws during the pre-Watergate period from 1954 to 1972. The explanatory or independent variables are largely the same as for the analysis of the first part of this chapter. The expectation is that the same factors that influenced states' decisions to adopt basic ethics codes also influenced the extensiveness of those codes. Details on the measurement of these explanatory variables can be found in appendix B. Two different types of models are used, one using linear regression and the other using ordinal regression.[61]

The results for the analysis of overall change in states' ethics codes yield some findings similar to the analysis of simple passage versus nonpassage of ethics codes. Sidebar 3.3 summarizes the regression results. The factors listed are those that are statistically significant, when controlling for other explanations. Table C.3 in appendix C presents the full regression results, and table C.4 in appendix C provides an interpretation of the quantitative impact of the key explanatory factors.[62]

The first result of note is that the occurrence of scandals led to the enactment of stronger substantive restrictions on legislators during this time. Recent scandals involving legislators, governors, and other state officials influenced the policy agenda by bringing the issue of legislative

---

Sidebar 3.3. Key Influences on Overall Change in State Ethics Laws, 1954–72

Scandal
Long-term history of corruption
Compensation
Political culture

Source: Regression results of table C.3 in appendix C. Factors listed are those that are statistically significant, controlling for other factors.

ethics reform to the forefront of the agenda and opening up a window of opportunity for reform advocates.

The states with the highest scandal scores for the period from 1953 to 1972 were, in order, New Jersey, Massachusetts, Texas, Louisiana, New York, Illinois, Alabama, Oklahoma, Wisconsin, West Virginia, and Florida. Of these eleven states, ten experienced an above-average change in their ethics laws during this time, compared with all the states. States that experienced no scandals during this period—such as Montana, Rhode Island, Idaho, and Vermont—tended to have below-average change in their ethics laws. As table C.4 shows, a state with no scandals during this period had only a 20.00 percent probability of enacting the strongest laws, whereas a state with the maximum scandal score (15) had a 92.69 percent probability of falling into the category of states that enacted the strongest laws (see appendix B for details on what constitute the "strongest" and "weakest" laws).

In addition, a long-term history of corruption was also a significant predictor of strengthened ethics laws. A state with the lowest score for its history of corruption had only a 9.91 percent probability of falling into the category of states that enacted the strictest laws during this time period, whereas a state with the maximum score had a 93.03 percent probability.

With regard to current and immediate scandals, the media served as the critical mechanism for linking scandal to reform success. Where scandals moved onto the media agenda, receiving sustained attention over a period of time rather than merely meriting a one-time notice, legislative ethics reform moved to a more prominent place on the policy agenda.

For example, in August 1963, the *New York Herald Tribune* ran a series of articles pointing out how Republican Senate majority leader Walter Mahoney—an attorney in private practice—had provided legal counsel to a financial institution for which he received a generous 3,000 shares of stock, and later helped pass legislation beneficial to small loan companies such as his former client. This was not illegal unless it could be shown that there had been an explicit quid pro quo—a direct exchange of favorable legislative action for financial benefits—which constitutes bribery. But the suggestion of the *Tribune* (and of the *New York Times*, which also reported on the majority leader's activities) was that such activities were undesirable and underscored the need to clarify ethical standards for state legislators: "Perhaps at the 1964 session," urged the *Times*, "they (state legislators and the governor) will write and pass the stronger code of legislative ethics that this newspaper has long urged and that previous sessions of the Legislature have turned down."[63]

Two months later, in October 1963, the *New York Times* reported on a six-day cruise to Nassau in the Bahamas enjoyed by seven legislators and their wives, paid for by the Savings Banks Association of New York State. One news story, headlined "Criticism Grows over Bank Cruise," pointed to criticism of the cruise by the Citizens Union and City Club of New York, two good-government groups. The *Times* itself joined in the criticism with editorials titled "Two Masters at Albany," suggesting that lawmakers were serving two different "masters"—the public and themselves. Additional ones followed, titled "Home from the Sea," "For Legislative Integrity," and "Watchful of the Public Interest." One editorial referred to Republican Assembly speaker Joseph Carlino as "an old hand at denying breaches of ethics." Another urged legislators to adopt the recommendations of a special committee appointed by the legislature to help strengthen the existing state code of ethics, noting that the speaker and majority leader had "turned" on the committee "violently and . . . called upon the Legislature to reject its key recommendations," such as barring representation by lawyer-legislators before all state agencies. Another editorial warned, "New York legislators had better begin to understand that the public is fed up with the easy conscience of many of them on ethical questions. This little cruise is only a minor daub in a vastly larger dark picture."[64]

Under this barrage of media criticism and beating of the drum for reform, the Legislature enacted new ethics laws in 1964 and then strengthened them slightly in 1965. These new laws strengthened the pioneering 1954 law, first, by prohibiting legislators from receiving gifts worth over $25 "if it could reasonably be inferred that the gift was intended to influence official actions" (a phrase that left substantial discretion for the individual legislator to draw or not draw such an inference). Second, the legislation expanded the financial disclosure requirements, for example, by requiring disclosure to the secretary of state of any financial interest in a business regulated by the state (previously, only interests over $10,000 had to be disclosed). In addition, the 1964 law included a two-year revolving-door limit on legislators becoming lobbyists after leaving office—the limit that the *Los Angeles Times* had urged to no avail that California legislators adopt in 1966.

The 1964 and 1965 laws also barred representation for a fee by lawyer-legislators before many state agencies, but not to the extent urged by the *Times* and the specially appointed committee chaired by Clyde LaPorte, the chair of the New York City Board of Ethics. A number of agencies were exempted from the ban, including the Department of Taxation and Division of Corporations. Also exempted were representation cases related to workers' compensation, disability benefits, and un-employment insurance. Attorneys populated well over half of each leg-islative chamber (41 of 58 Senate members and 90 of 150 Assembly members were lawyers), and they were not willing to accept an across-the-board ban.[65]

Most important, the Court of Claims—which hears claims against the state—was exempt from the ban. Approximately thirty lawyer-legislators had cases pending before the Court of Claims in March 1964, and the court represented a "substantial part of the practice of about fifteen legis-lators," according to the *Times*. The *Times* had urged lawmakers to include the Court of Claims in the ban, arguing that "there is no reflection on the integrity of anyone, judge or legislator, in bringing the standards of the State Court of Claims into line with those of the national Government, where for more than a century members of Congress have been prohib-ited from practicing in the United States Court of Claims. Nor should the state lag behind New York City, where City Council members are pro-hibited from appearing as counsel in cases to which the city is a party."[66]

While accepting the newspaper's call for new ethics provisions such as the $25 gift limit, legislators refused its entreaties to include the Court of Claims in its representation ban. It was excluded from the legislation passed by both houses in 1964, with both the Assembly speaker and Sen-ate majority leader going on record against it.

The incomplete but nevertheless substantial influence of the media becomes clear when we look at two sets of votes on ethics reform by New York legislators in May 1965. On May 4, Assembly members voted on two bills sponsored by liberal Democrat Daniel Kelly. The first bill aimed to expand the list of agencies covered in the 1964 ban to include the Court of Claims, and to further expand the requirements for disclosure of mem-bers' financial interests. The bill also changed the repository of financial disclosure statements from the clerk of the Assembly and secretary of the Senate to the nonlegislative office of the secretary of state. This bill failed by a narrow margin, 71–73.

A second bill, to establish a new independent ethics advisory com-mission, went down by a vote of 63–75. The *Times* coverage of the two votes noted that "only five . . . Assemblymen spoke in favor of the ethics bills (while) a score of Assemblymen, both Democratic and Republican, made vitriolic speeches against the bills. . . . One Democrat, Max M. Tur-shen of Brooklyn, rose and shouted, 'What are we worrying about these newspapers for? They don't run for election. We've got the greatest judges of all—the people. Let them decide whether we should be re-elected.'"[67]

To help the voters decide, the *Times* printed the roll-call of members' votes on the ethics bills. For good measure, the picture of Turshen, the vocal opponent, was printed under a later story discussing the legislature's failure to enact the bills. When a second vote on the bills came around twenty days later, support for the first bill limiting lawyer-legislators and expanding financial disclosure had increased dramatically. The bill passed 110–36 in what the *Times* called a "surprising turnaround" that was not so surprising given the embarrassment experienced by those who had been "outed" for voting against the bill the first time. Many legislators apparently responded to the newspaper's printing of the roll call by switching to a position of support—including the previously outraged Turshen.[68]

But the collective body was not so responsive with regard to the second bill. As they would twenty-two years later, lawmakers held firm when it came to the matter of enforcing legislative ethics, refusing to grant authority to an outside commission. The bill for an independent ethics advisory commission failed this time by an even wider margin than on the first vote—52–80. Democratic Assembly member Eugene Rodriguez of the Bronx spoke for the members who continued to oppose both bills, saying he would not give in to media pressure: "I care not what the press says so long as they spell my name right. I'm going to vote against. . . . Mrs. Rodriguez did not raise a stupid child." [69]

Thus some legislators responded to media pressure by coming around to support the first bill, but lawmakers did not give way with regard to the express wishes of the media and reform advocates when it came to the second bill. Clear limits existed, therefore, on how much legislators could be swayed by media pressure. Even with regard to the first Assembly bill that placed limits on lawyer-legislators, the final version signed by the governor was ultimately watered down due to opposition in the Senate. Although the Assembly voted to include the Court of Claims in its ban, the Senate refused to go along. The Senate Finance Committee, which was responsible for the bill, deleted the provision including the Court of Claims; thus it remained exempt from the ban. As in the cases of chapter 2, the Senate proved a less hospitable place for ethics reform than the lower house. And again, the governor played a potentially important role in the success—albeit only partial success—of ethics reform in 1965. Republican governor Nelson Rockefeller, in his annual address to the Legislature of January, called for a stronger ethics code to be passed later that year.[70] As in New York in 1954, Massachusetts in 1961, and California in 1966, gubernatorial attention to the issue of political ethics is likely to have helped the cause of ethics reform.

With regard to the influence of scandals on the extensiveness of reform, one potential methodological concern is worth noting here. It could be argued that scandals not only affect the passage of ethics laws but are also *affected by* the passage of these laws.[71] A statistical technique known as an "instrumental variables" approach was used to address this problem; the results were unchanged. Scandal was still a statistically significant predictor of stronger ethics laws.[72]

In addition to scandals, rising compensation also facilitated the enactment of more comprehensive ethics laws during this time, apparently helping to break down some of legislators' resistance to enacting such laws. States with the largest increases in real compensation during this period included Illinois (with the greatest increase, $67,500), New York ($56,000), Massachusetts ($38,340), Pennsylvania ($38,010), and California ($32,750). All these states enacted ethics laws that were well above average in stringency compared with all states. Table C.4 shows that a state with the minimum change in compensation (a decrease of $5,500 in real compensation) had only a 13.79 percent probability of enacting ethics laws that fell into the "strongest" category, whereas a state with the maximum change (+$67,500) had an 86.36 percent probability of enacting the strongest laws during this period. The notable exception to this pattern is Michigan, which increased its legislative compensation by $50,870. Despite this increase in legislators' salaries, Michigan enacted only a very weak code of ethics during this initial period.[73]

Of the seven states that saw a *decrease* in their real compensation for legislators during this period (Alabama, Arizona, New Hampshire, Oklahoma, Rhode Island, Utah, and West Virginia), four enacted ethics laws of below-average strength. The three that enacted relatively strong laws in the period despite decreasing real compensation—Arizona, Oklahoma, and West Virginia—each experienced at least one major scandal involving legislators and/or other elected officials. Other states that had very small increases in real compensation (well below the average change) but no major scandals, such as Virginia and Wyoming, enacted very weak ethics laws or no laws at all during this period.

Finally, states with nonindividualistic cultures were more likely to enact strong ethics laws during this period. A state with an individualistic culture had only a 1.96 percent probability of enacting the strongest laws, all else being equal, versus 63.64 percent for a state without such a culture. Thus there is some support for the hypothesis that states with more individualistic cultures are more tolerant of political corruption and are accordingly less likely to enact strong laws to prevent such corruption.

The Foundation for Post-Watergate Ethics Legislation

Several key points emerge with regard to the passage of legislative ethics laws prior to Watergate. First, the narrative makes clear that in certain important respects, the states were actually ahead of the federal government in their attention to the issue of legislative ethics and conflicts of interest. Second, the factors that catalyzed the enactment of ethics laws in this period were primarily *external* to legislatures, in particular scandals and a history of state corruption. Critical pressure on states to act was generated by the media, which publicized scandals and investigations into political corruption—and which took up the case of ethics reform and pressured legislators to act—and by governors using their positions as state policy leaders. Two additional factors external to state legislatures, namely liberal citizen ideology and political culture, provided facilitating background conditions for the passage of basic codes; culture also shaped the *content* of these codes.

At the same time, one factor internal to legislatures affected both the likelihood of legislative ethics code enactment and the extensiveness of the codes: the level of legislative compensation. States that increased their legislative salaries during this time were more likely to enact basic codes and to enact more extensive restrictions than states that professionalized less during this time.

This chapter has highlighted the fact that the states did not need Watergate to take action in the area of legislative ethics. The initial steps that states took during the years 1954–72 instead laid the foundation upon which the post-Watergate ethics statutes built. The next chapter carries the analysis of state legislative ethics regulation into the post-Watergate era.

four

Watergate and Beyond: Ethics Reform
Moves Forward, 1973–96

The backlash against the political corruption associated with Watergate sparked the quick enactment of new ethics and campaign finance laws at the state and national levels.[1] But even after the direct stimulus of Watergate had worn off, the states continued to enact new conflict-of-interest laws for legislators. What factors contributed to the passage of these new laws? Were the factors different from those that were important in the pre-Watergate period?

This chapter focuses on a twenty-year period that begins after the immediate catalyst of Watergate had faded into the background. The period is broken into two subperiods, 1977–88 and 1989–96. The first period ends in 1988 because that is when the first of a series of "sting" operations conducted by federal and local law enforcement agencies and aimed at exposing corruption in state legislatures became public.[2] These operations are discussed at greater length later in the chapter. For now, it is simply worth noting that the period that began in 1989 and went until roughly 1996 is considered to be unique because of these stings and the laws that were enacted in response to them. Carried out primarily by the Federal Bureau of Investigation—but also by state and local law enforcement agencies—the operations ensnared over fifty state legislators in eight years. The period from 1989 to 1996 also represents a new "wave" of ethics reform in the terms of the laws' *content*, which focused on restricting legislators from receiving things of value from lobbyists. In particular, gift and honoraria restrictions featured prominently in the reform efforts of this period.

Background: Overview of States' Efforts in the Immediate Post-Watergate Years, 1973–76

By the beginning of 1977, thirty-eight of the continental states had some legislative conflict-of-interest or disclosure provisions in either their statutes or their legislative rules. Because only twenty-seven of the continental states had such regulations as of 1972, this means that in the four years immediately following Watergate, a flurry of brand-new state-level conflict-of-interest regulation occurred. Eleven states that had not enacted any laws regulating legislative conflicts of interest before 1972 took decisive action during the short period from 1973 to 1976. These included Alabama, North Carolina, and Rhode Island.[3] Watergate, along with some state-specific scandals, seems to have prodded these states into action. In some cases, as in South Dakota, the only requirement of the new laws was financial disclosure. In other cases, such as Alabama, a range of substantive restrictions was enacted during this four-year time frame. Tennessee's 1975 law was particularly innovative with regard to its restriction on officials accepting anything of value from lobbyists. The Tennessee law, going beyond other laws of the time, specified that "anything of value" included hotel expenses and the use of lobbyist credit cards.[4]

Watergate also spurred states that had already enacted substantive ethics regulations to amend their existing laws by adding financial disclosure to their arsenal of ethics restrictions. Examples include California, Minnesota, and Wisconsin. Still other states added new substantive restrictions to their existing codes. For example, Kansas' original legislative ethics law in 1970 was a sparse code containing only general principles of ethical conduct with no substantive restrictions on legislators' behavior. In 1974, Kansas added a restriction on gifts worth more than $40 and began to require disclosure of representation before state agencies. Maine, described in the last chapter as having a weak pre-Watergate code, strengthened its code in 1973 and again in 1975, when it set up an independent ethics commission with jurisdiction over legislators. Michigan also strengthened its ethics code in 1973. Texas strengthened its ethics law in 1973 and 1975.

Although certain states—such as North Carolina and Texas—strengthened their bribery statutes between 1973 and 1977, bribery laws do not appear to have acted as a substitute for other conflict-of-interest regulation. Instead, changes in bribery law generally *accompanied* or supplemented changes in the "murkier" type of conflict-of-interest regulation examined here. Both states with weak conflict-of-interest regulations and states with strong regulations amended their bribery laws during the 1973–76 period. Ohio in 1973 strengthened its penalties for bribery at the same time as it enacted a civil statute requiring financial disclosure, a one-year revolving door limit for legislators, a ban on disclosure of confidential information, and a ban on representation by lawyer-legislators before state agencies.

Other states that strengthened their existing laws between 1973 and 1976 include Colorado, Kentucky, and Minnesota. Colorado, which had enacted financial disclosure requirements in 1971, added new requirements in 1973. Minnesota strengthened its relatively weak ethics code in 1974 by requiring the disclosure of representation by lawyer-legislators before state agencies. Though many states added to their existing ethics restrictions in this period, however, certain states were unmoved by the impetus of Watergate. Delaware, Idaho, Missouri, New Hampshire, North Dakota, Vermont, Virginia, and Wyoming still lacked even a simple code of legislative ethics at the end of 1976.

Another notable policy innovation of the 1973–76 period was the establishment of independent ethics commissions with the power to advise on, and investigate, potential violations of the state ethics laws. Prior to 1973, only Hawaii and Louisiana had such commissions (established in 1964 and 1968, respectively), and Hawaii's commission did not have jurisdiction over state legislators. The main enforcement mechanisms for legislative ethics prior to 1973 were legislative ethics committees—joint or separate by house—along with the secretary of state's office and the attorney general's office. Between 1973 and 1976, however, eight states, including California, Florida, and Kansas, set up independent commissions to monitor legislators' financial disclosure and to address alleged violations of substantive ethics restrictions. Additional states followed suit after 1976. The establishment of independent commissions during this period and afterward is the subject of the next chapter. For now, we continue with the analysis of changes in the content of state ethics laws, leaving the discussion of enforcement for later.

Legislative Ethics Regulation in the States, 1977–88: Types of Restrictions

States continued to revisit the question of legislative ethics even after the direct stimulus of Watergate had worn off. In a few cases, this meant repealing parts of their existing statutes. In 1977, for example, Colorado repealed portions of its legislative ethics code. In 1984, Alaska eliminated a 1974 restriction on lawyer-legislators representing clients before state agencies, watering down the law to require only disclosure of such representation. Other states eliminated certain mandatory disclosure requirements. However, the majority of states that changed their laws did so by strengthening them.

Also after 1977, some states that had no legislative ethics laws finally enacted them. One state that made its first foray into the regulation of legislative ethics during the 1977–88 period was Missouri. In 1978, Missouri legislators enacted an ethics law that restricted their activities in areas including gifts from lobbyists, postgovernment employment, and representation by lawyer-legislators. Financial disclosure was not required until 1990, however. Mississippi and New Hampshire also enacted their first legislative ethics laws in 1979 and 1987, respectively.

In addition, some states that already had an ethics law on the books placed additional substantive restrictions on legislators' activities. Massachusetts, as described in chapter 2, is one example. In addition to regulating lawyer-legislators and limiting gifts in 1978, it was one of several states that began to address the practice of legislators receiving fees for speeches, in this case by requiring disclosure of honoraria. Most states that limit honoraria today did not begin to do so until the 1990s. Other early innovators in the area of honoraria regulation that took action before 1980 included New Jersey and Wisconsin.

Pennsylvania also strengthened its ethics laws in the 1977–88 period; it instituted a one-year revolving door limit, tightened its representation limits, and limited total honoraria to $1,000 per year.[5] Oklahoma also strengthened its conflict-of-interest statute in 1986. The 1986 amendments strengthened Oklahoma's original 1968 law by adding financial disclosure requirements and shifting the power to enforce the state's ethics laws from the attorney general and legislative ethics committees to a new, independent ethics commission. Louisiana in 1979 also amended its ethics law, requiring financial disclosure of legislators for the first time. Maryland strengthened its ethics law in 1979 by requiring additional financial disclosure.

Explaining Change in State Legislative Ethics Laws, 1977–88

What explains variation in the changes states made to their legislative ethics laws between 1977 and 1988? As in chapter 3, an index is used to calculate change in each state's laws, based on six possible categories for which change could occur: the enactment of a basic ethics code, gift limits, postgovernment employment limits, honoraria limits, and financial disclosure limits.[6] Multiple regression analysis was used to examine the effects of various factors on the amount of change in states' laws. The outcome we want to explain, or the dependent variable, is the total amount of change in states' ethics laws. Two different types of regression analysis, linear and ordinal regression, were used (see appendix D). Forty-seven states were included in the data set.[7]

The factors that potentially explain change in states' laws, or the independent variables, are largely the same as in the previous chapter. The expectation is that the same factors that were considered to have possibly influenced states' decisions to enact laws in the pre-Watergate period may also have mattered after Watergate. The one modification is that I control for the recent passage of ethics legislation in each state.[8] Details on how the explanatory factors are measured can be found in appendix D.

The results suggest that three main factors influenced the enactment of new ethics laws for legislators during this period: scandals, party competition, and the presence of an initiative option. The factors listed in sidebar 4.1 are those that are statistically significant, when controlling for other explanations. The full regression results are presented in table E.1 in appendix E.[9] Table E.2 in appendix E provides an interpretation of the quantitative impact of the key factors.[10]

The first significant result, consistent with the findings for the pre-Watergate period, is that scandals had a positive impact on the enactment of new ethics laws. Below I discuss the impact of this factor at length, with attention to the ways in which the nature of scandals changed during this time period compared with the pre-Watergate period. Attention is then turned to the other factors that influenced the passage of ethics law during this time.

**Sidebar 4.1   Key Influences on the Passage
of Ethics Laws, 1977–88**

Scandal
Unified government
Initiative process

Source: Regression results of table E.1 in appendix E. Factors listed are those that are statistically significant, controlling for other factors.

Each one-unit change in a state's scandal score is associated with a change of 0.134 in the states' ethics index. This is not a large change (see appendix D for the scoring of the index). However, if a state experienced a combination of scandals equal to a ten-unit increase in its scandal score during this period, its ethics score increased by 1.34 points. That change is roughly equivalent to, for example, the enactment of a one-year post-government employment limit or an honoraria limit plus a small change in financial disclosure requirements.

Thus, while small scandals did not generally catalyze large reforms, a combination of larger scandals placed pressure on legislators to enact more substantial changes. Another way to understand the impact of scandal on reform is to consider the difference between a state that had no scandals during this period and a state that received the maximum score for the number and severity of its scandals. The probability that the first state would enact the maximum possible change in its ethics laws was only 13.79 percent. The probability that the second, scandal-ridden state would enact the maximum possible amount of change during this time was 66.10 percent (see appendix D for how these probabilities were calculated).

The Changing Nature of Scandal: Federal Prosecutors Target State Officials

The most interesting aspect of political scandals during this period was the heavy hand that government officials themselves, in particular federal prosecutors, played in the process of scandal production. During the pre-Watergate years, scandals were often the result of state investigations into the links between organized crime and public officials, which were in turn often a response to the activities of the Kefauver Committee in the U.S. Senate. During the 1977–88 period, the nature of state-level scandals and corruption shifted. In particular, many of the reported scandals that figured into the scandal measure during this later period were the result of a new trend: federal prosecution of political corruption at lower levels of government. Maass argues that beginning in the early 1970s, federal prosecutors began pursuing political corruption at the state and local levels with "unusual vigor."

In 1975, motivated largely by Watergate, President Gerald Ford and Attorney General Edward H. Levi announced that investigating and prosecuting official corruption would now be a priority of the Department of Justice. In 1976, the assistant attorney general, Richard Thornburgh, created the Public Integrity Section of the Department of Justice, giving it the "responsibility for overseeing the federal effort to combat corruption through the prosecution of elected and appointed officials at all levels of government."[11]

Figure 4.1 shows just how successful this effort was. The figure highlights the increase in federal prosecution of corrupt state and local officials from 1970 through 1995. Behind these numbers was a dramatic change in the activities of U.S. attorneys, who began in the early 1970s to make creative use of four federal statutes to prosecute elected state and local officials. This was a purpose for which they were arguably never intended. The four laws were the 1872 Mail Fraud Act, the 1946 Hobbs Act, the 1961 Travel Act, and the Racketeering Influenced and Corruption Organized Act (RICO), enacted in 1970. The first of these laws was aimed at combating lottery frauds perpetuated through the mail system, whereas the other three were aimed at fighting the racketeering activities of labor and organized crime. They were not designed to apply to cases of political corruption by state and local officials. But beginning in the early 1970s, ambitious federal attorneys began stretching the language of these laws—particularly the first, second, and fourth—to apply them to public officials. They began to prosecute bribery as mail fraud, as extortion, and as racketeering.

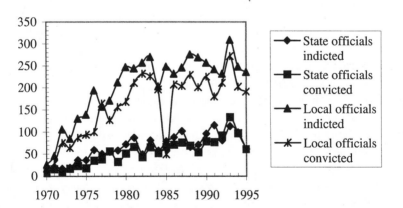

Figure 4.1   Increase in Federal Prosecution of Corrupt State and Local Officials, 1970–95 (number of officials)

Sources: Arthur Maass, "U.S. Prosecution of State and Local Officials for Political Corruption: Is the Bureaucracy Out of Control in a High-Stakes Operation Involving the Constitutional System?" *Publius* 17 (summer 1987): 202; U.S. Department of Justice, *Report to Congress on the Activities and Operations of the Public Operations Section for 1995* (Washington, D.C.: U.S. Government Printing Office, 1995).

For example, prosecutors argued under the Mail Fraud Statute that politicians who took bribes were guilty of mail fraud because they were defrauding citizens of their "'intangible right to conscientious, loyal, faithful, disinterested, and honest government.'" To obtain a conviction, it was simply necessary to show that some piece of documentation relating to the bribe had passed through the mails. Though lower-level courts upheld convictions obtained under the Mail Fraud Act, the U.S. Supreme Court was not so supportive. In 1987, the Court ruled 7–2 that the mail fraud statute was not intended to apply to politicians' defrauding citizens of their "intangible rights to honest and impartial government." But Congress gave federal prosecutors back their ammunition the following year when it passed a one-sentence amendment to an antidrug bill declaring that "the term 'scheme or artifice to defraud' includes a scheme or artifice to deprive another of the intangible right of honest services." As one commentator notes, the Mail Fraud Act remains the "pre-eminent weapon in the arsenal of any aggressive federal prosecutor. . . . Nothing is as broad, flexible, and powerful as mail fraud when it comes to putting public officials behind bars."[12]

RICO has been another important, though less frequently used, tool of federal prosecutors. To counter the infiltration of legitimate business enterprises such as trucking and warehousing by racketeers, RICO states that it is illegal for an individual who has received income from a "pattern of racketeering activity"—such as murder, arson, gambling, robbery, or bribery—to invest the income in any "enterprise" that affects interstate commerce, and for any person employed by or associated with any such enterprise to engage in such a pattern.[13] An enterprise is defined in the statute as an individual, partnership, corporation, association, or union. Federal prosecutors, however, devised an expansive interpretation of the term "enterprise" to include state legislatures, police departments, state and local executive agencies, and municipal courts. Thus a state legislator who received gifts from a racketeer could be prosecuted under the statute.

Using RICO has several advantages for prosecutors. First, they can avoid the normal five-year statute of limitations on prosecution of criminal acts. Second, they can introduce more incriminating evidence than under the other three statutes, such as evidence of prior crimes to prove a pattern of racketeering. And unlike the Mail Fraud and Travel Acts, which provide a maximum prison term of five years, a RICO conviction carries a twenty-year jail term. The fact that the law is relatively tough in these respects makes it easier for prosecutors to obtain cooperation from defendants.

Many successful prosecutions under these statutes in the 1970s and
1980s involved state legislators, governors, and other statewide officials.
They are therefore factored into the scandal variable calculated for this
period. Consider just two years from the period examined here: 1982 and
1985. In 1982, the Department of Justice reported that its U.S. attorneys
had convicted a former president pro tem of the Florida Senate of extortion and mail fraud in connection with a scheme to extort money from a
nightclub owner in exchange for assistance in obtaining a liquor license.
Department of Justice prosecutors also won the conviction of a former
Massachusetts state senator on extortion charges, a Michigan state representative for soliciting bribes, a South Carolina state representative for
defrauding the government under the Mail Fraud Statute, and a Tennessee
state senator for mail fraud and extortion.

This last case generated a landmark Supreme Court decision in which
the Court ruled that a state legislator cannot claim immunity concerning
his legislative activities in a federal prosecution. In 1985, the Department
of Justice reported the conviction of the president pro tem of the Mississippi State Senate under the Hobbs Act for extorting $50,000 to ensure
the passage of a horse racing bill, the indictment of a former New Jersey
state senator on RICO charges, and the conviction of a former Oklahoma
state senator on eighteen counts of mail fraud.[14]

Whereas state prosecutors may have been uninterested in pursuing
these officials under state bribery laws, federal prosecutors had no such
qualms. They were willing to use federal laws that were not intended for
that purpose to achieve their goal. Between 1975 and 1988, they went after
legislators in Alabama, Indiana, Kentucky, Pennsylvania, South Carolina,
and other states.

Thus although some of the scandals that catalyzed reform in this
period stemmed from state-level prosecutions of bribery, a considerable
number of scandals and the subsequent ethics laws that were enacted can
thus be traced to the efforts of federal prosecutors using federal statutes.
In Pennsylvania, the House speaker and a state senator were indicted in
1978, the first on charges of extortion and the second on charges of racketeering and mail fraud in connection with placing two no-show employees on the state payroll. Pennsylvania broadened the scope of its ethics
law considerably in response, adding a one-year revolving door provision, tightening its representation limits, and limiting honoraria to an
annual total of $1,000.

Another example of federal prosecution spurring ethics reform in this
period is Louisiana. There a federal bribery and racketeering investigation
implicated legislators, the lieutenant governor, and the former governor.
The 1979 ethics law followed closely on the heels of this scandal. Similarly,

Missouri's 1978 ethics law was a response to the mail fraud conviction of the former House speaker on fifteen counts of accepting kickbacks.[15]

ABSCAM—a Federal Bureau of Investigation (FBI) sting known primarily for entrapping seven members of the U.S. Congress—also catalyzed state ethics reform during this period because one New Jersey state senator was convicted on bribery charges in connection with the sting in 1980. The senator, who accepted $25,000 from FBI agents posing as Arab sheiks, told federal investigators that he wielded "considerable influence" over appointments to the Casino Control Commission that oversaw gambling in the state.[16] Specifically, he was involved in the sale of appointive positions to individuals willing to look the other way when it came to regulating the gambling industry. It was also revealed that other New Jersey state legislators had close ties to the gambling industry. Seven lawmakers were reported to own stock in casinos or companies that hoped to open casinos. Later that year, spurred by these allegations of influence peddling, the New Jersey legislature unanimously approved a strengthened code of ethics. It included a postgovernment employment provision prohibiting legislators and other state officials from working for the casino industry for two years after leaving office.

Yet another example of federal prosecution sparking ethics reform is New York. The 1987 ethics law discussed in chapter 2 was enacted largely in response to the prosecution of members of the state Assembly for placing no-show workers on their payrolls. And as the Massachusetts case study showed, a languishing ethics reform movement in that state finally found success in 1978 after the indictment and conviction of two powerful state legislators by federal prosecutors using the Hobbs Act. Finally, Oklahoma's strong ethics law was enacted in 1986 in the wake of several convictions of state legislators on charges of mail fraud, abuse of office, and vote fraud.[17]

The targets of federal prosecutors were not limited to legislators. Prosecutors also pursued the chief executive in some states, and in at least two cases these prosecutions appear to have contributed to the enactment of state ethics laws. One example is Maryland, where the U.S. attorney obtained the conviction of Governor Marvin Mandel under the mail fraud statute for receiving payoffs for favorable action on racetrack operations in 1977 (Illinois governor Otto Kerner had been convicted for the same thing in 1973, in a pioneering use of the mail fraud law by federal prosecutors). In the wake of Mandel's conviction, Maryland strengthened its ethics law.

Other governors who were targets of federal prosecution for corruption during this period include Louisiana governor Buddy Roemer, Oklahoma governor David Hall, West Virginia governor Arch Moore, and Louisiana governor Edwin Edwards. Though not every one of these federally prosecuted cases of gubernatorial or legislative corruption led to stronger legislative ethics laws, a significant number of them did make such a contribution.[18]

Unified Government and the Initiative: Additional Factors Facilitating Ethics Reform

Two other factors besides scandals influenced the passage of ethics laws during this time. First, states in which government was more frequently unified under one party during this time tended to enact stronger ethics laws. The probability of enacting the maximum change in ethics laws went from 2.91 percent for a state where control of government was divided during the entire time period to 53.76 percent for a state with unified government during the entire time period (see table E.2 in appendix E). This finding contradicts the theory that party competition should facilitate the passage of ethics legislation. Instead, it provides some support for the argument made by Ripley and Sundquist that unified governments are more likely to get things done because they are able to avoid interparty conflicts that block action.[19]

However, there may be another more subtle reason why states with more unified government enacted stronger laws in this period. The majority of states with unified government during these years were dominated by Democrats. It may be that Democratic leaders were especially likely to take up the cause of ethics reform after Watergate because it was a scandal involving a Republican presidential administration. There is evidence that in some states Watergate led to the election of "reformist" Democrats who enacted strong ethics laws in the immediate post-Watergate years (1973–76).[20] Although the analysis of this chapter begins in 1977, after the immediate fervor of Watergate had worn off, it is plausible that the new cohort of Democrats may have continued to push for additional legislation. Indeed, some of the reformist Democrats elected after Watergate— such as Tom Loftus, who later became the Democratic speaker of the Wisconsin House of Representatives—were first elected in 1976 and did not start serving until 1977.

Another plausible but quite different explanation for why the change in ethics laws was greater in unified Democratic states during this period is suggested by Meier and Holbrook's analysis of political corruption in the states between 1977 and 1987, essentially the same years examined here. The authors find evidence of partisan targeting by federal prosecutors of elected officials under the Reagan administration during the years

1981 to 1987. Specifically, they argue that federal "prosecution of corrupt officials was more intense in Democratic states than in Republican states during the Reagan years."[21] The greater rate of convictions of Democratic officials on public corruption charges during this time may have spurred those states, which generally had unified Democratic governments, to pass new ethics regulations.

In addition, some scandals are not picked up by the scandal measure used here, and these may have been disproportionately associated with states whose politics were dominated by the Democratic Party. As shown in figure 4.1, convictions of public officials at the local level grew exponentially during this period. However, I only measure scandals involving *state* officials. I do not count convictions of local officials, which make up the majority of convictions by federal prosecutors because of the sheer number of local officials compared to state and federal officials. The reason these convictions are not counted is because the guiding hypothesis is that only scandals involving *state* officials will catalyze state legislative ethics reform. However, in this period, federal prosecutors engaged in several large-scale efforts to target local officials that may have contributed to the success of ethics reform. Two states that experienced numerous convictions of county officials for taking kickbacks during this period were Oklahoma and Mississippi.[22] These scandals immediately preceded the enactment of strong ethics laws in those states and are likely to have bolstered the legitimacy of the ethics reform cause.

Finally, there is some evidence that the initiative process facilitated the enactment of new ethics laws. The probability that a state with an initiative option would enact the strongest possible laws during this time was 33.33 percent, versus only 5.66 percent for a state with no initiative. States that used the initiative to enact new ethics restrictions for legislators during this period include Missouri (1978), Montana (1980), Arkansas (1988), and Colorado (1988). In Montana, for example, voters supported an initiative mandating financial disclosure for legislators and disclosure for lobbyists by a 3–1 margin. In Arkansas, the state Common Cause organization and the League of Women Voters turned to the initiative process after a special legislative session called in 1988 failed to pass a financial disclosure bill. Later that year, with the support of then-governor Bill Clinton, several civic-minded groups such as Common Cause and the League of Women Voters took the proposal to the voters. The ballot question won by a 64 percent margin.[23]

In other states that had an initiative option, Common Cause and other good-government groups wielded the threat of its use to push legislators to enact strict new ethics regulations. The Massachusetts case study is one such example; Oklahoma is another. In Oklahoma in 1983, Common Cause failed to get enough signatures to put an ethics measure on the ballot. By 1986, with a recent scandal involving several legislators and the strong support of Governor George Nigh, the group was able to make successful use of the threat of initiative to get the legislature to approve a strong ethics law.[24] It seems plausible that this threat would be taken seriously, particularly in states where the initiative had already been used to enact legislative conflict of interest and disclosure proposals, as Oregon in 1974 or Michigan and Florida in 1976.

Certain factors that were significant in the 1954–72 period were not influential in the period from 1977 to 1988. For example, increasing compensation did not have a strong influence on the passage of new laws during this second period. Nor did political culture have a strong effect.[25] A different, more timely measure of political culture was also used, to take advantage of a 1983 survey that measured each state's Common Cause membership per capita.[26] This measure reflects public support for Common Cause, an organization devoted to good government and the moralistic view of politics. However, it had no influence on the passage of ethics laws.[27] Thus, culture was not an important factor in this period, based on two different measures.

This is not to suggest, however, that Common Cause as an *organization* was insignificant in the enactment of legislative ethics laws during this period. In fact, as noted above, Common Cause played an important role. The group was active in pushing for ballot initiatives related to the regulation of political ethics in general and legislative ethics in particular. As in Massachusetts in 1978, a key function served by Common Cause was to generate attention to scandals and use them to create a window of opportunity to push through reforms that legislators had been unwilling to enact earlier. The Oklahoma case discussed above is another example of how Common Cause was an important player in the passage of new ethics laws, gathering signatures and using the initiative process as a tool in its arsenal.

Common Cause also had an important influence on the passage of ethics laws in another way. In the mid-1970s, it began disseminating a "model ethics law" for the states that was used by reform advocates within state government when they drafted ethics legislation. The text of the laws that have been enacted across the states since 1974 closely mirrors and often replicates the language of the Common Cause model law. The second political culture measure tried, however, does not measure the impact of Common Cause's strategies and efforts; it simply reflects popular support for Common Cause in the different states.

Finally, ethics laws did not diffuse among neighboring states during this period as they had prior to Watergate. The passage of new laws during this period, instead, was greater in states with more corruption scandals, that had unified government, or that had an initiative option.

Reform Moves Forward, 1989–96

During the brief period from 1989 to 1996, thirty-six states strengthened their legislative ethics laws. The range of states' efforts varied widely. Idaho finally enacted a simple ethics code but no substantive restrictions or financial disclosure requirements, while Kentucky and South Carolina added substantive restrictions in every category considered here (gift limits, honoraria limits, revolving door limits, and representation limits) and increased their financial disclosure requirements. In addition, many states also began to enact bans on legislators accepting campaign contributions during a legislative session.[28]

Of the three periods examined in this book, overall change in states' legislative ethics laws was greatest during this last period. Average change in the ethics index was 1.85 for the 1989–96 period, versus 1.73 for the 1953–72 period and 1.22 for the 1977–88 period (see appendix A). Of particular note was the extent to which states during the years 1989–96 tightened their restrictions on gifts and honoraria. State action on honoraria stemmed in part from the decisions by the U.S. House and Senate to ban honoraria in 1989 and 1991, respectively. The issue of honoraria became a matter of major public controversy at the federal level in 1988, when U.S. senator David Durenberger and then-House speaker Jim Wright became embroiled in controversies involving their honoraria earnings.[29] State-level attempts to ban honoraria did not simply follow the federal bans, however; honoraria bans were considered as early as 1987 in Maryland and Tennessee (though they did not pass), two years before the U.S. House instituted its ban.[30]

Seventeen states banned honoraria for legislators between 1989 and 1996. These included Pennsylvania and Tennessee in 1989; Arkansas and California in 1990; Connecticut, South Carolina, and Texas in 1991; Kentucky and Ohio in 1993; and Maryland in 1995. Only Arkansas and California did so through the initiative process. Though the majority of states established honoraria bans by statute, others such as Indiana and Tennessee only incorporated a ban into their legislative rules.[31] Several important loopholes were retained by virtually all the states that chose to limit honoraria. First, lawmakers could generally accept travel reimbursement, though not direct monetary compensation, for speaking at a conference on a matter pertaining to legislation. Second, they could accept honoraria if they donated it to charity or returned it to the giver, a loophole that parallels the congressional honoraria restriction.[32]

Also between 1989 and 1996, fifteen states joined Wisconsin in enacting a "no cup of coffee" ban on gifts (recall that Wisconsin passed its pioneering ban on gifts in 1957). These states included Kentucky, Massachusetts, Minnesota, and South Carolina. Other states placed numerical restrictions on gifts where before there were none or where the law had been vague about what gifts were acceptable. Iowa, for example, went from a $35 limit, enacted in 1987, to a $3 limit per gift or meal in 1993 following a conflict-of-interest case involving the senate president. Florida's 1990 law prohibited legislators from accepting gifts worth over $100 from lobbyists, their principals, or political action committees, and it required disclosure of gifts over $25. Lawmakers in Florida can still accept all the food and drink they can consume in a single sitting. Ohio placed a $75 limit on gifts from lobbyists in 1994 and placed a restriction on lobbyist-funded trips. Texas banned pleasure trips funded by lobbyists in 1990. However, Texas still allows lawmakers to accept $500 worth of entertainment and $500 worth of gifts from an individual lobbyist in one year.[33]

Ohio and Texas are rare among the states in their explicit inclusion of trips in their gift limits. Many states have a loophole exempting trips. Also, most state laws contain an exemption for lobbyist-funded meals when they are consumed out-of-state. This loophole continues to be a bone of contention for advocates of strong ethics regulation. In Maryland, for example, as of February 2004, the state Common Cause chapter was working to eliminate it.[34]

Analysts of the changes in state ethics laws during the late 1980s through the mid-1990s tend to stress one explanation for the reform efforts: the catalyzing effect of scandal.[35] Were recent scandals the *only* factor that influenced the enactment of legislative ethics regulations during this period? Or did factors that were significant in earlier periods—such as the initiative process, ideology, political culture, compensation, unified government, or regional diffusion—play a role?

Explaining Ethics Reform in the Final Period, 1989–96: Scandal and the Continued Role of Federal Prosecution

Multiple regression analysis is used here to analyze the effects of various factors on the passage of new legislative ethics laws during this final period. The models are the same as the ones used in the first part of this chapter. The explanatory or independent variables are measured in basically the same way as for the 1977–88 period.[36] Appendix D provides details on measurement of the dependent and independent variables. Sidebar 4.2 summarizes the regression results, showing the factors that were statistically significant when controlling for other factors. In appendix E, table E.3 shows the full results of the regression analysis, and table E.4 provides an interpretation of the quantitative impact of the key independent variables.[37]

As in the previous two periods, scandal proved to be a critical influence on states' efforts to strengthen their legislative ethics restrictions.[38] A scandal involving three or more legislators was associated with a nearly 1-point increase in the state's ethics index, roughly equivalent to the enactment of an honoraria limit or a one-year revolving door limit. The occurrence of a sting operation targeted at the state legislature was associated with a 1.6-unit change in the ethics index, roughly equivalent to the enactment of a numerical gift limit in a state that previously placed no limits on the receipt of gifts, or a one-year revolving door limit plus some financial disclosure requirements. Interpreted in a different way, a state that experienced no scandals during this period had only a 20 percent probability of enacting the maximum change possible in its ethics laws, while a state with the highest scandal score had a 98.66 percent probability of enacting the maximum change in its ethics laws.

As from 1977 to 1988, many of the corruption scandals in this period resulted from aggressive federal prosecution efforts by the Department of Justice, often working with the FBI. Seven states were the subject of FBI sting operations that caught state legislators taking bribes from federal agents. These were California, Illinois, Kentucky, Louisiana, South

---

**Sidebar 4.2   Key Influences on the Passage
of Ethics Laws, 1989–96**

Scandal
Long-term history of corruption
Majority party control
Political culture

Source: Regression results of table E.3 in appendix E. Factors listed are those that are statistically significant, controlling for other factors.

Carolina, Tennessee, and West Virginia. In most cases, the undercover agents pretended to be representatives of companies involved in horse and dog racing and offered bribes in exchange for favorable legislation. In California, they presented themselves as businesspeople working for a fictitious seafood company (hence the scandal's name, Shrimpgate). In Illinois, in Operation "Silver Shovel," agents offered bribes to legislators to entice them to propose legislation beneficial to cemetery owners. These stings marked a "major escalation of the federal war against public corruption." In two other states, Arizona and New Mexico, local law enforcement officials carried out similar stings against state legislators.[39]

The 1989–96 period was not the first time that a sting operation involving state legislators was carried out. As suggested above, the 1980 ABSCAM sting, which drew New Jersey state legislators into its net, received considerable publicity, but the main target was members of the U.S. Congress. In the 1989–96 period, however, the emphasis shifted to *state* legislators. In California, five current and former legislators were convicted, including the former Assembly minority leader. Fifteen legislators were convicted in Kentucky's BOPTROT scandal—eight senators and seven representatives, including the House speaker, who accepted a $1,500 bribe; other legislators accepted bribes as low as $500 to promote legislation on behalf of the horse-racing industry. West Virginia's sting operation implicated two powerful legislators, the current and former Senate presidents. In South Carolina, seventeen current and former legislators were indicted in connection with "Operation Lost Trust" after taking cash in return for their votes on a gambling measure. All but one were convicted of extortion under the Hobbs Act.[40]

Every state that faced such a highly publicized exposure of legislative corruption enacted major changes in its legislative ethics laws, although their specific responses varied. New restrictions were placed on legislators' activities, and, in some cases, independent ethics commissions were established with the power to police legislators. West Virginia even gave its new ethics commission the power to appoint a special prosecutor in any county where a public official was on trial, a significant power given that West Virginia does not have a state prosecutor and must rely on county prosecutors to bring cases of alleged unethical behavior to court.[41] Lawmakers in Kentucky voted unanimously to enact a law that vaulted the state to the number one spot as of the end of 1996 in terms of the stringency of its legislative ethics regulations, up from the fortieth spot as of 1988 (see appendix A). The law enacted by South Carolina lawmakers in response to their sting operation catapulted that state into the number two spot from the eighteenth spot in 1988. According to Common Cause of South Carolina's executive director, John Crangle, state legislators there would not have considered "reform of this magnitude without the sting." Arizona Common Cause executive director Dana Larsen agreed: "The indictments (which resulted from the sting) raised the interest in our issues and that makes my job easier."[42] The job was not as easy for reform advocates in states with no scandals during this period, such as North Dakota and Wyoming. Such states generally did not enact new ethics laws for legislators.

Other states experienced nonsting scandals that also grew out of federal prosecution of legislators, governors, and other statewide elected officials. Beginning in early 1993, for example, Michigan faced a major political scandal that involved lax oversight and fraud at the House Fiscal Agency. Seven former legislative staffers and a state representative pleaded guilty to felonies including mail fraud. Michigan enacted a new ethics law in the wake of this scandal. This law banned honoraria, required lawmakers to report free trips valued at over $100, prohibited members who left in midterm from becoming lobbyists during the remainder of their terms, and ended officeholder expense funds that had historically been used as slush funds. Common Cause of Michigan's executive director, Karen Holcomb-Merrill, was quoted as saying, "Negative publicity regarding the scandal made the legislature feel they had to address governmental ethics in some respects."[43]

However, Michigan failed to act on a number of changes desired by reformers, such as the establishment of an independent ethics commission, a one-year revolving door limit, and financial disclosure of members' business interests (the state had, and continues to have, no financial disclosure requirements). Thus lawmakers did not accept wholesale the recommendations of reformers who had been waiting in the wings when the scandal broke.

Scandals that occurred as a result of state, not just federal, prosecution also helped reformers win enactment of new laws. For example, the Arkansas attorney general, who was running for governor in 1990, was convicted of felony theft for spending money from his office operating account on "wine, women and entertainment."[44] He dropped out of the race when the charges were first reported. The state Common Cause chapter and other observers suggest that this scandal helped the 1990 initiative effort that created an independent commission and banned honoraria. Fallout from the scandal also facilitated a 1991 effort—by sympathetic legislators this time, rather than by initiative—to expand financial disclosure.

Ethics reform also followed state prosecution of unethical behavior in Minnesota. The Minnesota House majority leader and the speaker of the House resigned in 1994 after the "Phonegate" investigation into the use of state phones by Majority Leader Alan Welle to make $90,000 worth of personal calls. Welle was indicted and pleaded guilty to a gross misdemeanor to avoid prosecution on a felony charge. The speaker, who had not made any illegal phone calls herself, resigned after criticism of her handling of the affair, including her refusal to turn over phone records to the press.[45] In the immediate wake of this highly publicized scandal, Minnesota enacted a no-cup-of-coffee gift law. The vote was 64–0 in the Senate and 117–13 in the House. The legislative resistance to such laws that exists in "normal" times was thus highly subdued.

In Texas, House Speaker Gib Lewis was indicted in 1990 on misdemeanor charges of violating state ethics laws by failing to report certain gifts.[46] The next year, Texas lawmakers voted unanimously to ban honoraria, institute a one-year revolving door ban for legislators and other officials and limits on lawyer-legislators, restrict gifts, add new disclosure requirements, and strengthen its bribery law. The new ethics law also reinvigorated the Texas Ethics Commission, which had gone unfunded for the previous four years.

Alabama was yet another state that enacted strong new regulations in the wake of state prosecution of unethical behavior. After Governor Guy Hunt was convicted in April 1993 of diverting $200,000 in inaugural funds for personal use, a new law placed limits on the personal use of office equipment and facilities, expanded financial disclosure, and established a two-year postgovernment employment limit for legislators and other state employees.[47]

Massachusetts is another example of how state investigations and prosecution helped spark ethics reform in this period. In Massachusetts, ten former and current legislators were fined by the State Ethics Commission for violating state conflict-of-interest laws by accepting gratuities from insurance industry lobbyists. The commission's action followed newspaper revelations about legislators going on an island vacation that was partly financed by lobbyists. In December 1992, the *Boston Globe* had sent a team of investigative reporters to follow seven Massachusetts state legislators—including the speaker of the House and several committee chairs—as they spent four days at a posh resort in Puerto Rico. The lawmakers soaked up the sun, played golf, and drank and ate in style, according to the *Globe*. Their entertainment bill was footed by some of the state's most powerful lobbyists, representing the hospital, insurance, and automobile industries, as well as doctors and attorneys. Though the legislators paid for their airfare and hotel bills, the lobbyists covered all their other expenses, including one dinner bill for $1,500. The *Globe* reported that as soon as Democratic speaker Charles Flaherty Jr. and his fellow legislators arrived at the resort, the lobbyists took turns picking up the bar and dinner tabs. A lobbyist for the Massachusetts Medical Society even hand-delivered the drinks to the speaker.

Four months after the Puerto Rican getaway, the *Globe* noted, the Health Care Committee chaired by a legislator at the resort approved two bills that had been requested by a medical industry lobbyist who had also been there. These bills substantially weakened the state medical board that disciplines doctors. The clear implication of the newspaper stories that ran on the vacation was that legislators had been "bought" by the lobbyists, if not through an explicit bribe then through the influence of the free drinks, food, and golf. Its reputation under attack, the Massachusetts Legislature responded in 1994 by passing a gift ban.[48]

However, the precise meaning of what constitutes an allowable gift continues to be debated in Massachusetts, as in other states, even where a gift ban is in place. In January 2004, the Massachusetts State Ethics Commission was asked to rule on legislators receiving special access to tickets for sold-out events like sports playoff games. Again, the *Boston Globe* shone the spotlight on legislators' activities, reporting that several politicians—including Democratic Senate president Robert E. Travaglini and Democratic House speaker Thomas Finneran—got tickets to the Red Sox playoffs at face value, even though the games had already sold out. At the time, tickets were selling online for as much as $2,000 each. The commission ruled that allowing public officials to pay face value under these circumstances was "not acceptable" and "constituted an unwarranted privilege."[49] At the same time, the commission said the politicians can attend games for free as part of their official duties, for example, if they are invited to throw the first pitch at a baseball game.

Wisconsin is still another example of state scandals prompting ethics reform during this period. An investigation of twelve state lawmakers and six lobbyists by the state Ethics Commission and the Dane County district attorney resulted in the House majority leader and ten other legislators being fined for accepting a lobbyist-financed trip. Another legislator pleaded guilty to five misdemeanor charges under the state ethics laws, resigned, and served ninety days in jail. Wisconsin, which already had a relatively strong ethics law, clarified and tightened its statute with regard to legislators accepting gifts in the wake of this scandal (e.g., one sentence specified that legislators could not accept discount sky boxes at the local stadium from lobbyists). In 1989 the legislature also transferred regulation of lobbyists from the secretary of state to the independent ethics board.[50]

Certain scandals clearly led to new laws that addressed the very problems that had been highlighted by the scandals, for example, in Florida,

Massachusetts, and Wisconsin. In other states, the response was more sweeping and went beyond the scope of the scandal that had catalyzed it. For example, the scandal involving misuse of public resources in Alabama led to a postgovernment employment limit as well as a limit on the use of public resources and facilities. In Michigan, the scandal involving the House Fiscal Agency led most directly to an audit of the agency, changes in its bookkeeping methods, and the removal of the House committee chair who oversaw the agency.[51] However, the honoraria ban and revolving door limit of the new law were not direct responses to the wrongdoing uncovered by the scandal. Rather, they were changes that reformers had been seeking for years. Groups like Common Cause took advantage of the window of opportunity opened by the scandal to press for their enactment as part of a broader reform package.

The new laws in Kentucky and South Carolina, as suggested above, were the most sweeping of the period. In response to the bribery convictions of numerous legislators, both states increased the penalties for bribery, but they also instituted postgovernment employment limits, strengthened financial disclosure, and banned gifts and honoraria. The strengthening of financial disclosure and honoraria limits for legislators in many states during this time was often a generalized response to abuses of power, even though in some cases (e.g., Alabama, Arkansas, and Pennsylvania), the scandals did not involve honoraria and the main culprits in the scandals were governors, attorney generals, and treasurers. Indeed, it was rare for a state to enact only regulations directly related to a scandal, as with a scandal over honoraria practices in Ohio.

Not only immediate scandals but also a long-term tendency to corruption had an influence on the enactment of new ethics laws. States with a greater long-term history of political corruption were more likely to strengthen their ethics laws during this time. A state with the lowest possible score for its long-term history of corruption had only a 27 percent predicted probability of enacting the maximum positive change in its ethics laws during this period. The probability was 74.87 percent for a state with the highest score.

Other Factors That Shaped Legislative Ethics Reform, 1989–96

Several additional factors influenced change in state legislative ethics laws during the 1989–96 period. First, states with greater majority party control of the legislature enacted fewer new ethics restrictions for legislators.

Where the majority party controlled fewer seats and interparty competition was higher, states enacted more new ethics regulations. This is consistent with the theory, outlined in chapter 3, that party competition should facilitate ethics reform success.

States with individualistic cultures were marginally less likely to enact strong new laws during this period. Culture therefore had a weak impact on the passage of ethics reform during this time. I tried using the alternative political culture measure that was also employed in the 1977–88 regressions (see note 26). Recall that this measure equals each state's Common Cause membership per capita in 1983, so it has the advantage of being less dated than the Elazar measure of political culture. Because it reflects public support for Common Cause's progressive agenda, in which good-government reform features prominently, it can be seen as a proxy for moralistic culture. However, this factor did not have an influence on the passage of ethics laws.[52] Again, this does not imply that Common Cause was unimportant as a *political actor* on the ethics reform front. As the discussion of the previous section indicated, Common Cause was active in the reform process—for example, in Arizona, Arkansas, and South Carolina. When major scandals were reported, Common Cause was ready to take advantage of their occurrence and to use them in negotiations with legislators once the passage of reform became all but certain.

Increasing compensation did not influence the enactment of new ethics laws. As in the 1977–88 period, rising compensation was not necessary in the presence of major scandals, which alone provided enough of a stimulus in many cases. In fact, during the years 1989–96, many states experienced a significant decline in real legislative compensation, due to a combination of inflation and voters' hostility to legislators attempting to raise their pay.[53] The average change in real compensation during this period was –$690. Half the legislatures experienced declines in real compensation during these years. For example, Pennsylvania legislators saw their compensation fall $45,200 in real terms. The drop was $23,650 in Massachusetts and $17,030 in Illinois.

Perhaps most illuminating is the fact that the two states that strengthened their legislative ethics laws the most actually experienced a fall in real legislative compensation. Real compensation during this time fell by $21,600 in South Carolina and $3,690 in Kentucky. This suggests that increasing compensation was far from necessary in cases where states experienced major scandals involving state legislators. With the exception of California, all the states that experienced legislative stings and followed up with ethics reform started the period with relatively low salaries and did little if anything to increase legislators' pay. California was unique in that, as in 1966, limits on outside income were tied to a legislative salary increase in 1990. Real compensation increased $18,570 during this time there. But this link was the exception to the rule.

Thus, even though Rosenthal suggests that extremely low compensation hindered ethics regulation in some states during this time, the effect did not show up in the regression analysis.[54] For example, Rosenthal argues that poor pay for legislators made the New Mexico legislature unwilling to substantively limit representation by lawyer-legislators when it considered ethics reform in 1993. Legislators in that state decided only to prohibit members from using their titles or legislative stationary in connection with their legal work. However, poor pay for the unprofessionalized New Mexico legislature clearly did not present an insurmountable barrier to restricting outside income. In the wake of the sting operation that occurred there, New Mexico legislators banned honoraria, placing a significant limit on their own outside income potential. Indeed, many of the states that banned honoraria during this period were "category 3" states, meaning those with part-time, low-paying legislatures, as classified by the National Conference of State Legislatures. Among the states in that group that banned legislative honoraria during this period were Arkansas, Louisiana, Nevada, and West Virginia. These states all took strong action despite relatively low compensation, in the wake of major scandals involving legislators and other high-level state officials.[55]

In contrast to the previous period, the initiative process did not emerge as a strong predictor of new ethics laws. Certain states did use the initiative process during this period to enact new legislative ethics restrictions. California, Arkansas, and Florida are three examples. And in another state, Massachusetts, Common Cause used the threat of initiative to get ethics and campaign reform through the legislature. In 1994, using a similar strategy as in 1978, the organization dropped its proposed ballot initiative question to tighten campaign finance and ethics regulation after the legislature enacted campaign finance reform and banned gifts from lobbyists.[56] But the initiative was not a *statistically* significant factor, probably for the same reason that compensation was not significant: A large number of states experienced scandals big enough to propel ethics reform forward in state legislatures. Scandal clearly dwarfs all other explanatory variables in this period.

Although the regression analysis of this chapter cannot tell us about the impact of governors on the ethics reform process, there is some evidence that governors made legislative ethics reform a campaign issue in certain states during this period and that their attention to the issue facilitated the passage of new laws. Governor Mike Foster of Louisiana, for example, promised ethics and lobby law reform on the campaign trail in 1995. Foster called a special legislative session in March of the next year and succeeded in getting legislators to approve ethics law changes "that had been recommended for years." Perhaps most important, he won the legislature's approval for the merger of the separate ethics boards that oversaw the enforcement of legislative and executive branch ethics. The new board was given the power to launch its own investigations and to impose stiffer fines than either of the separate boards had possessed.[57] While Foster pushed hard for strong ethics reform, however, it appears that the driving factor behind legislators' willingness to enact new regulations was the FBI sting that surfaced in the summer of 1995.

In 1991, a gubernatorial election year in Kentucky, every candidate for governor was found "pushing some version of ethics and campaign reform."[58] But it was not until after the FBI probe became public in the closing days of the 1992 session that legislators became interested in enacting sweeping changes in the state's ethics laws. Thus it was not so much gubernatorial attention to the problem of legislative ethics as it was a legislative scandal of major proportions that lit the fire under smoldering reform efforts. Similarly, in Texas, Governor Ann Richards pushed for strong ethics reform in 1991. However, it was the scandal involving the House speaker's failure to report gifts from lobbyists that pushed legislators to strengthen the existing ethics statute in 1993.

By the end of 1996, the states collectively had much stronger legislative ethics laws on the books than they had in 1988, albeit with important loopholes, particularly with regard to gifts from lobbyists. Judging from the breadth and depth of the laws, it seems that the states were on a march forward to delineate legislative standards of conduct and restrict various activities. But stronger laws do not always go hand in hand with strong enforcement. The next chapter turns to the enforcement side of ethics regulation, again with an aim to explaining variation in states' policies.

five

The Mostly Toothless Tiger: The Authorization of Independent Ethics Commissions, 1973–96 and Beyond

The previous two chapters looked at variation in the content of state legislative ethics laws. However, strong laws and strong enforcement of good-government laws are often two different things. They do not necessarily go hand in hand. A state may enact a set of relatively stringent restrictions on legislative behavior. But without strong enforcement, the laws may end up having little impact.[1] This chapter focuses on variation in states' enforcement mechanisms. Just as states choose to enact strong or weak legislative ethics laws (or no laws at all), they also differ in how they enforce these laws. Most important, they can leave enforcement up to legislators themselves or grant authority over enforcement to an outside body.

All fifty states today except Colorado and Connecticut have permanent (standing) legislative ethics committees in one or both chambers to consider violations of the legislative rules and ethics statutes. In Colorado and Connecticut, the speaker of the House and the Senate president appoint a committee upon receipt of a complaint.[2] Some states have both an ethics committee within each chamber and also a joint committee to consider issues pertaining to the whole legislature. In conjunction with legislative ethics committees, some states also use the office of the attorney general or secretary of state to pursue allegations that the ethics laws have been violated. Some states also use independent commissions, bodies composed of individuals appointed by various political actors such as the governor or legislators but who are not themselves legislators.

The last form of enforcement, the independent commission, has received particular attention from political scientists. A manifestation of the Progressive legacy with its emphasis on creating neutral, objective bodies outside politics, the independent commission raises the same question that has been addressed in earlier chapters: Why do legislators support ethics policies that seem to go against their self-interest? As Thompson notes, the independent commission is perhaps the ethics policy that legislators are *most* resistant to adopting.[3]

For example, though New York legislators have put in place a relatively strong gift limit, a two-year postgovernment employment statute for legislators, and increasingly extensive financial disclosure requirements, they have for four decades resisted pressure from good-government reformers, the media, governors, and some of their own members to authorize an independent commission with jurisdiction over legislative ethics. Although there is an independent commission with jurisdiction over the executive branch, lawmakers have refused to relinquish autonomy to judge *legislators'* ethics violations to an outside body, keeping that authority instead firmly within the legislature itself.

In June 2003, New York's Republican governor George Pataki added his voice to the call for an independent commission to oversee legislative ethics, to replace the enforcement body created in 1987 that consists of four senators and four members of the Assembly. This body had not brought a complaint against a sitting member of the Legislature in six years. Pataki's call fell on deaf ears, however, even in the aftermath of the bribery conviction of a prominent Democratic assemblywoman and evidence that other legislators had received gifts from a contractor that did business with the state prison system.[4]

In other states, lawmakers have been willing to authorize independent commissions to oversee legislators' ethics. Twenty-six states had set up such commissions as of January 2004. Twenty-five of these were established before 1997; Illinois authorized its commission in late 2003. The adoption of these commissions, as suggested above, involves delegation of authority in a highly sensitive area for legislators. This delegation entails a host of well-known concerns centering on what is known as the "principal–agent problem," which results when one entity gives power to another entity to carry out certain tasks.[5] Most significantly, the creation of an independent commission entails uncertainty for legislators, the principals, over whether the commission, the agent, will carry out the principals' wishes, which in this case are for less strict enforcement of state ethics laws that many legislators are ambivalent about to begin with.

So why have some states authorized such commissions, knowing that the commissions may levy punishments more onerous than what they could expect from a legislative ethics committee composed of lawmakers themselves? The first half of this chapter addresses this question. Regression analysis is used to examine the influence of different factors on the authorization of commissions. The second half of the chapter turns to a consideration of the difficulties these commissions have faced in carrying out their mission. The focus is on two dimensions of commission strength: (1) independence from the legislature as measured by the method of appointment of commission members; and (2) advisory, investigative, and adjudicatory powers of the commissions. In the second section, I consider variation in the powers of the ethics commissions and the implications of the limits that have been placed on their powers. Before turning to the empirical evidence, however, it is worthwhile to lay out the normative argument that is often made in favor of the independent commission, in contrast to legislative ethics committees, as the means of enforcing legislative ethics laws.

The Argument for Independent Ethics Commissions

Scholars generally part ways with legislators in their preference for the independent ethics commission over other forms of ethics enforcement. Numerous academics and practitioners in the field of public ethics argue that ethics laws should be enforced by an independent commission composed of nonlegislators rather than by ethics committees composed of legislators themselves.[6] These analysts generally laud the decision of some states to authorize such commissions and lament the refusal of the U.S. Congress to do so. Congress has opted to keep regulation of legislative ethics solely within its own jurisdiction, eschewing calls from outside and inside the institution for an independent commission. The exception to this congressional avoidance of outside regulation is bribery law, which is generally part of the criminal code.

Dennis Thompson states the case for the independent commission succinctly in his discussion of congressional ethics:

> No matter how much the ethics committees are strengthened and their procedures improved, the institutional conflict of interest inherent in members judging members remains. Most other professions and most

other institutions have come to appreciate that self-regulation of ethics is not adequate and have accepted at least a modest measure of outside discipline. Congress should do the same.[7]

Stern suggests that the verdicts of an independent commission have more credibility with the public and the press, and that commissions with the power and willingness to impose fines will serve as a strong deterrent to unethical behavior.[8] Although some state legislative ethics committees have the power to impose fines, they tend to do so very infrequently. The reason why is simple, stated clearly in the words of a legislator (and former chair of the New Jersey legislative ethics committee) himself: "A lot of legislators believe they are appointed to these ethics committees to protect their own. I'm sure many legislators think 'I might be in that situation someday myself' and take it easy on their fellow lawmakers."[9]

The existence of an independent commission, argues Thompson, should provide greater accountability and "help restore the confidence of the public in the ethics process," a claim echoed by Weber. An additional advantage, Thompson suggests, would be the reduction of the time that members now spend on ethics regulation, leaving them more time to spend making public policy. It is worth noting, however, that Thompson's proposal for an independent national legislative ethics commission is actually *weaker* than the model adopted by some of the states since 1973; indeed, his proposal is actually for a "semi-independent" commission composed of seven "distinguished citizens with a knowledge of legislative ethics and (legislative) practice."[10] The main difference between his proposed commission and those that exist in many states is the method of appointment. The majority leader or speaker and the minority leader of each chamber would each choose three members of Thompson's commission; the chair would be appointed by the other six. Though some states allow legislators to select all or most of the members of independent commissions, others do not, as demonstrated later in the chapter.

There is another way in which the states have gone beyond Thompson's proposal. Thompson suggests that a semi-independent commission should take over the advisory and educational functions of the current ethics committees, but that it should not have full investigative and decision-making power. It would investigate charges against members to determine whether substantial, credible evidence exists that a member has violated the chamber's ethics rules, but the committees would still make the final judgment and recommendation to the full chamber.

By contrast, in the states that have authorized independent commissions, the commissions generally conduct an initial investigation *and* make a final decision. Though legislative ethics committees in these states also conduct their own investigations and render decisions side-by-side with the commissions, they do not have the sole authority to decide whether a member has violated the state's ethics laws. There is an overlap of authority, with the commissions providing a critical alternative mechanism to the ethics committees in terms of investigating and punishing alleged ethics violations.

Explaining the Authorization of Independent Commissions

As suggested above, the states rather than the federal government were the pioneers of a new ethics enforcement mechanism to oversee legislators.[11] Louisiana was the first state to authorize an independent commission in 1964. Twenty-five states followed suit in the aftermath of Watergate, and many also set up campaign finance commissions with jurisdiction over legislators. Prior to Watergate, some states—such as Connecticut, Indiana, Iowa, Maine, and New York—had established standing legislative ethics committees to enforce their new conflict-of-interest laws. Watergate sparked the establishment of independent commissions in some states as a stronger mechanism of overseeing political ethics.

Although some of these new commissions were granted jurisdiction over legislators, a number of states authorized ethics commissions to oversee executive branch ethics only. Examples are Indiana (1974), South Carolina (1976), Maryland (1979), and New York (1987), as well as Illinois, Michigan, North Carolina, and Ohio. These executive branch commissions were, like the legislative committees, pioneered by the states rather than the federal government, which did not establish the Office of Government Ethics until 1978.[12] Thus the authorization of state ethics commissions was not simply an imitation of federal policy.

This section focuses on the decision of twenty-two states to authorize independent commissions with jurisdiction over *legislative* ethics during the period 1973–96. Sidebar 5.1 shows the states that authorized independent commissions and the years of authorization. An independent commission is defined as a body whose members are all nonlegislators, although some may be *appointed* by legislators.[13] Only commissions that have jurisdiction over legislators' standards of conduct are counted. I do not count commissions with authority only over legislators' financial disclosure because agencies without the power to look into allegations of unethical conduct, beyond the failure to file disclosure forms, tend to be

---

Sidebar 5.1   The Establishment of Independent Legislative Ethics Commissions, 1973–96

1973	Alabama, Wisconsin
1974	California[a] (by initiative), Kansas, Oregon
1975	Maine, Michigan[b] (both by initiative)
1976	Florida (by initiative)
1977	Connecticut, Nevada
1978	Massachusetts, Pennsylvania
1979	Mississippi
1983	Texas
1986	Oklahoma, Rhode Island
1989	West Virginia
1990	Arkansas (by initiative)
1991	Missouri
1993	Kentucky
1994	Minnesota
1995	Montana

Note: Hawaii, Louisiana, and Nebraska all have independent legislative ethics commissions but are not included in the data set used here. Illinois established an independent commission with jurisdiction over legislators' ethics in 2003.

[a]California legislators took away this commission's jurisdiction over legislative ethics in 1996.

[b]Declared unconstitutional.

Sources: Council on Governmental Ethics Laws 1990, 1993; Council of State Governments 1996; and state conflict-of-interest statutes.

---

bodies with very limited power.[14] Monitoring of financial disclosure is a more routine, less intrusive form of ethical control than monitoring of legislators' standard of conduct; thus it does not fit the description of a strong form of ethics enforcement. Because the question of interest is why states choose strong enforcement mechanisms, I do not include commissions that only monitor legislators' financial disclosure. However, if a commission had jurisdiction over *both* legislators' ethics and financial disclosure, it is included.[15]

The outcome we want to explain, or the dependent variable, is the decision to authorize or not authorize a commission. Multiple regression analysis is used to explore how this decision was influenced by various factors.[16] The same factors that were considered in chapters 3 and 4 are considered here as well: (1) party competition, (2) ideology / political culture, (3) policy diffusion, (4) scandal/corruption, (5) economic self-interest, (6) direct democracy, and (7) policy legacies. Appendix F provides details on measurement and data sources for the independent variables (and the model used).

In addition, I consider three additional theories that address the particularities of administrative enforcement. As suggested at the beginning of this chapter, enactment of strong laws and enactment of strong enforcement mechanisms are not necessarily the same thing. Additional factors come into play in terms of policymakers' decisions about what type of enforcement mechanism to use. Opheim, looking at the stringency of state lobby laws and the stringency of enforcement, suggests that while there are similarities, there are also some differences.[17] In particular, it is relevant to know whether or not the state can afford, and has the capacity to manage, an independent commission, and how such a commission would affect the balance of power between the legislative and executive branches. These concerns can be thought of as "bureaucratic factors," in contrast to ideological, cultural, electoral, or other factors.

State Wealth

First, the level of state wealth may affect the choice of enforcement mechanism. Ethics commissions cost tax dollars; thus their most obvious cost is a financial one. Setting up a new bureaucracy and paying for staff and office space is not free. Though the budgets of ethics agencies are typically small, the fact that some costs are involved may deter poorer states from using this method of ethics enforcement.[18] It is cheaper to delegate ethics enforcement to existing agencies such as the attorney general or secretary of state, or to the state legislature's ethics committees.

Although there are financial costs associated with these alternative enforcement mechanisms, they tend to be lower than if an entirely new agency were created. Legislators who staff the ethics committees and those who staff the attorney general's or secretary of state's office do not generally receive additional payment for their work. Similarly, when attorneys general or secretaries of state are given responsibility for the enforcement of legislative ethics laws, some of the costs are typically subsumed under the existing budget. Also, these alternative mechanisms entail fewer start-up costs than establishing a new agency.

Wealthier states are therefore expected to be more likely to authorize independent commissions, just as they tend to spend more money on costly policies in areas such as education and welfare.[19] This is especially the case with regard to programs that states fund largely without federal assistance; enforcement of state ethics laws is one such area.

Bureaucratic History

The history of a state's bureaucratic development may also affect its decision about whether or not to authorize a commission. A lack of bureaucratic development can hinder institutional formation in later years, both because of bureaucratic start-up costs and the lack of institutional advocates.[20] Thus, states with a less developed bureaucratic-institutional base (more limited technical and intellectual capacities) on which to build may be less likely to choose a bureaucratic solution to the problem of ethics enforcement, relying instead on legislative ethics committees.

Legislative–Executive Relations

Finally, the decision about commission establishment may also be influenced by the existing balance of power between the legislative and executive branches. State legislators view the governor as their main competitor for power. Governors have important formal powers that enable them to take a leadership role in the policy process.[21] These include appointment, budgetary, and veto powers. I hypothesize that in states where governors have greater formal powers, legislators will be wary of enacting policies that would further increase the power imbalance between the two branches. More precisely, the governor typically has some appointive control over independent commissions, and legislators in states with powerful governors may be more concerned about further increasing the chief executive's power. States with relatively weak governors may be more willing to delegate some new appointment authority to the chief executive.

A summary of the regression results is presented in sidebar 5.2, which highlights the factors that are statistically significant, when controlling for other factors. The full regression results are presented in table G.1 of appendix G. Table G.2 in appendix G provides a quantitative interpretation of the impact of the significant variables, known as "mean effects."

The regression results suggest that ethics commission establishment is explained by some of the same factors that explain variation in the content of ethics laws. In addition, one factor specific to the dynamics of delegation to administrative agencies played a role. The most influential variable, measured by the mean effects, was the scandal variable. The probability of a state with the maximum scandal score (15) authorizing a

Sidebar 5.2   Key Influences on the Establishment of Independent Ethics Commissions, 1973–96
Scandal Actions by other states Political culture Governors' powers History of corruption
Source: Regression results of table G.1 in appendix G. Factors listed are those that are statistically significant, controlling for other factors.

commission was 71.84 percentage points higher than the probability for a state with a scandal score of 0. Put another way, the likelihood that a state with no scandal in the previous two years would authorize a commission was only one-tenth of 1 percent, whereas the likelihood for a state with the maximum cumulative scandal score for the previous two years was 71.94 percent.

As with the passage of ethics laws between 1977 and 1996, many of the scandals that led to commission authorization resulted from federal prosecutors using the mail fraud statute, the Travel Act, and other federal laws to pursue corrupt state officials. Chapter 4 detailed how federal and local prosecutors worked together with the Federal Bureau of Investigation and local law enforcement agencies to conduct legislative sting operations. Two examples of sting operations that led to ethics commission establishment occurred in Kentucky in 1992, where fifteen legislators were convicted on bribery charges, and in West Virginia in 1989, where the current and former Senate presidents were implicated on bribery charges. In Massachusetts, as discussed in chapter 2, the 1977 convictions of the Senate majority leader and assistant minority whip on extortion charges led legislators to authorize an ethics commission in 1978, a proposal that had languished in committee for six years.

However, the link between scandals and commission authorization was not automatic. Every scandal did not lead to the establishment of an independent commission. For example, although the sting operation that targeted the South Carolina legislature in the early 1990s resulted in the indictment of seventeen current and former legislators, the state still failed to authorize such a commission. However, lawmakers there did enact other legislative ethics laws, such as a ban on honoraria and an expansion of the existing gift limit. This same pattern, where legislative scandals led to some reform, but not to commission establishment, also occurred in Arizona, New Mexico, and Tennessee.

Other states that experienced numerous scandals involving legislators and other state officials during the study period—such as Illinois, New Jersey, and New York—also failed to authorize legislative ethics commissions. Thus, though scandals made commission authorization much more likely, they did not make it inevitable. As shown in previous chapters, scandals are best conceived of as a powerful resource that can be used by ethics reformers to help set the agenda for the enactment of new ethics policies, but not as a resource powerful enough to assure their passage.

The actions of neighboring states also influenced a state's chances of establishing a commission. The estimated probability of a state establishing a commission if it had four neighbors that had already done so (the maximum number in the data set) was 1.59 percentage points greater than that of a state with no neighbors that had established one. Though the effect of regional diffusion considered by itself was small, in combination with some other key independent variables its impact was more substantial. For example, a state with four neighbors with commissions and the maximum scandal score was 97.09 percentage points more likely to authorize a commission than one with the minimum values of these two variables. This pattern of regional diffusion suggests a similarity between ethics policy and other policies such as the adoption of state lotteries and tax policy, welfare, and abortion policies.[22]

Traditionalistic political culture also influenced the likelihood of commission authorization, though the impact was small. A traditionalistic state was one-fourth of 1 percentage point more likely to authorize a commission than a nontraditionalistic state. Though political culture mattered here, as it did in the analysis of previous chapters, it is important to note that the impact of traditionalist culture was not consistent over time. For example, while traditionalistic states were *more* likely to adopt ethics codes, they were less likely to authorize independent commissions. It may be that independent commissions represent a greater loss of power for legislators compared with the simple enactment of a basic code, which as noted in chapter 3 may be very vague and of limited practical impact. By contrast, authorizing an independent commission involves a greater threat to legislators' political and economic power, something that legislators in traditionalistic cultures may be more resistant to doing.

The likelihood of commission authorization was also shaped by the extent of the governor's powers. States with more powerful governors were marginally less likely to establish a new administrative agency over which the chief executive would likely exert some appointive power. Among the states with relatively powerful chief executives were Colorado, Illinois, New York, Ohio, Utah, and Washington (see appendix F for details on the measurement of gubernatorial power). Legislators apparently viewed the establishment of independent commission in part through the lens of its potential impact on legislative–executive power relations. Lawmakers in such states may have been highly attuned to the balance of legislative–executive power and hence less willing to do something that could shift power even further in the governor's favor.

Even if a commission were established over which legislators retained complete appointment power, it would still represent a reduction in legislators' power, compared with using a legislative ethics committee as the sole enforcement mechanism, because the commission members would be nonlegislators. In states where legislators were already relatively weak compared with their main competitor for power, it makes sense that they would be less willing to accede to a further diminution of their autonomy, particularly in an area as sensitive as ethics.

This dynamic was played out in the case study of New York in chapter 2. The *New York Times* account of the ethics reform battle that took place in 1987 suggests that it was fundamentally a power struggle between the two branches, which had manifested itself on other issues. Faced with a governor whom they saw as overreaching his already substantial powers, legislative leaders banded together to oppose his proposal for an independent commission to monitor their ethics, and they prevailed.

The one unexpected finding was that states with more ongoing political corruption or a long-term tendency to corruption were *less* likely to authorize commissions. This contrasts with the positive impact of this factor in the analysis chapters 3 and 4. The mean effect, however, is small, under 1 percentage point (see table G.2 in appendix G).[23]

Contrary to the common wisdom, having an initiative process did not make commission authorization more likely. Though political reform advocates used the initiative to enact term limits and campaign finance reform during the 1990s, they apparently did not make similar use of the initiative with regard to ethics laws. Four states did use the initiative to authorize commissions (see sidebar 5.1), and the initiative played an indirect role in the decision of at least one other state—Massachusetts—to establish a commission. But for the remaining seventeen states in the data set that authorized commissions, it did not appear to play a significant role.

It is also notable that higher legislative compensation did not make states more likely to authorize independent commissions. Several of the states that paid the highest legislative salaries during this period—for example, Illinois, New York, and Ohio—declined to establish independent commissions. Higher legislative pay did not make states more willing to adopt stronger ethics enforcement mechanisms, even if it did facilitate stronger laws in the pre-Watergate years. When this fact is combined with the results of chapter 4, there were clearly limits to which higher compensation could facilitate strong ethics policy.

Controlling Commissions by Appointing the Members

As suggested above, when legislators delegate power to an agency, a principal–agent problem arises in that the legislature, the principal, has given over authority to an agent who may fail to carry out the principal's wishes. Legislatures, like other principals, do not simply relinquish control and hope for the best, especially where the new agency has jurisdiction over an area so close to their own interests. Lawmakers want to make sure that unelected bureaucrats comply with their policy preferences.[24]

Legislators use various means to assure that agencies carry out the desired policies, including budgetary control, oversight, and appointments. Of these, perhaps the most effective means of influence is control over appointments. It is therefore important to know who appoints members and what the criteria for appointment are. For example, the federal Equal Employment Opportunity Commission has been more or less aggressive in carrying out its mandate to combat discrimination depending on whom the president has chosen to head the agency. Similarly, the National Labor Relations Board has been more prolabor or promanagement, depending on whom the president appointed to head it.[25] With regard to state ethics commissions, legislators themselves often play an important role in appointing, not just confirming, members.

Table 5.1 shows the range in legislative control over appointments to the independent ethics commissions that were established between 1973 and 1996.[26] Specifically, it shows the percentage of commission members appointed by legislators in each state that had a commission as of 1996. A lower percentage indicates greater independence from the legislature in appointments. In some states, such as Massachusetts, Missouri, and Wisconsin, legislators did not appoint any of the commission members. In those states, the governor appointed every member. By contrast, in Alabama and Kentucky, legislators appointed every member. For the Illinois commission established in November 2003, legislators also appoint

Table 5.1   Legislative Appointments
to Independent Commissions, 1996

State	Total Appointments (%)	No. of Appointments
West Virginia	0.00	0 of 12
Nevada	0.00	0 of 8
Minnesota	0.00	0 of 6
Missouri	0.00	0 of 6
Wisconsin	0.00	0 of 6
Hawaii	0.00	0 of 5
Massachusetts	0.00	0 of 5
California[a]	0.00	0 of 5
Louisiana	0.00	0 of 5
Montana	0.00	0 of 1
Nebraska	22.22	2 of 9
Mississippi	25.00	2 of 8
Arkansas	40.00	2 of 5
Florida	44.44	4 of 9
Texas	44.44	4 of 9
Rhode Island	55.55	5 of 9
Pennsylvania	57.14	4 of 7
Connecticut	57.14	4 of 7
Oregon	57.14	4 of 7
Oklahoma	66.66	6 of 9
Kansas	80.00	4 of 5
Maine	85.70	6 of 7
Alabama	100.00	5 of 5
Kentucky[b]	100.00	9 of 9

Note: Appointments made by the governor from lists submitted by key legislators (e.g., the speaker) are counted as legislative appointments.

[a]California legislators removed its jurisdiction over legislative ethics in 1996.

[b]The nine members were originally appointed by the governor from lists submitted by nonlegislative state officials (e.g., the attorney general and auditor). In 1996, the legislature changed the appointment process. Members are now appointed by the Senate president, the House speaker, and the joint leadership of the legislature.

Sources: State statutes, commission websites, and commission staff.

all the members. The other commissions fell in between these extremes, with legislators appointing some members and governors or other nonlegislators appointing the rest.[27]

Table 5.1 suggests several things about the independent commissions. First, only ten of the twenty-four commissions were fully independent from the legislature in terms of who appointed their members. In another five states, nonlegislators appointed a greater percentage of commission members than did legislators, so there was some significant degree of independence. For the remaining nine commissions, legislators appointed over 50 percent of the members, compromising the commissions' independence.

Thus slightly over one-third of the commissions were clearly stacked in favor of legislators with regard to member appointments. As suggested above, Kentucky and Alabama were at one extreme, with legislators appointing all members. In Kansas and Maine, legislators appointed all but one member. The Oklahoma commission, though powerful in other ways (e.g., its power to promulgate regulations and levy heavy fines), was also stacked strongly toward the legislature in terms of appointments, with only three of nine members being appointed by nonlegislators. In Pennsylvania, Connecticut, and Oregon, legislators had a one-member edge over the governor, appointing four of seven members. In Florida and Texas, the one-member edge was reversed, with legislators appointing four of nine.

The overall picture that emerges is that a majority of commissions were at least nominally independent, if one uses the method of appointment as the primary measure. Fifteen of the twenty-four had members appointed primarily by nonlegislators. In only two cases did legislators retain full authority over appointments. However, the method of appointment is only one way of gauging the strength of the commissions. We turn now to a second measure, statutory powers of the commissions.

Doing the Job: Powers of the Commissions

Appointments and budgetary control are important ways that legislators control the behavior of regulatory agencies. Another way is through the formal tools that are given to or denied to the agencies. McCubbins, Noll, and Weingast refer to "deck-stacking" in terms of how an agency is initially structured and how its procedures empower or disempower both the agency and its various constituencies.[28]

One way to assess how the deck is stacked is to examine the powers the agency is given. Sidebar 5.3 shows the investigative and adjudicatory powers of the independent commissions that were in place as of 1996. These powers—to conduct hearings, subpoena witnesses and documents, levy fines, request prosecution, and file court actions independently—all bolster a commission's ability to carry out the mission of enforcing the

---

Sidebar 5.3. Powers of the Independent Commissions, 1996

5 powers: California,[a] Kentucky, Massachusetts, Montana, Nebraska, Nevada, Pennsylvania, Wisconsin

4 powers: Arkansas, Connecticut, Kansas, Maine, Minnesota, Mississippi, Oklahoma, West Virginia

3 powers: Alabama, Florida, Hawaii, Louisiana, Missouri, Oregon, Rhode Island, Texas

Note: Each state received one point for each of the following powers that its ethics commission could possess: (1) can conduct administrative hearings, (2) can impose fines/penalties, (3) can subpoena records and witnesses, (4) can request prosecution on a discretionary basis, and (5) can file court actions independently.

[a] California legislators removed its jurisdiction over legislative ethics in 1996.

Sources: Public Integrity Annual (Council of State Governments 1996), state statutes, and commission websites.

---

states' legislative ethics laws. If these powers are lacking, the deck is stacked against the commission being able to carry out its mission.

Sidebar 5.3 shows that the twenty-four commissions in place as of 1996 were split equally among those with all five powers, those with four of the five powers, and those with only three powers. To the extent that all these powers are essential to a strong commission, only one-third of the commissions in place as of 1996 can be considered strong (and one of the "strong" eight, California, no longer has jurisdiction over legislative ethics). Thus, in terms of powers, there was significant room for improvement among the commissions.

We can combine powers and independence to yield a single measure of commission strength. Sidebar 5.4 shows this combined measure. Commissions with no appointments made by legislators and full (all five) powers were given a score of 1, or "strong." If legislators appointed fewer than 50 percent of commission members and the commission fell in the high or middle range for commission powers (4 or 5), the commission was assigned a score of 2, or "moderately strong." The rest were given a score of 3, or "weak."

This combined measure of commission strength suggests that only five of the twenty-four commissions considered fit into the "strong" category, and of these, one (California) no longer has jurisdiction over leg-

---

Sidebar 5.4   Commission Strength: Independence and Powers Combined, 1996

Strong Commissions (score of 1)
California,[a] Massachusetts, Montana, Nevada, Wisconsin

Moderately Strong Commissions (score of 2)
Arkansas, Minnesota, Mississippi, Nebraska, West Virginia

Weak Commissions (score of 3)
Alabama, Connecticut, Florida, Hawaii, Kansas, Kentucky, Louisiana, Maine, Missouri, Oklahoma, Oregon, Pennsylvania, Rhode Island, Texas

[a]Since 1996, California's ethics commission has not had jurisdiction over legislators.
Sources: Table 5.1 and sidebar 5.3.

---

islative ethics. Five were moderately strong, while fourteen (over 50 percent of all commissions) were categorized as "weak" because they fell short on one of the two dimensions of strength, independence or powers, or both.

Other Difficulties Faced by the Commissions

In addition to authorizing many commissions that were weak to begin with, as a general rule legislators have further weakened these commissions over time, rather than strengthening them. For example, in 1989 West Virginia established an independent ethics commission with jurisdiction over legislators, but a year later, legislators took away its power to initiate investigations in the absence of a sworn complaint.[29]

Kentucky, where the Legislative Ethics Commission was created in 1993 to oversee legislators only, is another example of this gradual weakening. In its first annual report, the commission reported that it had conducted eighteen investigations, fourteen instigated by the commission itself, a record that former commission director Earl Mackey said sent a "clear message to legislators, lobbyists, and the public that the commission intended to enforce the law." Two years later, during the next legislative session, lawmakers retaliated against the commission, taking "deadly aim at [its] independence." The commission's power to initiate investigations was rescinded, and legislative leaders also gave themselves more control over the appointment of commission members. The authorizing legislation had required legislative leaders to appoint members from lists submitted by selected state officials, but a new law put the power to appoint all the members solely in the hands of the legislative leadership, with no outside input. These actions sparked a round of resignations from the commission. Today the commission is much less active, both with regard to investigating alleged ethics violations and in issuing advisory opinions. The conclusion of former commission director Mackey is that active commissions quickly come under attack by legislators, and it is hard to sustain public interest in strong ethics enforcement after the initial shock of a scandal has subsided.[30]

Another example of a commission that has been weakened over time is Rhode Island, where the State Ethics Commission was established in 1986. As in Kentucky, a once-strong commission's decline can be traced to assertive action against legislators. In 1996, the commission voted to ban legislators from holding seats on boards and commissions that control many state agencies. Lawmakers responded by attacking the commission, according to former commission director Richard Morsilli, using their power to put forward nominees for committee members. Though the governor appoints the nine members, five must be chosen from lists submitted by the Senate president, Senate minority leader, House speaker, House majority leader, and House minority leader. These lawmakers decided to "load the commission up with . . . well-connected lawyers" who had close ties to lobbyists. Another former commission director, Sarah Quinn, suggests that members in recent years have been chosen by the leadership "by design to gut the effectiveness of the agency."

In 2000, the lobbyist-friendly Rhode Island commission voted 5–4 to repeal the state ban on gifts from lobbyists to legislators and other public officials. The change allowed lobbyists to give up to $450 per year to each legislator in meals, liquor, sports tickets, golf outings, and other things of value. One of the commission members voting to repeal the gift ban and replace it with the $450 annual limit was the brother of the former Senate minority leader and a prominent State House lobbyist. As of February 2004, the commission had not initiated any conflict-of-interest complaints against a public official in over five years, though it had pursued a number of complaints from citizens. Though weakened in certain ways, the commission has still shown some teeth with regard to legislative ethics—for example, fining a state legislator $10,000 in January 2004 for voting on a contract from which his law firm would benefit.[31]

In 1991, in retaliation for strong action against several lawmakers and lobbyists, the Connecticut legislature took away the Ethics Commission's authority to render a final decision in an enforcement action. Similarly, the Hawaii Ethics Commission's willingness to fine legislators for violating state conflict-of-interest laws led to the introduction in 1996 of two bills, one to prevent the commission from issuing advisory opinions and another to increase the number of commission members appointed by the legislature.[32] In some states, such as Pennsylvania, the process of sunset review has been used to threaten the state ethics commission with extinction.

In addition to controlling the commissions through appointments and the limitation of commission powers, legislators have also attempted to exert control through the courts. In virtually all states where independent commissions have been established, legislators have mounted challenges to their constitutionality both before and after authorization. The challenges have been made on several bases: that the commissions violated the constitutional power granted to the legislature to determine its own rules and punish members, that they violated the right to trial by jury, and that they impinged on the constitutional separation of powers.[33] In other cases, ballot questions asking voters to establish independent commissions have been challenged on technical grounds, for example, having to do with question wording. These legal challenges have rarely succeeded, however.[34]

In general, state courts have upheld the establishment of independent commissions with the power to monitor legislators' ethics. Michigan is the one exception. Constitutional challenges have generally failed because states that authorized these agencies at the same time kept in place their permanent legislative ethics committees (or if they did not already have them, authorized them). Thus the legislature retained the power to discipline its own members. The commissions therefore serve as enforcement bodies in conjunction with, rather than instead of, legislative ethics committees. Thus the constitutional issue of the legislature's right to judge and punish its members becomes moot.

Beyond legal challenges to the commissions' basic right to exist, there have also been numerous court challenges regarding the scope of the commissions' jurisdiction and powers. The Oklahoma and Rhode Island ethics commissions are unique in that they were given the power to promulgate ethics rules on their own. In Oklahoma, the legislature and governor must approve the rules, but in Rhode Island this additional step is unnecessary. Both commissions, however, have faced numerous court challenges by legislators regarding the scope of their powers. For example, in 1992, the governor and legislative leadership in Rhode Island initiated a lawsuit challenging the commission's power to write ethics rules. In June 1992, the Rhode Island Supreme Court ruled that the Ethics Commission had the constitutional authority not only to enforce but also to promulgate a code of ethics.[35] In other court battles, however, independent commissions did not fare so well. In 1986, for example, attorneys for the Massachusetts legislature argued before the State Supreme Court that the Ethics Commission was overstepping its statutory authority by enforcing certain parts of the state conflict-of-interest law. In this case, legislators won their court battle.[36]

In other states, the main method of emasculating the commissions has been through the legislature's power of the purse. The Texas Ethics Commission, established in 1983, was not funded at all for four years. In Oregon, after the Government Ethics Commission investigated a state senator in the 1990s, a bill was introduced (by the same senator) to abolish the commission. Although that bill failed, the Oregon legislature cut the commission's budget by 25 percent, and it also restricted its ability to conduct investigations. Another bill, which did not pass, would have abolished the commission entirely and transferred its functions to the secretary of state and attorney general. The Massachusetts Ethics Commission has also suffered retaliatory budgetary action for its willingness to levy serious fines against state legislators. After the commission fined several legislators in 1992, including the Senate president, its budget was promptly slashed. Two years later, in 1994, House Speaker Charles Flaherty, under investigation by the commission, sponsored a bill to transfer the commission's adjudicatory powers to the Division of Administrative Law, limit its investigative powers, and strip the commission of its authority to issue subpoenas.[37] This bill did not pass, however.

In most states with independent commissions, bills have been introduced to eliminate the commission at one time or another, as in the Oregon case mentioned above. In most states, these bills do not go far. For example, in Nebraska a recent proposal to eliminate the Accountability and Disclosure Commission never made it out of committee. In Alabama in 1990, a proposal to eliminate the State Ethics Commission did come to a vote in the State Senate, but it failed 18–10, with seven members abstaining.[38] In California in 1996, legislators succeeded in stripping the Fair Political Practices Commission of its jurisdiction over legislative ethics, leaving the joint legislative ethics committee as the sole possessor of that authority. This unusual action followed the commission's decision to fine a former state senator $15,000 for failure to disclose his sources of income and some loans.

In rare cases, the ethics commissions have actually been strengthened over time. Rhode Island's commission was first established in 1976 with jurisdiction over financial disclosure only. Ethics jurisdiction was added in 1986, and the commission was further strengthened in 1992, when it gained the power to levy increased fines for ethics violations. Today, it can impose fines of up to $25,000. Florida's commission was also granted an increase in the maximum fine it could levy, from $5,000 to $10,000. The Arkansas Ethics Commission, established by initiative in 1991, did not originally have the power to administer fines or other sanctions, but it was granted those powers in 1995. And in Texas, in April 2003 the House Ethics Committee passed a bill making it easier for the state Ethics Commission to take action, by eliminating the requirement that the commission needs at least six members to initiate an investigation. Advocates continue to try to bolster commissions in their states. For example, in January 2004, reformist legislators in Connecticut, allied with the state attorney general, secretary of state, and public interest groups, were attempting to strengthen the state's ethics commission by increasing its maximum fine from $2,000 to $5,000.[39]

However, though some commissions have been strengthened in certain respects, as a general rule the commissions have found themselves under constant threat by legislators in terms of their budgets, their authority to conduct investigations, and their ability to punish violators. Legislative action toward the commissions, as suggested above, is generally nonsupportive and often downright hostile.

The Principals Retain Control over Their Agents

The creation of independent ethics commissions applied the Progressive era innovation of the independent regulatory commission to the area of political ethics. The impetus of Watergate, combined with state-level scandals and policy diffusion, helped stimulate roughly half the states to authorize commissions between 1973 and 1996. Since then, one more state, Illinois, has authorized an independent commission. But consistent with theories of legislative control, legislators have not simply abdicated authority to the new commissions. Instead, lawmakers have exercised various means of control and deck stacking, using their budgetary power, appointment authority, legal challenges, and amending legislation that circumscribes the authority of these commissions beyond the initial limits placed on their operation.

Where commissions have taken strong action against legislators, as in California, Connecticut, Massachusetts, and Oregon, legislators have responded quickly and firmly to maintain control. They have done so by reducing the commissions' budgets and powers or even, in rare instances, by eliminating their jurisdiction over legislators, as in California. Thus though state legislators have been willing to create these commissions under certain circumstances, they have retained a fairly tight rein on their discretion. The commissions are not nearly as powerful as they might be.

six

Ethical Self-Regulation
and Its Limitations

Between 1954 and 1996, the American states made important strides in the regulation of legislative ethics. In some cases they preceded—and in others they went beyond—the federal government, for example, with regard to financial disclosure, gift bans, and the authorization of independent ethics commissions. This book has outlined how these efforts to regulate legislative conflicts of interest came about, and why some states have enacted stronger ethics laws than others. In particular, it has emphasized how the ethics reform process is an externally driven one. Political actors and institutions outside the legislature such as federal prosecutors, the media, public interest groups, and governors play a critical role in bringing the issue of legislative ethics to the center of the policy agenda. They have a major influence on the timing and content of new laws. Though certain features internal to legislatures, such as members' positions in the institutional hierarchy and the level of compensation, influenced legislators' support for ethics reform, the primary factors that moved the reform process forward were external.

Like other policies, legislative ethics policy is characterized by "partial equilibria" that are upset by changes in the attention of governmental elites.[1] One important difference, however, is that the equilibrium state tends to persist for longer periods of time in the case of ethics policy than other policy areas. Change comes infrequently and nonincrementally. When it does come, it often resembles a "big bang" involving the addition of numerous regulations that appear to significantly circumscribe allowable behavior.

Yet below the surface appearance of comprehensive and strong ethics laws, there are important limits on the extent to which legislators are willing to self-regulate in the domain of conflict-of-interest law. Substantive restrictions that on their face appear strict generally have important exemptions and gaps that blunt their impact. Thus whereas legislators are willing under certain circumstances to enact ethics measures that challenge the perks of power and their economic self-interest, they do so in a constrained manner. They balance their perception of a need for new regulations, on the one hand, against a host of other interests and concerns, on the other: their desire to retain individual political power and the freedom to pursue economically beneficial activities, their wish to maintain the legislative institution as an attractive place to serve, and their drive to protect the collective autonomy of the legislature to set and enforce standards of conduct. Because many lawmakers are dubious about the very concept of regulating ethics through law, they do not adopt in full the proposals of outside reformers.

Modern ethics laws thus reflect both the desires of outside reform advocates such as Common Cause and the assessments of legislators themselves about what sorts of limits on behavior are acceptable. The loopholes that lawmakers build into the laws they enact are an important part of the puzzle "Why do legislators self-regulate in the area of ethics?" This book has called attention not only to the "why," or the circumstances under which they do so, but also to the "how," or the *manner* in which they do so. Legislators design conflict-of-interest laws in a way that is attentive to their own political and economic interests. Thus they enact laws that do not go too far in restricting outside activities and requiring disclosure of such activities, and they oppose powerful and unfettered enforcement.

In sum—as with civil service reform in the nineteenth and twentieth centuries and campaign finance reform in the late twentieth century—ethics laws are shaped and delimited by the institutional power-holders whose interests they most directly affect.[2] Thus, to understand the content of ethics and other political reform measures, specifically why they often seem partial and incomplete, we must focus on the interests and fears of the power-holders who draft the laws and whose interests are challenged by them.

Agenda Setting and the Electoral Incentive

This account of state legislative ethics reform from 1954 to 1996 has emphasized an agenda-setting process in which scandals catalyzed reform by affecting the policy agenda. Conflict-of-interest scandals, especially those involving legislative leaders or a large number of legislators, served as "rapid-onset" or "focusing" events that catapulted the issue of legislative ethics to the top of the media agenda, whereas before it had languished on the periphery. As Kingdon argues, scandals "reinforce some preexisting perception of a problem, focus[ing] attention on a problem that was already 'in the back of people's minds.'" Ethics policy in a sense is always "in the back of people's minds," because concern about political corruption is a constant in American politics. The challenge is bringing it to the forefront of the policy agenda. Baumgartner and Jones's portrait of the influence of media attention on policymaking fits nicely with the case of modern ethics reform: "Media attention tends to follow a pattern of either feast or famine. Important political questions are often ignored for years, but during certain periods almost every general media outlet features similar stories prominently. . . . Each time there is a surge of media interest in a given topic, we can expect some degree of policy change."[3]

The sustained barrage of media coverage typical of the major scandals highlighted in this book creates pressures on lawmakers to enact new ethics laws. In New York, for example, legislators agreed to enact Governor Mario Cuomo's ethics package in 1987, only a year after Senate leaders had adamantly refused to support similar legislation. The intervening variable that made the difference was a major scandal that implicated numerous lawmakers in a scheme to defraud the public by placing no-show employees on the payroll. From the time the first story on the scandal broke in October 1986 to the passage of Cuomo's reform package in July 1987, the *New York Times* ran twenty-four stories about the scandal and ten editorials supporting ethics reform.[4] This media attention (and note that we are only considering the attention of one media outlet among many) put legislators under tremendous pressure to support reform out of a fear of potential electoral retaliation by voters and a sense that the reputation of the legislative institution was suffering.

In addition to having a direct influence on elites (policymakers), the media agenda can also have an *indirect* impact by influencing the public, which then leads to elite action. We do not know the extent to which citizens become increasingly concerned with legislative ethics due to the various scandals that occur. Good-government groups often argue that new ethics laws are necessary because of public outcry and citizen demand. For example, the head of the Illinois Campaign for Political Reform commented that the new ethics law was passed in November 2003 in the aftermath of corruption charges against Illinois governor George Ryan because "people were really fed up. They were sick of it (corruption). It became an issue that couldn't be dodged anymore."[5]

There are few if any data, however, to tell us what the public really thought about that particular scandal. But in a sense it does not matter whether the claim about public outrage leading to reform is true. What matters is that policymakers acted as if they believed there was some latent public outrage to which they needed to respond, and that if they did not pass new ethics laws soon, voters might one day hold it against them. Even inattentive and unorganized publics can have an influence if policymakers believe that their failure to act on a problem may have negative electoral consequences at some unspecified point in the future.[6] In 1965, as described in chapter 3, a significant number of New York lawmakers responded to the media publicity that followed their votes against an early version of ethics reform by switching to support in a later vote. These legislators could not know which citizens were paying attention or how many of them, if any, cared. Yet they responded as if they thought that at least *some* voters knew and cared, and they took action in part to put an end to the ongoing and negative media attention.

Voting against ethics reform is a potentially "wrong" and costly choice from the perspective of the rational, forward-looking legislator concerned about the electoral implications of his actions. In contrast to other policies, voters tend to be more uniform in their preferences about clean government. They generally prefer more rather than less regulation of the influence of special interests and potential conflicts of interest.[7] Ethics policy (and how legislators vote on it) is a nontechnical issue that is relatively easy for voters to assess, and it is one that can easily be used by political opponents in a campaign due to the politicization of ethics charges.[8] Thus the electoral incentive, and concerns about the overall image of the legislature—for example, in the wake of stings in California, Kentucky, or South Carolina—led legislators to take action on ethics in many instances. But there are clear limits to this legislative self-regulation.

Limits to Reform

Media attention to the problem of legislative ethics and lawmakers' responsiveness to scandal coverage does not mean that legislators enact wholesale the reform proposals of Common Cause, Public Citizen, and newspaper editors. Because ethics laws threaten the economic and political interests of legislators, and because many lawmakers find them demeaning and nit-picky, they tend to enact them only when compelled to do so. Even then, they do so in a bounded fashion, building in loopholes and gaps that allow them substantial latitude to supplement their official salaries, to protect their privacy, and to maintain control over their own standards of conduct.

A recent example of this boundedness is the 2003 ethics law enacted in Illinois, which has been touted as a major step forward by ethics-in-government advocates. The law contains what is referred to as a "gift ban," but the ban includes exemptions for up to $75 in meals per day and for items worth under $100. Further, although the new ethics commission established by the law has jurisdiction over legislators, closer examination shows that all the members are to be appointed by the legislative leadership, which severely compromises the agency's "independent" status.[9]

Even in cases where states enacted relatively strong ethics laws, the final reform packages that emerged from the bargaining between legislators and governors, and from the pressure of the media and public interest groups, generally involved important concessions to lawmakers. In New York, for example, legislators ultimately rejected Governor Cuomo's proposal for an independent legislative ethics commission. In Michigan in 1994, a legislative scandal led to the regulation of honoraria and other new ethics restrictions, but legislators refused to accept Common Cause's proposals for financial disclosure and an independent commission. In Massachusetts and New York, where legislators enacted limits on lawyer-legislators, they held the line on disclosure of client names. This exemption for client names also applies in many states to the financial disclosure of members' sources of income.

Further, the seventeen states that banned representation before state agencies between 1954 and 1996—on its face a tough restriction—generally exempted numerous agencies from their bans. In sixteen states during the same period, legislators only went part of the way in terms of limiting representation, requiring the disclosure of representation rather than placing a substantive limit on the practice. Similarly, only nineteen states banned honoraria between 1954 and 1996, whereas an additional seven placed a cap on the amount of honoraria allowed. As of 2002, four additional states had banned honoraria.[10] Thus in 2002, fewer than half the states had honoraria bans similar to the one enacted by the U.S. House and Senate in 1989 and 1991, respectively. In this regard, the states have lagged behind the federal government.

The limitations of legislative ethics laws also show up in restrictions on gifts. For example, gift limits often exempt travel that is paid for by lobbyists. In general, lobbyists have significantly more leeway in entertaining lawmakers out of state than they do inside state boundaries. Thus a 2003 newspaper editorial in Maryland blasted state cable lobbyist Bruce Bereano, who had hired a 103-foot clipper to take Maryland lawmakers

around San Francisco Bay, calling the trip a "cruise on the *SS Loophole*."
When lobbyists entertain legislators inside Maryland, the invitation must
be extended to the full General Assembly, a particular committee, or a
recognized delegation, rather than individual legislators. However, when
lawmakers are out of state, lobbyists are free to choose individual members to entertain.[11] The media increasingly scrutinizes such out-of-state
jaunts because they make for good news copy, and thus legislators have
become increasingly cautious about participating in them. Still, the fact
that such activities are exempt from state law is a significant loophole.

Postgovernment employment statutes are also limited in their scope.
In 2002, twenty-seven states had revolving door statutes limiting legislators from becoming lobbyists after leaving office. Of those twenty-seven,
six had two-year limits, nineteen had one-year limits, one had a six-month
ban, and one had a limit until the end of the conclusion of the session after
a member left office.[12]

Perhaps most important, independent ethics commissions, promoted
as a tough form of ethics enforcement by advocates, are kept on a tight
rein by legislators through their powers of appointment and appropria-
tions and through strict delineation of commission powers. Just as the Federal Election Commission was designed to be a "toothless tiger," state
ethics commissions have been hobbled by their initial design and the
ongoing hostility of legislators.[13]

Explaining Ethics Reform Success

This book has suggested that several factors contributed to the success of
ethics reform. Between 1954 and 1996, the most consistent factor in
explaining the enactment of ethics restrictions and the authorization of
independent ethics commissions was scandals involving legislators and
other high-level state officials. The reforms enacted, however, were not
always—and not only—direct responses to the unethical behavior highlighted by the particular scandals that they followed.

In many states, the new laws addressed a wide range of behavior, going
beyond the specific activities involved in a given scandal. For example, federal prosecution of state legislators on bribery, mail fraud, and other
charges led to the passage of laws banning honoraria and gifts, to postgovernment and representation employment limits, and to mandatory
financial disclosure. The sting operations in Kentucky, South Carolina, and

other states that exposed legislators taking bribes could have led simply to stronger bribery laws. Instead, they catalyzed a broad range of conflict-of-interest laws that became part of the civil, not criminal, statutes. There are parallels in this regard to Watergate. As Calvin Mackenzie and Michael Hafkin suggest, "Watergate was about burglary, cover-ups, lying, and campaign irregularities. [Yet] nothing in the Ethics in Government Act [passed in its wake] would have added new deterrents to, or punishments for, those behaviors."[14] As with Watergate, reformers seized the opportunity presented by scandal to push for a variety of new restrictions.

In emphasizing the role of scandal, this book has argued that scandals should not be seen merely as isolated instances of misbehavior by public officials. Rather, they arise out of a broader political context. The nature of scandal has changed over the years, and the government itself plays an increasingly important role in the scandal production process. In the pre-Watergate years, scandals often came out of state investigations into the link between politicians and organized crime figures. These investigations were in turn a response to the national spotlight shone on organized crime by a U.S. Senate investigating committee in the early 1950s.

In the post-Watergate years, an important development was the targeting of corrupt state officials, especially legislators, by federal prosecutors. In response to Watergate, a new Public Integrity Section was set up within the Department of Justice in 1976 and was given the mission of fighting corruption at all levels of government. At times working with the Federal Bureau of Investigation, these federal prosecutors were responsible for many highly publicized indictments and convictions of legislators, governors, and other statewide officials during this period. Without this shift in federal priorities and federal resources to fighting corruption at lower levels of government, we would not have seen as many scandals, which often resulted in new ethics laws.

The scandals that sparked ethics reform in many states thus had an important institutional origin: the restructuring of federal prosecutorial capacities. The increase in federal prosecutions of state and local officials after the 1970s did not necessarily mean, however, that public officials became more corrupt in this period. Instead, the hand of federal prosecutors pursuing their own agenda, and using new legal tools, weighed heavily in the production of the scandals.

The scandal-driven nature of the ethics reform process is problematic.[15] Perhaps the most powerful criticism of scandal-motivated reform is that laws enacted in response to scandal are often not well thought out, not narrowly tailored to existing problems, and lacking in deep support from legislators themselves. Scrambling to respond to media criticism, legislators enact laws that many are highly skeptical about. Only later, when the barrage of media criticism has subsided, do they try to correct what many perceived of as excesses to begin with. In January 2003, for example, the Iowa House Ethics Committee was working on rewriting the state law restricting gifts from lobbyists to legislators, enacted in 1994 in the wake of a scandal involving the former Senate president and his ties to a state investment fund. The law prohibited lawmakers from accepting gifts of $3 or more. One representative told reporters that it was absurd and insulting to argue that a legislator can be influenced by a meal or drink, and that the law had stifled social life at the State House. "It's got to be changed," said Representative John Connors (D–Des Moines).[16]

In linking scandal to ethics reform, the media plays a critical and controversial role. This role goes beyond simply reporting prosecutions by law enforcement authorities as they occur. The media also engages in investigative reporting that sometimes results in the pursuit of ethics charges against legislators and other public officials, and that often puts pressure on lawmakers to enact new ethics laws because it portrays them and other public officials in a negative, sleazy light. In the California case study, the *Los Angeles Times* conducted its own investigative report on conflicts of interest in the legislature. Supporters of ethics reform used the information revealed in this special section to bolster their claim that new laws were needed.

The print media has also made frequent use of editorial pages to advocate for new ethics laws. Journalists generally take the side of reform advocates, although they do not always line up neatly on the side of public interest groups. For example, in the Massachusetts case study, the *Boston Globe* criticized Common Cause's petition as flawed and inserted itself firmly into the legislative debate on the side of a Senate bill it felt was fairer. The *Globe*'s criticism appeared to have influenced both Common Cause and lawmakers to accept certain changes.

In New York in 1965, as described above, after the *New York Times* "outed" legislators who voted against an early version of ethics reform, some switched to support the bill. However, though lawmakers ultimately enacted representation limits and financial disclosure, they held firm in their opposition to an independent ethics commission. They also put a significant exemption in for representation before the State Court of Claims, before which many lawmakers appeared in their capacity as private-sector attorneys. Thus the interaction between the media and legislators was complex. Journalists had some influence on the content of reform, but their influence was limited in important ways by legislators' own assessments of what reforms were acceptable.

Besides scandal, other factors played a limited role in the ethics reform process. However, unlike scandal, these factors were not significant in all the periods examined, which suggests that their impact was not as consistent or central as that of scandal, which played a role across all time periods and for all types of ethics reform considered. Increased legislative compensation had a positive impact on reform success in two of the three case studies. And it appeared to be significant in the regression analysis of change in ethics laws prior to Watergate, where it was associated with a greater willingness of legislators to enact basic ethics codes and substantive restrictions such as gift and representation limits. Beyond this, however, the effect of increasing legislators' salaries was limited. In the post-Watergate period, increasing compensation was not important in facilitating the passage of new ethics laws. Strong laws were enacted in its absence in many cases, and strong enforcement mechanisms were also enacted in states with low compensation.

Thus the link between higher compensation and ethics reform that has been found at the national level and in isolated state cases does not appear to hold over time and across states. One reason may be that most state legislatures pay low salaries and the increases that do occur are generally not sufficient to induce a trade-off between higher pay and outside income limits. It is illuminating that the California case study involved a substantial pay raise (166 percent). The 33 percent increase in New York that secondary-source accounts linked to reform success in 1987 was also significant. But in many states, salaries are low to begin with and increase only slightly over time in real terms, if at all. Due to statutory and cultural barriers that reinforce the notion of a "citizen" legislature, legislators' salaries in many states are stuck at a low level. Many states actually saw a drop in real compensation in the last period considered. But though many states were actually "deprofessionalizing" between 1989 and 1996 in terms of their legislative compensation, thirty-two of them still enacted new ethics laws. Where scandals were big enough, as in Arizona, Kentucky, or South Carolina, some type of reform resulted regardless of the level of legislative salaries.

Overall, then, the strategy of linking higher salaries to ethics reform at the state level—as has been done frequently at the national level—does not appear to be an option that has been exercised much, nor is there reason to expect it to be exercised much in the future. California in 1990 was an isolated recent example, in which limits on honoraria were again tied explicitly to a pay raise. However, this is the exception to the rule.

Ideology was another factor that did not have a strong or consistent effect on variation in states' ethics reform efforts. At the level of the individual lawmaker, liberal ideology is associated with greater support for legislative ethics reform.[17] At the aggregate, cross-state level, it helped to explain the passage of basic ethics codes in the pre-Watergate period. But beyond that, in the other periods, it had no significant impact. Thus, though liberal ideology helps to explain how members vote once ethics reform is on the policy agenda, it does not explain how it *gets* on the agenda. Instead, external factors are key—such as scandals, the actions of other states, and gubernatorial attention.

Political culture had an inconsistent influence on the passage of ethics laws. States with individualistic cultures were, as expected, less likely to enact ethics laws before Watergate, and were less likely to enact strong new ethics regulations in the final post-Watergate period examined here. Traditionalistic states were also less likely to authorize independent commissions, as expected. But traditionalistic states were actually *more* likely to be early innovators in enacting basic codes, contrary to expectations. Thus though political culture mattered, it did not matter in a straightforward way consistent with the expectations stemming from Elazar's typology. Culture seemed to come into play not so much as a belief system in the minds of citizens and elites but primarily to the extent that moralistic beliefs were translated into organizational form—namely, into state chapters of Common Cause, which waged a concrete battle for new ethics laws.

One similarity between modern ethics reform and earlier political reform movements is the role played by outside public interest groups. In this book, I have highlighted the role played by Common Cause, the group with the most active and sustained interest in good-government reform. Common Cause did not achieve much success in the absence of scandals that propelled the issue of legislative ethics to the front of the agenda. But in the aftermath of scandal, it worked effectively with sympathetic legislators and with the media to build support for reform, taking advantage of the window of opportunity presented by scandal.

In the tradition of Progressive era groups such as the National Civil Service Reform League (NCSRL), Common Cause relies on publicity and education and uses the media as a key ally to build support for clean government legislation. However, the group has relied less on electoral tactics, such as endorsing or even running candidates, than do groups such as the NCSRL. This is most likely due to the fact that these tactics were more effective in the earlier era of intense party competition.

Common Cause has also made strategic use of the initiative process, particularly in the aftermath of scandals, to win passage of new ethics laws in several states. However, the initiative process was only statistically significant in explaining change in the 1977–88 period, and in some isolated cases where states authorized independent commissions by initiative. Where scandals were big enough, the initiative was not necessary to compel legislators to act. Where they were absent, the initiative was generally not sufficient to compel them to act. Thus the initiative did not have a strong independent impact on ethics reform success.

The influence of Common Cause on state legislative ethics regulation is evident when we compare the text of the group's model ethics law and the conflict-of-interest statutes that have been enacted since 1972. Common Cause clearly sets the standard that state policymakers have followed in crafting their ethics laws. Still, as the Massachusetts case study showed, Common Cause does not dictate the details of reform to legislators, who put the brakes on proposals they consider too intrusive and excessive.

Another outside group that has had an influence on the content of state ethics laws is the Council on Governmental Ethics Laws (COGEL), a nonprofit organization that provides information on government ethics. COGEL disseminates a model ethics law that is very similar to that of Common Cause, and it also sponsors annual ethics education seminars for legislators. Its role is more one of informational resource or information clearinghouse, however, not that of an active participant in the reform process.

In contrast to studies of political reform during the Progressive era and other earlier periods of American history, the research described here did not find party competition to have a strong impact on the passage of modern ethics laws. In general, party competition neither facilitated nor hindered the passage of new ethics laws. Again, where big enough scandals occurred, factors such as party competition or increasing compensation were not necessary to spur legislators to act on ethics reform. They were essentially irrelevant, because reform generally passed by unanimous or near-unanimous votes.

Although the centrality of scandal to ethics policymaking makes it somewhat distinctive, one important similarity between ethics policy and other policy areas did emerge. This is the role of policy diffusion among the states, which has been found to occur in areas such as education, tax policy, and state lotteries. Specifically, basic ethics codes were found to diffuse among neighboring states in the pre-Watergate period, and independent commissions diffused among neighboring states in the post-Watergate period. Thus whereas ethics policy is different from other policy areas in certain ways, it is not *that* different to the extent that it follows some familiar diffusion patterns. There is also evidence that diffusion occurred in a more complex way as well, with states copying other non-neighboring states' ethics laws, for example on representation limits.

With regard to the role of elite policymakers, the position of power-wielding legislators—such as House speakers, Senate presidents, and committee chairs—was not always straightforward, consistent with prior research.[18] In some cases, institutional power-holders worked to block or water down strong reform proposals, but they did not do so universally. For example, California Assembly speaker Jesse Unruh was a vocal proponent of California's pioneering ethics law of 1966. However, his interest in ethics reform appears to have been secondary to his interest in legislative modernization and in strengthening the Legislature in its competition with the executive branch. Thus the support of legislative leaders for ethics reform is contextual, depending in part on perceived electoral and political gains. While their tendency is to oppose ethics reform, this response is not purely automatic and can vary depending on the circumstances.

Governors were also found to be active proponents of ethics reform in two of the three case studies—California and New York—where they used the bully pulpit to promote new ethics laws both in their campaigns and in office. In the other states discussed in later chapters, such as Texas in the early 1990s or Louisiana in 1996, governors played a similar and important role in lobbying for stronger versions of ethics reform than many legislators wanted. More recently, in June 2003, Democratic governor Rod Blagojevich of Illinois used the amendatory veto to tighten up loopholes in an ethics reform bill passed by lawmakers. Their version had allowed public officials and state workers to accept unlimited golf and tennis perks from special interests. The governor eliminated this loophole and put a $75 limit on gifts from each lobbyist per day.[19]

Enforcement remains the biggest challenge for ethics reform advocates. Even states with strong ethics laws (laws that contain many substantive restrictions on behavior) often lack strong enforcement. For example, neither New York nor South Carolina has an independent ethics commission with jurisdiction over legislators. Further, many nominally independent commissions lack all the tools that are necessary to do the job, such as the power to subpoena witnesses and documents. This book has highlighted how legislators use a variety of means, ranging from the power of the purse to legal action to the threat of dissolution, to manage the principal–agent problem that is inherent in creating independent commissions. Again, the puzzle of why legislators self-regulate in the area of ethics is best understood by paying close attention to the *how* as well as the why, in this case how ethics laws and their enforcement are delimited and constrained by the lawmakers who enact them.

Implications for the Future

The general trend in state legislative ethics regulation has been a forward march since New York enacted the first general conflict-of-interest law in 1954. Most states continue to tighten their ethics laws over time, although a few—such as South Dakota, Vermont, and Wyoming—still have basically blank slates in regulating legislative conflicts of interest beyond bribery statutes.

As at the federal level, however, there has been some backlash against ethics laws in the states, and resistance by legislators to new regulations.[20] In Rhode Island, for example, a gift ban was repealed in 2000. In Maryland in January 2004, the General Assembly continued to resist five years of pressure by the state Common Cause chapter to enact a bill placing its members' financial disclosure forms online. The aim of this proposal, according to Common Cause, is to make it easier for those who want to obtain that information but now have to visit the legislative ethics committee offices and sign in. Legislators can also request to be notified whenever their records are pulled, which advocates say has a "chilling effect on the public's access to public records." One lawmaker, John Arnick (D–Baltimore County) explained his opposition to the Common Cause proposal, "I don't want (my information) out there for every kook to read."[21] Even in the wake of recent scandals involving revelations of lobbyist influence on Maryland legislators, lawmakers were holding the line with regard to this particular ethics reform proposal, citing their interest in maintaining some degree of privacy.

Despite this resistance to expanding the scope of existing ethics laws, some states do continue to add new restrictions for legislators and to fill in gaps in their existing laws. Since 1996, many states have added new laws of the type detailed in this book. For example, as noted above, four additional states have banned honoraria, and five additional states have instituted a revolving door limit for legislators who want to become lobbyists.[22]

What does the future hold? Most likely, it will see continuation of the forward march to enact new laws, but also continuing debate over whether existing laws go too far in certain respects. Although it is important to pay attention to the enactment of new laws, it is also essential to be aware of less-publicized changes that loosen the restrictions of existing law. And as this book suggests, when evaluating new ethics laws that appear strong on the surface—and are touted as such by credit-claiming legislators, governors, and good-government advocates—we must look closely at the fine print of those laws to see what loopholes they contain.

Future research will have to sort out the effects of these laws and whether they have had beneficial or harmful effects, for example, on the recruitment and retention of legislators, on public trust, and on other aspects of American democracy. The limits of even the strongest laws detailed here suggest that the practical impact of the laws—both good and bad—may be minimal. The laws may be largely symbolic, serving primarily as evidence that legislators are doing *something* about corruption, even if that something is of limited practical consequence.

Conversely, some recent research suggests that there are important costs to ethics reform. For example, ethics laws seem to deter some individuals from pursuing public service, in both the legislative and executive branches.[23] If these are otherwise qualified individuals who could make a valuable contribution to public life, this must be counted in some sense as a cost. More broadly, typical conflict-of-interest laws aim low in their expectations. Dennis Thompson refers to them as "minimalist," and indeed they are in that their primary focus is on setting minimal standards for what legislators should *not* do.[24] Although this is a valuable and necessary undertaking, it also leaves a lot unsaid about the types of action and leadership to which public servants should aspire. Thus ironically, though lawmakers often complain that ethics laws go too far, in a certain sense they do not go very far at all. Their very existence can generate the illusion that legislators and the public do not need to think further about the issue of political ethics, for example, about qualities such as political courage or integrity more broadly conceived.

On the positive side, the existence of ethics laws forces legislators to be sensitive to situations and to think about potential conflicts of interest in ways they might not otherwise do. Most states offer some form of "ethics training" for state legislators. More than forty states include ethics training in their new-member orientation programs, while nine offer "continuing education" programs. Though the majority of these programs simply include instruction on ethics statutes and rules, some states go further and provide a forum for discussion of general ethical principles. At least eleven states in 2002 had programs that incorporated "principle-based discussions" on topics such as honesty, integrity, and value conflicts. In some states, such ethics programs are voluntary. In thirteen states in 2002, it was a statutory mandate that legislators attend such programs. In some states, these training efforts are conducted by ethics commissions; in others, the legislature itself conducts the sessions. An increasing number of states are also providing ethics training for legislative staff members, lobbyists, and other public officials.[25]

In addition to examining how ethics laws affect legislative recruitment and retention, and legislative behavior more generally, future research might apply the theories advanced in this book about why legislators self-regulate in the arena of ethics policy to other issues on which legislators display a lack of enthusiasm about acting. For example, the push for federal campaign finance reform received a major boost from the Enron scandal, which helped force the issue to the front of the congressional agenda.

At the state level, we can test more systematically whether scandals, regional diffusion, and other factors shown to be important to the passage of ethics laws have also been important catalysts for campaign finance reform. And if scandals matter, do the reforms respond directly to the issues raised by the scandals? Or, as this book suggests, do they go beyond those issues? In other words, are there common patterns in the process and outcomes of self-regulatory legislation more broadly conceived?

Other types of laws that legislators are generally loath to enact include limits on their own salaries, the elimination of official perks (e.g., free haircuts for members of Congress), and sunshine laws. Why then have such laws been enacted at various times, against the apparent self-interest of legislators? The agenda-setting process, with its modification of legislators' self-interest calculus, may help to explain policymaking in these areas as well.

The findings of this book also suggest that researchers need to look closely at the loopholes and limits of self-regulatory legislation. It is clear that legislators do enact such laws under certain circumstances. But they do so in a way that is sensitive to their own concerns and interests. Most centrally, these include concerns about institutional maintenance, privacy, economic well-being, and political power.

Many lawmakers remain deeply skeptical about the very concept of ethics laws, finding them offensive and insulting. Legislators are also highly aware of the fact that good-government laws can have unintended consequences. For example, the Federal Elections Campaign Act fueled the growth of special interest groups in the form of political action committees, and partisan prosecutors and politicians have used ethics laws as weapons of attack. Thus although ethics reform is primarily an externally driven process, it is necessary to pay close attention to the perspective of those who are both doing the regulating and being regulated: the legislators themselves. It is through their interests and concerns that ethics reform is channeled.

appendix A

Appendix to Chapter 1 and General Appendix for 1996 Ethics Index

The index used in table 1.1 in chapter 1 measures the stringency of state legislative ethics laws as of 1996, based on six categories of legislative ethics restrictions. This appendix explains in detail how the index was constructed, and it shows the breakdown of scores by category for each state. In selecting the categories that make up the index, I relied on both scholarly and nonacademic discussions of state legislative ethics laws. Scholarly sources include Goodman, Holp, and Rademacher 1993; Rosenthal 1996; and Zimmerman 1994. Nonscholarly sources include the key groups that have provided information and/or advocacy on legislative ethics over the past thirty years, including the Council of State Governments, the Council on Governmental Ethics Laws, and Common Cause (see the references section for full citations). I chose the categories that have been emphasized by scholars and nonacademic analysts as important components of ethics regulation. The categories therefore reflect the types of restrictions believed to be important by those concerned with defining and promoting ethical legislative behavior.

Four of the six categories represent substantive restrictions on the activities of legislators: (1) limits on legislators receiving honoraria (fees for speechmaking); (2) limits on legislators receiving gifts that might influence their official action, votes, or judgment; (3) limits on representation by lawyer-legislators of clients before state agencies; and (4) limits on the postgovernment employment of legislators as lobbyists ("revolving door" restrictions). The fifth category—personal financial disclosure—is a keystone of state and federal ethics-in-government laws. The sixth category is a "baseline" category that measures whether the state has an ethics code for legislators in its statutes or its legislative rulebook.

States were given scores ranging from a possible 0 to 11 points for the stringency of their legislative ethics restrictions. They could get two points in each of five categories and one point in the sixth, baseline category. In looking at each state's laws, I consulted the index under "conflict of interest," "ethics," "financial disclosure," "legislature," and "public employees/ officials." In some states, ethics laws are part of the criminal codes, so I also looked under the section of the codes containing statutes on bribery and official misconduct. For some states, legislative ethics restrictions were concentrated in one section of the statutes. For others, they were spread out across several different sections. Some states also had ethics restrictions in their legislative rules, so I used each state's legislative rulebooks. Finally, I also relied on the *Public Integrity Annual* (Council of State Governments 1996) to confirm the information found in the statutes and rules. The breakdown of points given to states by category is as follows.

Ethics code: States received 1 point if they had a code of ethics in their statutes or legislative rules. A code of ethics need not include any substantive restrictions such as prohibitions on receiving gifts or honoraria. It only requires a general statement of purpose or general principles of ethical conduct.

Honoraria: A state received 0 points if it had no limit at all, 1 point if it had a numerical limit or limited honoraria to a "reasonable" or "customary" amount, and 2 points if it banned honoraria for legislators. States that scored 2 in 1996 included Arkansas, California, and Pennsylvania.

Gifts: A state received 0 points if it did not limit legislators in the receipt of gifts from lobbyists and others based on any understanding that their vote, official action, or judgment would be influenced; 1 point if it required disclosure of gifts; 1.5 points if it had a numerical limit on gifts (e.g., no gifts worth over $100 each) or limited the receipt of gifts of "substantial value"; and 2 points if it had a "no cup of coffee" law banning legislators from taking anything of value from lobbyists or legislative agents, or otherwise said legislators shall not take anything of value with no numerical or "substantial value." Qualifier language varies greatly in this category, so a state was coded according to which of the four subcategories it fit into most closely. States that scored 2 in 1996 included Kentucky, Minnesota, and Wisconsin.

Postgovernment employment / revolving door limit: A state received 0 points if it did not place any restrictions on legislators working as lobbyists after they leave office; 1 point if there was a one-year "revolving door" restriction for legislators; and 2 points if there was a two-year restriction. States that scored 2 in 1996 included Kentucky, Massachusetts, and New York.

Representation by lawyer-legislators before state agencies: A state received 0 points if it did not substantively limit lawyer-legislators in their appearances before state agencies; 1 point if it required lawyers-legislators to disclose the clients they represent before state agencies; and 2 points if it restricted appearances by lawyer-legislators before any state agencies. States that scored 2 points in 1996 included Alabama, Massachusetts, and New York.

Personal financial disclosure: Public Integrity Annual (Council of State Governments 1996) provides information on the fifty states' personal financial disclosure (PFD) requirements at the end of 1995. State codes were used to supplement this information for 1996. In scoring states for PFD, I considered nineteen possible areas in which legislators could be required to disclose information (two of those catalogued by *Public Integrity Annual* were excluded because they overlap with other categories in the index). The nineteen were tax returns, sources of personal income, investments, sources of income of business of a partner or shareholder, ownership interest in a business, real estate interests, offices and/or directorships held, creditor indebtedness, leases or other contracts with state entities, retainers, professional/occupational licenses held, reimbursement of travel expenses from private sources, deposits in financial institutions, cash surrender value of insurance, private employer or nature of private employment, professional services rendered, identification of trusts by trustee, identification of trusts by beneficiary, names of immediate family members, and financial interests of spouse.

A state received 0 points if it had no financial disclosure requirements; 1 point if it required disclosure in four areas or fewer; 1.5 points if it required disclosure in five to nine areas; and 2 points if it required legislators to disclose information in ten areas or more. States scoring 2 points in 1996 included California, Illinois, and New York. The state with the highest score was Ohio, which had nineteen requirements as of 1996.

Here are the statute sources for each state as of 1996:

(1) Alabama: *Ala. Code* § 36-25-1 to § 36-25-27 (Alabama Code of Ethics for Public Officials).

(2) Arizona: *Arizona Rev. Stat. Ann.* § 38-3-501 to § 38-3-543 (Arizona Conduct of Office, Arizona Standards for Financial Disclosure).

(3) Arkansas: *Ark. Stat. Ann.* § 21-8-101 to § 21-8-903 (Arkansas Ethics and Conflict of Interest).

(4) California: *Cal. Government Code* § 2-2-8920 to § 2-2-8926, § 2-2-8940 to § 2-2-9955, § 9-7-86201 to § 9-7-86205, § 9-7-87100 to § 9-7-87504 (California Political Reform Act, Regulations of the Fair Political Practices Commission).

(5) Colorado: *Colo. Rev. Stat.* § 24-18-101 to §24-18-113 (Colorado Code of Ethics).

(6) Connecticut: *Conn. Gen. Stat.* § 1-10-80 to § 1-10-91, § 2-16a (Connecticut Code of Ethics).

(7) Delaware: *Delaware Code Ann. Tit.* § 29-10-1002 to § 29-10-1004, § 29-10-5812 to § 29-10-5815 (Laws Regulating the Conduct of Officers, Legislative Conflicts of Interest).

(8) Florida: *Fla. Stat. Ann.* § 10-112-311 to § 10-112-324, § 10-112-3135 to § 10-112-3151 (Code of Ethics for Public Officers and Employees).

(9) Georgia: *Ga. Code* § 45-10-1 to § 45-10-28, § 21-5-1 to § 21-5-11, § 21-5-50 (Georgia Ethics in Government Act).

(10) Idaho: *Idaho Code* § 59-6-701 to § 59-6-705, § 18-381-1352 to § 18-381-1360 (Ethics in Government, Gifts to Public Servants by Person Subject to their Jurisdiction).

(11) Illinois: *Illinois Rev. Stat.* Ch. 5 § 420/1 to 5 § 420/4, § 720-645/01 to § 720-645/2 (Illinois Governmental Ethics Act, State Gift Ban Act).

(12) Indiana: *Ind. Code* § 2-2.1-3-1 to 2-2.1-3-7 (Legislative Ethics).

(13) Iowa: *Iowa Code* § 2-68B.1 to § 2-68B.7, § 2-68B21 to § 2-68B35.A (Iowa Public Officials Act).

(14) Kansas: *Kan. Stat. Ann.* § 75-43-4301 to § 75-43-4306, § 46-2-201 to § 46-2-263 (State Governmental Ethics).

(15) Kentucky: *Ky. Rev. Stat.* § 45A.340, § 45A.990, § 6.601 to § 6.849 (Code of Legislative Ethics).

(16) Louisiana: *La. Rev. Stat.* § 42:1101 to § 42:1121 (Code of Governmental Ethics).

(17) Massachusetts: *Mass. Gen. Laws Ann.* § 268A§1 to § 268A§23, § 268B§1 to § 268B§8 (Conflict of Interest Law for Public Officers and Public Employees, Financial Disclosure Laws).

(18) Maine: *Me. Rev. Stat. Ann.* § 1-25.1002 to § 1-25.1020 (Governmental Ethics).

(19) Maryland: *Md. State Government Code Ann.*, § 15-101 to § 15-904 (Maryland Public Ethics Law).

(20) Michigan: *Michigan Comp. Laws* § 15.301 to § 15.342c (Conflict of Interest Act, Standards of Conduct for Public Officers and Employees).

(21) Minnesota: *Minn. Stat.* § 10A.01 to § 10A.10 (Ethics in Government).

(22) Mississippi: *Miss. Code. Ann.* § 25-4-1 to § 25-4-31, § 25-4-101 to § 25-4-119 (Ethics in Government).

(23) Missouri: *Mo. Rev. Stat.* § 8.105.450 to § 8.105.485, § 8.105.955 to § 8.105.961 (Public Officers and Employees: Ethics Laws).

(24) Montana: *Mont. Code. Ann.* § 2-2-101 to § 2-2-304, § 13-37-101 to § 13-37-131, § 45-7-104 (Code of Ethics).

(25) Nebraska: *Neb. Rev. Stat.* § 49-1404 to § 49-14,126, § 49-1401 to § 49-14,133 (Political Accountability and Disclosure Act).

(26) Nevada: *Nev. Rev. Stat.* § 281.411 to § 281.625 (Ethics in Government Law).

(27) New Hampshire: *N.H. Rev. Stat. Ann.* § 15-A:1 to § 15-A:3, § 15-B:1 to § 15-B:6 (Ethics Guidelines).

(28) New Jersey: *N.J. Rev. Stat.* § 52:13D-12 to § 52:13D-25 (New Jersey Conflicts of Interest Law).

(29) New Mexico: *N.M. Stat. Ann.* § 10-16-1 to § 10-16-18 (Governmental Conduct).

(30) New York: *New York Public Officers Law* § 73, § 74 (Public Officers Law).

(31) North Carolina: *N.C. Gen. Stat.* § 120-85 to § 120-105, § 14-234.1 to § 14-247 (Code of Legislative Ethics).

(32) North Dakota: *North Dakota Criminal Code* § 12.1-13-01 to § 12.1-13-02, § 2C:27-6.

(33) Ohio: *Ohio Rev. Code Ann.* § 101.01 to § 101.99 (Ohio Ethics Law).

(34) Oklahoma: *Oklahoma Statutory Laws* § 74.4222 to § 74.4248 (Constitutional Ethics Rules).

(35) Oregon: *Or. Rev. Stat.* § 244.010 to § 244.390 (Government Standards and Practices).

(36) Pennsylvania: *Pa. Const. Stat. tit.* § 46.143.1 to § 43.145.8, § 65§401 to § 65§413 (Legislative Code of Ethics, Conflicts of Interest).

(37) Rhode Island: *R.I. Gen. Laws* § 36-14-1 to § 36-14-21 (Code of Ethics in Government and Regulations).

(38) South Carolina: *S.C. Code Ann.* § 8-13-100 to § 8-13-1130 (Ethics, Government Accountability and Campaign Reform).

(39) South Dakota: *S.D. Codified Laws Ann.* § 3-1A-1 to § 3-1A-6.

(40) Tennessee: *Tenn. Code Ann.* § 2-10-116 to § 2-10-505, § 3-6-108 to § 3-6-110 (Financial Disclosures, Lobbying).

(41) Texas: *Texas Government Code Ann.* § 110A-6252-9, § 5-553.001 to § 5-553.023, § 5-571.001 to § 5-571.137, § 5-572.001 to § 5-572.058 (Texas Ethics Commission, Personal Financial Disclosure, Standards of Conduct and Conflict of Interest).

(42) Utah: *Utah Code Ann.* § 67-16-1 to § 67-16-14 (Public Officers' and Employees Ethics Act).

(43) Vermont: None.

(44) Virginia: *Va. Code* § 2.1-639.1 to § 2.1-639.61 (The General Assembly Conflicts of Interest Act).

(45) Washington: *Washington Rev. Code* § 42.17.240 to § 42.17.400, § 42.20.010 to 42.20.090, § 42.22.010 to § 42.22.120 (Ethics in Public Service, State Legislative Ethics Board Rules).

(46) West Virginia: *W. Va. Code* § 6B-1-1 to § 6B-2-10 (Governmental Ethics Act).

(47) Wisconsin: *Wis. Stat.* § 19.41 to § 19.58 (Code of Ethics for Public Officers and Employees).

(48) Wyoming: None.

Individual State Scores and Years of Passage of Ethics Laws

Below are the total scores for each state (excluding Alaska and Hawaii), and also a breakdown of the scores for the six different categories of ethics restrictions. The following abbreviations are used for the different categories: BC = basic ethics code, HL = honoraria limit, GL = gift limit, PGE = postgovernment employment limit, RL = representation limit, and PFD = personal financial disclosure. The year that the restriction was established by law or by legislative rule is also included in the second row for each state. In some cases, more than one year may be included for a given category—for example, in the case of Alabama, the state first passed financial disclosure requirements in 1973 and then strengthened them in 1995.

(1) Alabama = 8.0

	BC	HL	GL	PGE	RL	PFD
Score	1	0	1	2	2	2
Year passed	'73		'73	'95	'73	'73, '95

(2) Arizona = 5.0

	BC	HL	GL	PGE	RL	PFD
Score	1	0	1	1	0	2
Year passed	'67		'74	'92		'67,'74

(3) Arkansas = 8.0

	BC	HL	GL	PGE	RL	PFD
Score	1	2	1	0	2	2
Year passed	'71	'90	'88		'71, '88	'71, '88

(4) California = 9.5

	BC	HL	GL	PGE	RL	PFD
Score	1	2	1.5	1	2	2
Year passed	'66	'90	'66	'90	'66	'74, '82

(5) Colorado = 4.0

	BC	HL	GL	PGE	RL	PFD
Score	1	0	1	0	0	2
Year passed	'71, '88		'88			'72, '85

Note: Colorado's basic code was first enacted in 1971, repealed in 1977, and enacted again in 1988.

(6) Connecticut = 9.0

	BC	HL	GL	PGE	RL	PFD
Score	1	2	1.5	1	2	1.5
Year passed	'71	'91	'82	'93	'71	'77

(7) Delaware = 4.0

	BC	HL	GL	PGE	RL	PFD
Score	1	0	1	0	0	2
Year passed	'89		'83			'83

(8) Florida = 9.5

	BC	HL	GL	PGE	RL	PFD
Score	1	2	1.5	2	1	2
Year passed	'67	'90	'67, '90	'74	'67	'67, '74

(9) Georgia = 4.5

	BC	HL	GL	PGE	RL	PFD
Score	1	0	1.5	0	0	2
Year passed	'68		'68			'86

(10) Idaho = 1.0

	BC	HL	GL	PGE	RL	PFD
Score	1	0	0	0	0	0
Year passed	'90					

(11) Illinois = 8.5

	BC	HL	GL	PGE	RL	PFD
Score	1	2	1.5	0	2	2
Year passed	'67	'95	'67		'67	'67, '72

(12) Indiana = 6.0

	BC	HL	GL	PGE	RL	PFD
Score	1	2	1	0	1	1
Year passed	'74	'91	'74		'74	'74

(13) Iowa = 8.5

	BC	HL	GL	PGE	RL	PFD
Score	1	2	1.5	2	1	1
Year passed	'67	'92	'67	'92	'93	'93

(14) Kansas = 4.5

	BC	HL	GL	PGE	RL	PFD
Score	1	0	1.5	0	1	1
Year passed	'70		'74		'74	'70

(15) Kentucky = 10.5

	BC	HL	GL	PGE	RL	PFD
Score	1	2	1.5	2	2	2
Year passed	'72	'93	'72	'93	'93	'93

(16) Louisiana = 7.0

	BC	HL	GL	PGE	RL	PFD
Score	1	0	2	2	1	1
Year passed	'64		'64	'79	'64	'79

(17) Maine = 4.0

	BC	HL	GL	PGE	RL	PFD
Score	1	0	1	0	1	1
Year passed	'61		'73		'73	'73

(18) Maryland = 8.5

	BC	HL	GL	PGE	RL	PFD
Score	1	2	1.5	1	1	2
Year passed	'71	'95	'71, '95	'95	'71	'71, '79

(19) Massachusetts = 8.0

	BC	HL	GL	PGE	RL	PFD
Score	1	1	2	0	2	2
Year passed	'61	'78	'62, '77,	'78, '94	'77, '78	'61, '77, '78

Note: Massachusetts enacted financial disclosure in 1961 but repealed it in 1962; disclosure was not required again until 1977.

(20) Michigan = 6.0

	BC	HL	GL	PGE	RL	PFD
Score	1	2	2	1	0	0
Year passed	'68	'94	'73, '94	'73		

Note: Financial disclosure was enacted in 1975, but the Michigan Supreme Court declared the law—which would also have established a state ethics commission—unconstitutional.

(21) Minnesota = 5.5

	BC	HL	GL	PGE	RL	PFD
Score	1	0	2	0	1	1.5
Year passed	'61		'94		'74	'74

(22) Mississippi = 3.5

	BC	HL	GL	PGE	RL	PFD
Score	1	0	0	0	1	1.5
Year passed	'79				'79	'79

(23) Missouri = 7.0

	BC	HL	GL	PGE	RL	PFD
Score	1	0	1	1	2	2
Year passed	'78		'78	'78	'78	'91

(24) Montana = 4.0

	BC	HL	GL	PGE	RL	PFD
Score	1	0	1.5	0	0	1.5
Year passed	'77		'77			'80

(25) Nebraska = 5.5

	BC	HL	GL	PGE	RL	PFD
Score	1	1	1.5	0	0	2
Year passed	'76	'91	'76			'76

(26) Nevada = 6.5

	BC	HL	GL	PGE	RL	PFD
Score	1	2	1	0	1	1.5
Year passed	'77	'91	'77		'77	'77

(27) New Hampshire = 3.0

	BC	HL	GL	PGE	RL	PFD
Score	1	0	1	0	0	1
Year passed	'87		'87			'87

(28) New Jersey = 9.0

	BC	HL	GL	PGE	RL	PFD
Score	1	1	1.5	2	2	1.5
Year passed	'67	'88	'67	'81	'67	'71, '88

(29) New Mexico = 5.5

	BC	HL	GL	PGE	RL	PFD
Score	1	1	1	1	0	1.5
Year passed	'67	'93	'93	'93		'93

(30) New York = 8.5

	BC	HL	GL	PGE	RL	PFD
Score	1	0	1.5	2	2	2
Year passed	'54		'64	'64	'65	'54, '64, '87

(31) North Carolina = 3.0

	BC	HL	GL	PGE	RL	PFD
Score	1	0	1	0	0	1
Year passed	'75		'75			'75

(32) North Dakota = 0

	BC	HL	GL	PGE	RL	PFD
Score	0	0	0	0	0	0
Year passed						

(33) Ohio = 8.5

	BC	HL	GL	PGE	RL	PFD
Score	1	1	1.5	1	2	2
Year passed	'74	'94	'74	'74	'74	'74

(34) Oklahoma = 8.5

	BC	HL	GL	PGE	RL	PFD
Score	1	1	1.5	1	2	2
Year passed	'68	'86	'68	'86	'82	'86

(35) Oregon = 5.0

	BC	HL	GL	PGE	RL	PFD
Score	1	1	1.5	0	0	1.5
Year passed	'74	'93	'74, '93			'74

(36) Pennsylvania = 9.0

	BC	HL	GL	PGE	RL	PFD
Score	1	2	1.5	1	2	1.5
Year passed	'68	'78, '89	'68	'78	'68, '78	'78

(37) Rhode Island = 7.5

	BC	HL	GL	PGE	RL	PFD
Score	1	0	1.5	1	2	2
Year passed	'76		'86	'92	'92	'86

(38) South Carolina = 10.0

	BC	HL	GL	PGE	RL	PFD
Score	1	2	2	1	2	2
Year passed	'75	'91	'75, '91	'91	'75	'91

(39) South Dakota = 1.0

	BC	HL	GL	PGE	RL	PFD
Score	0	0	0	0	0	1
Year passed						'76

(40) Tennessee = 7.5

	BC	HL	GL	PGE	RL	PFD
Score	1	2	2	0	1	1.5
Year passed	'77	'89	'75, '89		'89	'72, '89

(41) Texas = 9.5

	BC	HL	GL	PGE	RL	PFD
Score	1	2	1.5	1	2	2
Year passed	'57	'91	'57	'91	'73, '93	'73

(42) Utah = 5.0

	BC	HL	GL	PGE	RL	PFD
Score	1	0	1.5	0	1	1.5
Year passed	'69		'69		'89	'89

(43) Vermont = 0

	BC	HL	GL	PGE	RL	PFD
Score	0	0	0	0	0	0
Year passed						

(44) Virginia = 5.5

	BC	HL	GL	PGE	RL	PFD
Score	1	0	1.5	1	1	1
Year passed	'87		'87	'94	'94	'87

(45) Washington = 7.0

	BC	HL	GL	PGE	RL	PFD
Score	1	2	1.5	0	1	1.5
Year passed	'67	'94	'94		'67	'67

(46) West Virginia = 6.0

	BC	HL	GL	PGE	RL	PFD
Score	1	2	2	0	0	1
Year passed	'68	'89	'68, '89			'89

(47) Wisconsin = 9.0

	BC	HL	GL	PGE	RL	PFD
Score	1	1	2	1	2	2
Year passed	'67	'73	'57	'73	'73	'73, '89

(48) Wyoming = 0.0

	BC	HL	GL	PGE	RL	PFD
Score	0	0	0	0	0	0
Year passed						

appendix B

Models and Data Sources for Chapter 3

Event History Analysis of the Enactment of Basic Ethics Codes, 1954–72

The Model and the Dependent Variable

Event history analysis, a type of logistic regression, is used to analyze the likelihood of states' enacting an ethics code during this time. Forty-six states are included in the data set. The excluded states are Alaska, Hawaii, Minnesota, and Nebraska, for which certain independent variables could not be measured. Observations are annual, with a state coded as 0 if it does not enact a code in a given year and 1 if it does. Once a state enacts a code, it drops out of the data set. The likelihood of code enactment, or the "hazard rate," is determined by the independent variables in the model. To control for duration dependence, year dummies are included for every year for which data were measured; the first year dummy is excluded and used as the reference category. Data for the dependent variable came from state statutes, legislative rule books, and a 1971 survey prepared by the Council of State Governments that asked states about their conflict-of-interest laws and rules. See Committee on Legislative Rules of the National Legislative Conference, Council of State Governments, *Conflict of Interest and Related Regulations for State Legislatures* (Lexington, Ky.: Council of State Governments, 1972).

Independent Variables

Political Culture

States were divided into three categories following the classification by Elazar (1970). Dummy variables were created to represent states with *moralist*, *individualist*, and *traditionalist* cultures. The *moralist* variable was omitted and used as the reference category.

Ideology

To measure *ideology*, I used the data from Berry and others (1997), available on the Florida State University website (http://www.pubadm.fsu .edu/archives/). The authors constructed a measure of citizen ideology for each state and year from 1960 to 1993. Higher values indicate a more liberal ideology. Since no data were available for the first six years examined in this analysis, I was unable to use observations for individual years. Instead, I computed the average ideology score for each state for the period 1960–72. While it would be ideal to have information relating to the years 1954–59, the measure I use covers a large portion of the time frame examined here and is preferable to employing other commonly used state ideology measures that were constructed from information gathered after 1972 (e.g., Wright, Erikson, and McIver 1987).

Party Competition

Unified government equals 1 if the governor's office and two branches of the legislature are controlled by the same party, 0 otherwise. Data came from the Council of State Governments, *Book of the States* (Lexington, Ky.: Council of State Governments), for the years 1953–72 and from a data set provided by Morris Fiorina to the author.

Majority party control equals the percentage of legislative seats controlled by the party that dominated the legislature in a given year (i.e., the party that controlled over 50 percent of the seats). Data came from the *Book of the States.*

Scandal/Corruption

Scandal is a continuous variable that measures the presence and severity of a recent conflict-of-interest scandal or scandals in a given state during the two years immediately preceding a given year and the first six months of that year. Data came from the *New York Times Index* for the years 1952–72. Obviously, there was some discretion involved in which events to classify as a scandal. I did not count sexual scandals or scandals related to vote fraud. Instead, I focused on the type of scandal most likely to lead to ethics reform (i.e., bribery, embezzlement, misuse of state funds, or other uses of public office for personal financial gain). I also did not count scandals related to campaign funds. Thus the focus is on scandals relating to what Thompson (1995) calls individual corruption rather than institutional corruption. Mere "allegations" of a conflict between an official or state employee's public and private duties were not sufficient to count as a scandal. There had to be a reference to an indictment or conviction, an official investigation by law enforcement authorities, or an official report on corruption involving state officials. A media "report" of a scandal without any official investigation was not counted. However, if the reporting led to an official investigation, it was counted.

For each year, I searched the *Index* under each state's heading and also under the heading "Crime." A state received a score of 0 if no scandal was reported in the two years prior to a given year or the first six months of that year. Points were given for scandals of two types: (1) those involving legislators and (2) those involving the governor, other statewide officials (e.g., the secretary of state or the state auditor), or state employees. A state received 1 point for each scandal involving one legislator; 2 points for a scandal that involved two legislators; 3 points for a scandal involving the speaker of the House, House majority leader, Senate president, or Senate majority leader in the state legislature; and 4 points for any scandal involving three or more legislators. Two points were given for any scandal involving the governor, and 1 point for a scandal involving any other statewide official (e.g., the attorney general or state treasurer). One point was given for an investigation or report regarding corruption in state politics (e.g., by a special commission, legislative investigating committee, or other official body). If more than one type of scandal was reported, the points for the scandals were added together for that year's scandal value. The minimum score was 0 points and the maximum score was 9 points.

To measure ongoing or enduring corruption, I used the variable *TPO*, equal to the traditional party organization scores for each state from Mayhew (1986). The *TPO* scores are based on Mayhew's analysis of state politics in the 1960s, a time frame appropriate for the time period being studied here. States received scores ranging from 1 to 5 points based on the extent to which they had traditional party organizations, or organizations with the following features: (1) substantial autonomy, (2) longlasting, (3) organized hierarchically, (4) nominate candidates for public office, and (5) rely heavily on material incentives to motivate support. There are important similarities between TPOs and political machines that make this measure potentially relevant to the passage of ethics laws.

Most particularly, both rely on material incentives such as appointive positions in government, business opportunities, and exemptions from law enforcement to motivate support and action. The use of such incentives is argued to be conducive to political corruption (Benson 1978; Johnston 1982). States with high *TPO* scores should therefore have more ongoing corruption than states with low *TPO* scores, and should be more likely to enact ethics codes in response.

Legislative Compensation

Compensation equals the biennial compensation for legislators (total compensation for a given year and the year preceding it). It is measured in real (1982) dollars. Data came from a data set provided to the author by Morris Fiorina and used in Fiorina 1994. Data for the states not in Fiorina's data set came from the *Book of the States* for the years 1953–72.

Attorneys

Attorneys equals the percentage of state legislators (senators and house members) who listed their occupation as attorney. Data came from state legislative manuals and *Blue Books* for the states in 1965.

Policy Diffusion

Neighboring states was measured according to the methodology described in Berry and Berry (1990, 1992). It is a count of the number of neighboring states that had already enacted an ethics code.

Direct Democracy

Initiative process is a dichotomous variable equal to 1 if the state had an initiative process and 0 otherwise. Data came from Ross (1987). Wyoming, which does have an initiative process, was coded as zero because the process was never used between 1898 and 1979. For all practical purposes, the state did not have an initiative process during the period examined here. See Ross (1987, 71).

Preexisting Laws

Campaign finance laws ranges from 0 to 2 points. States received 1 point if they had contribution limits on corporations, 1 point if they had contribution limits on unions, and 2 points if they had both limits. States with no limits were scored as 0. Data came from the *Book of the States* for each biennial session.

Linear Regression Analysis of Change in States' Ethics Laws, 1954–72

The Model and the Dependent Variable

Ordinary least squares regression was used to analyze change in states' ethics laws. Forty-six states are included in the data set. The excluded states are Alaska, Hawaii, Minnesota, and Nebraska, for which certain independent variables could not be measured.

The equation that measures change between the two time points, 1954 and 1972, is

$$Y_2 = \beta_0 + \beta_1 Y_1 + \beta_2 X_1 + \beta_3 X_2 + \beta_4 X_3 + \ldots + \beta_{13} X_{12} + e_2$$

X_1 through X_{12} represent the independent variables, which are described below. Y_2 equals a state's ethics index score in 1972, and Y_1 on the right-hand side of the equation equals the state's score at the beginning of the period or 1954. Y_1 is included because it is necessary to control for the initial level of the dependent variable (Markus 1979; McAdams 1986; Mooney 1995). However, Y_1 drops out of the equation because all states started the period with a score of zero on the index. Because Y_1 is zero for all states, it therefore has no effect on Y_2. The time frame here is unique because the starting point is a true starting point, uncontaminated by earlier enactments of restrictions.

The dependent variable, change in state ethics laws, trends upward over the time period examined here (change is positive for all states). Some of the independent variables also trend upward during this period. For example, change in real compensation is positive for forty-one of the forty-six states in the data set. To avoid spurious findings about the impact of any of these explanatory variables, the raw value of Y_2 is transformed to equal the number of standard deviations from the mean value of Y_2. This transformed variable therefore measures deviation from the average change; thus some states have positive and some have negative values. This means that the hypotheses are being tested with regard to relative change, not absolute change.

To measure Y_2, an additive index reflects the number and extent of the legislative ethics restrictions that each state had in place as of 1972. This index score is based on five categories: (1) a baseline category that reflects the presence or absence of a legislative code of ethics in the statutory codes or legislative rules; (2) limits on legislators receiving gifts that might influence their official action, votes, or judgment; (3) limits on representation by lawyer-legislators of clients before state agencies; (4) limits on postgovernment employment of legislators; and (5) personal financial disclosure requirements.

One point was given for a basic code and up to 2 points for each of five substantive ethics restrictions. For the formula used to assign scores, see appendix A.

Data for the dependent variable came from state statutes, legislative rule books, and a 1971 survey prepared by the Council of State Governments that asked states about their conflict-of-interest laws and rules. See *Conflict of Interest and Related Regulations for State Legislatures.*

Independent Variables

Political Culture

States were divided into three categories corresponding to the classification by Elazar (1970); see above.

Ideology

Ideology is the average of the citizen ideology scores for the years 1960 through 1972, using Berry and others' (1997) data (see above for details).

Party Competition

Unified government equals the percentage of the twenty years from 1953 to 1972, during which one party held unified control of state government. Data came from the *Book of the States* and from a data set provided by Morris Fiorina to the author.

Majority party control equals the average percentage of legislative seats held by the party which dominated the legislature (i.e., the party that controlled over 50 percent of the seats), for the years 1953–72. Majority party control is calculated for each biennial session and the numbers are averaged over the total number of sessions in the period. Data came from the *Book of the States.*

Scandal/Corruption

Scandal was calculated using the same method of scoring as for the event history model (see above). *Scandal* for the linear regression, however, equals the sum of all reported scandals for all years between 1952 and the first six months of 1972. Each scandal is counted only once. *Scandal* scores ranged from 0 to 15.

TPO equals the traditional party organization score for each state (see above for details). The data came from Mayhew (1986).

Change in Compensation

Change in compensation equals the change in biennial compensation for legislators between 1953–54 and 1969–70. It is calculated as compensation in 1969–70 minus compensation for 1953–54, so if compensation increases over the period, the value is positive. Compensation is measured in 1982 dollars. Data came from a data set provided by Morris Fiorina and used in Fiorina 1994. Data for the states not in Fiorina's data set came from the *Book of the States* for the years 1953–72.

Attorneys in Legislatures

Attorneys equals the percentage of state legislators (senators and house members) who listed their occupation as attorney. The data came from state legislative manuals and *Blue Books* for the states in the year 1965.

Policy Diffusion

Diffusion was measured by summing the amount of all ethics law changes in all the state's neighbors during the period 1954–71. Change in ethics laws is calculated as described above. Thus each state is assumed to be affected by the aggregate amount of change in all its neighboring states.

Direct Democracy

Initiative process is a dichotomous variable that equals 1 if the state had an initiative process and 0 otherwise. See above.

Preexisting Laws

Campaign finance laws ranges from 0 to 2. States received 1 point if they had contribution limits on corporations and 1 point if they had contribution limits on unions. States with no limits were scored as 0. The data came from the *Book of the States* and are for the 1953–1954 biennium, the beginning of the period examined here.

Ordinal Regression and the Analysis of Change in States' Ethics Laws, 1954–72

The ordinal model is the same as the linear model detailed above, except that the dependent variable is construed as ordinal rather than continuous in nature. Forty-six states were included in the data set. The excluded states are Alaska, Hawaii, Minnesota, and Nebraska, for which certain independent variables could not be measured. The dependent variable,

Y_2, takes on three possible values. $Y=0$ when there is no change in ethics laws during this period, $Y=1$ when there is a change that is less than or equal to 2 on the additive index (see above for the scoring of the index), and $Y=2$ when there is a change greater than 2 on the additive index. Of the forty-six states in the data set, nineteen had scores of 0, nine had scores of 1, and eighteen had scores of 2. As in the linear regression, Y_1 drops out of the model. For purposes of estimating the impact of statistically significant variables in this model (see table C.4 in appendix C), states that scored 2 are considered to have the "strongest" laws.

Independent Variables

The independent variables are identical to those used in the linear regression (see above).

appendix C

Regression Tables for Chapter 3

Table C.1 presents the results of the event history analysis. Because it is difficult to interpret the coefficients in logistic regression, table C.2 presents a more intuitive way of understanding the impact of key explanatory variables. It shows how the probability that a state will enact an ethics code changes as the values of key variables (those that are statistically significant in the regression) change. Specifically, it shows the "mean effects," or the difference between the likelihood of code enactment when a key variable is set at its maximum and its minimum values.

For example, the mean effect of scandal is the difference in the predicted probability of code enactment for a state that experienced the maximum amount (and severity) of scandals for the data set and a state that experienced no scandals. All other variables are set at their mean values. Mean effects are calculated using the coefficients from Model 2 in table C.1. The formula used to calculate the predicted probabilities is $1/(1 + e^{-L})$, where $L = B_0 + B_1 X_1 + B_2 X_2. \ldots$

Table C.3 presents the results of the linear regression and the ordinal regression. Table C.4 uses the ordinal regression results to show the effect on the probability that the state will experience the maximum amount of change in its ethics laws during this time as key predictors are varied in value. Specifically, it shows the predicted probability that a state will enact the maximum amount of change in its ethics laws during this period ($Y = 2$), given different values for the independent variables indicated in the left-hand column. All other variables are set at their means. Predicted probabilities are calculated using the coefficients from Model 4 in table C.3. The formula is $P(Y = 2) = 1 - 1/(1 + e^{-m2} + \beta_2 X_1 + \beta_3 X_2 \ldots)$.

Table C.1   Event History Analysis:
The Passage of Legislative Ethics Codes, 1954–1972

Variable	Model 1	Model 2
Culture/Ideology		
Individualist	−1.895* (1.118)	−1.097+ (.731)
Traditionalist	1.286+ (.932)	1.461+ (.877)
Ideology	0.077** (.028)	0.066** (.024)
Party competition		
Unified government	0.409 (.519)	
Majority party control	0.005 (.024)	
Scandal/Corruption		
Scandal	0.564** (.223)	0.562** (.218)
TPO (traditional party organization)	0.286 (.293)	
Economic self-interest		
Compensation	0.028+ (.018)	0.032* (.016)
Attorneys	0.029 (.027)	0.019 (.024)
Policy diffusion		
Neighboring states	0.447+ (.291)	0.482* (.284)
Direct democracy		
Initiative	0.847 (.700)	0.446 (.585)
Preexisting laws		
Campaign finance laws	0.312 (.439)	
Year dummies	Yes	Yes
Constant	−10.492** (3.441)	−8.339** (2.022)
−2 log likelihood	146.121	147.914
PRE (proportional reduction in error)	.19	.19
No. of observations	711	711

Note: $+ p < .10$; $* p < .05$; $** p < .01$, one-tailed tests. Standard errors in parentheses. Model 1 includes all independent variables. Model 2 keeps only those variables for which the coefficients exceed the standard errors. PRE = (errors in predicting the dependent variable, DV, using the modal value of the DV − errors using the model) / errors using the modal value of the DV.

Sources: Dependent variable from state conflict-of-interest statutes, legislative rule books, and Committee on Legislative Rules of the National Legislative Conference, Council of State Governments, *Conflict of Interest and Related Regulations for State Legislatures* (Lexington, Ky.: Council of State Governments, 1972). See appendix B for details on measurement of the dependent and independent variables.

Table C.2 Mean Effects for Key Independent Variables

Variable	Mean Effect (%)
Scandal	+ 16.41
Compensation	+ 12.52
Ideology	+ 1.60
Diffusion	+ 1.05
Scandal, diffusion	+ 62.41
Scandal, ideology	+ 69.92
Scandal, compensation	+ 95.25

Note: Mean effects are calculated for variables for which the coefficient is statistically significant at the .05 level or greater. The mean effect represents the difference between the predicted probabilities of support when the variable of interest is at its maximum and minimum values, setting all other variables at their means. Where there is more than one variable, the mean effect equals the difference between the predicted probability when each of the variables is at its maximum and when each is at its minimum. Calculations are made using the coefficients from Model 2 in table C.1. The formula used to calculate the predicted probabilities is $1/(1 + e^{-L})$, where $L = B_0 + B_1X_1 + B_2X_2 \ldots$

Table C.3 Explaining Overall Change in State Legislative Ethics Laws, 1954–72

Variable	Model 1, Linear Regression	Model 2, Linear Regression	Model 3, Ordinal Regression	Model 4, Ordinal Regression
Culture/Ideology				
Individualist	−1.015* (.507)	−0.784* (.347)	−5.989** (2.281)	−4.377** (1.606)
Traditionalist	−0.109 (.561)		−1.071 (1.587)	
Ideology	0.009 (.015)		0.041 (.045)	
Party competition				
Unified government	0.487 (.699)		1.802 (2.048)	
Majority party control	0.009 (.015)		0.007 (.041)	
Scandal/Corruption				
Scandal	0.096* (.049)	0.109** (.031)	0.212 (.176)	0.261* (.115)
TPO (traditional party organization)	0.319* (.146)	0.304* (.098)	0.947+ (.596)	1.190** (.465)
Economic self-interest				
Change in compensation	0.016+ (.011)	0.022** (.007)	0.039 (.031)	0.053* (.025)
Attorneys	0.008 (.014)		0.002 (.039)	
Policy diffusion				
Neighboring states	−0.004 (.037)		0.085 (.097)	
Direct democracy				
Initiative	0.171 (.307)		0.893 (.854)	0.695 (.709)
Preexisting laws				
Campaign finance	−0.016 (.206)		0.501 (.649)	
Constant	−1.204 (1.488)	−1.089 (.206)		
Threshold $Y = 0$			6.478+ (4.614)	2.350* (1.021)
Threshold $Y = 1$			7.728+ (4.667)	3.606** (1.103)
Adjusted R^2	0.32	0.47		
Pseudo R^2 (Nagelkerke)			0.46	0.42
−2 log likelihood			71.79	78.35
No. of observations	46	46	46	46

Note: $+ p < .10$; * $p < .05$; ** $p < .01$, one-tailed tests. Standard errors in parentheses. Model 1 and Model 3 include all independent variables; Model 2 and Model 4 keep only those variables for which the coefficients exceed the standard errors.

Sources: Dependent variable from state conflict-of-interest statutes, legislative rule books, and Committee on Legislative Rules of the National Legislative Conference, Council of State Governments, *Conflict of Interest and Related Regulations for State Legislatures* (Lexington, Ky.: Council of State Governments, 1972). See appendix B for details on measurement of the dependent and independent variables.

Table C.4   Effects of Changes in Key Variables on the Predicted Probability of a State Enacting Maximum Change in Ethics Laws

Variable	Probability $(Y_2 = 2)$
Change in compensation = minimum	.1379
Change in compensation = maximum	.8636
Individualist culture	.0196
Nonindividualist culture	.6364
TPO = minimum	.0991
TPO = maximum	.9303
Scandal = minimum	.2000
Scandal = maximum	.9269

Note: TPO = traditional party organization. The figures in the right-hand column show the predicted probability that a state will enact the maximum amount of change in its ethics laws, or the strongest laws $(Y = 2)$ during this period, given the different values for the independent variables indicated in the left-hand column. All other variables are set at their means. Predicted probabilities are calculated using the coefficients from Model 4 in table C.3, using the formula $P(Y = 2) = 1 - 1/(1 + e^{-m2} + \beta_2 X_1 + \beta_3 X_2 \ldots)$.

appendix D

Models and Data Sources for Chapter 4

Linear Regression Analysis of Change in States' Ethics Laws, 1977–88

The Model and the Dependent Variable

Ordinary least squares regression is used to analyze change in states' ethics laws. Forty-seven states are included in the data set. The excluded states are Alaska, Hawaii, and Nebraska, for which certain independent variables could not be measured.

The equation that measures change between the two time points, 1977 and 1988, is

$$Y_2 = \beta_0 + \beta_1 Y_1 + \beta_2 X_1 + \beta_3 X_2 + \beta_4 X_3 + \ldots + \beta_{15} X_{14} + e_2$$

X_1 through X_{14} represent the independent variables, which are described below. Y_2 equals a state's ethics index score in 1988, and Y_1 on the right-hand side of the equation equals the state's score at the beginning of the period or 1977. Y_1 is included because it is necessary to control for the initial level of the dependent variable (Markus 1979; McAdams 1986; Mooney 1995).

To measure Y_1 and Y_2, an additive index was constructed to reflect the number and extent of the legislative ethics restrictions that each state had in place at the beginning of 1977 and end of 1988, respectively. This index score is based on six categories: (1) a baseline category that reflects the presence or absence of a legislative code of ethics in the statutory codes or legislative rules; (2) limits on legislators receiving gifts that might influence their official action, votes, or judgment; (3) limits on representation by lawyer-legislators of clients before state agencies; (4) limits on post-government employment of legislators; (5) honoraria limits; and (6) personal financial disclosure requirements.

One point was given for a basic code and up to 2 points for each of the other categories of ethics restrictions. For the formula by which points were assigned, see appendix A.

Data for the dependent variable came from state statutes, legislative rule books, and *Public Integrity Annual* (Council of State Governments 1996).

Independent Variables

Political Culture

States were divided into three categories corresponding to the classification by Elazar (1970). See appendix B.

Ideology

Ideology is the average of the citizen ideology scores for each state for 1977 to 1988, using Berry and others' (1997) data. See appendix B for details.

Party Competition

The variable *unified government* equals the percentage of the years from 1977 to 1988 that one party held unified control of state government. Data came from the Council of State Governments, *Book of the States* (Lexington, Ky.: Council of State Governments, various years).

The variable *majority party control* equals the average percentage of legislative seats controlled by the party that dominates the legislature (i.e., the party that controlled over 50 percent of the seats), for the years 1977–88. Majority party control is calculated for each biennial session and the numbers are averaged over the total number of sessions in the period. Data came from the *Book of the States*, various years.

Scandal/Corruption

The scandal variable was calculated using the same method as in chapter 3 (see appendix B). *Scandal* here equals the sum of all scandals for all years between 1975 and the first six months of 1988. Each scandal is counted only once. Sources were the *New York Times Index* (used as described in appendix C), and the U.S. Department of Justice, *Annual Report to the Congress on the Activities and Operations of the Public Integrity* Section (Washington, D.C.: U.S. Government Printing Office) for each year from 1976 to 1988 (1976 was the first year these reports became available). I relied on the section at the end of each Department of Justice report for incidents involving prosecution of state officials; the scandals were scored in the same way as the scandals reported in the *New York Times Index.* Scandal scores ranged from 0 to 12.

The variable *TPO* equals the traditional party organization score for each state (see appendix B for details). Data came from Mayhew (1986).

Change in Compensation

Change in compensation equals the change in real biennial compensation for legislators between 1977–78 and 1987–88. Compensation is measured in 1982 dollars. Data came from a data set provided to the author by Morris Fiorina and used in Fiorina 1994. Data for the states not in Fiorina's data set came from the *Book of the States.*

Attorneys in Legislatures

Attorneys equals the percentage of state legislators (senators and house members) who listed their occupation as attorney. The data came from Bazar (1987) and were calculated for the year 1976.

Policy Diffusion

Diffusion was measured by summing the amount of change in ethics laws for all the state's neighbors during the period 1977–87 (see appendix B). Thus each state is assumed to be affected by the aggregate amount of change in all its neighboring states. *Change in ethics laws* was calculated using the index as described above.

Direct Democracy

Initiative process is a dichotomous variable that equals 1 if the state had an initiative process and 0 otherwise. The data came from Ross (1987). See appendix B for details.

Preexisting Laws

The variable *campaign finance laws* ranges from 0 to 2. States received 1 point if they had contribution limits on corporations and 1 point if they had contribution limits on union. States with no limits were scored as 0.

Data came from the *Book of the States*, 1976–77, and were calculated for the beginning of the period.

Last Passed Laws

The variable *last passed laws* controls for the amount of time since a state last enacted a law regulating legislative ethics. The variable was coded as 0 if it was between one and five years, as 1 if it was between six and ten years, as 2 if it was eleven years or more, and as 3 if the state never passed a legislative ethics law or legislative ethics rules. It is expected to have a positive coefficient, because states that have not enacted ethics laws or have not enacted them in a long time should be more likely to enact new laws.

Ordinal Regression and the Analysis of Change in States' Ethics Laws, 1977–88

In the ordinal model, the dependent variable is construed as ordinal rather than continuous in nature. Forty-seven states are included in the data set. The excluded states are Alaska, Hawaii, and Nebraska. The dependent variable in the ordinal specification takes on three values. $Y = 0$ if there was no change in ethics laws during the period, $Y = 1$ if there was a change less than or equal to 2 points on the additive index, and $Y = 2$ if there was a change greater than 2 in the index. For twenty-seven states, Y was equal to 0. For five states, it was equal to 1. For fifteen states, it was equal to 2. For purposes of estimating the impact of statistically significant variables in this model, states that scored 0 are considered to have the "weakest" laws and states that scored 2 are considered to have the "strongest" laws (see appendix E, table E.2).

Independent Variables

The independent variables are identical to those used in the linear regression (see above).

Linear Regression Analysis of Change in States' Ethics Laws, 1989–96

The Model and the Dependent Variable

Ordinary least squares regression is used to analyze change in states' ethics laws. Forty-seven states are included in the data set. The excluded states are Alaska, Hawaii, and Nebraska, for which certain independent variables could not be measured.

The equation that measures change between the two time points, 1989 and 1996, is

$$Y_2 = \beta_0 + \beta_1 Y_1 + \beta_2 X_1 + \beta_3 X_2 + \beta_4 X_3 + \ldots + \beta_{15} X_{14} + e_2.$$

X_1 through X_{14} represent the independent variables, which are described below. Y_2 equals a state's ethics index score in 1996 and Y_1 on the right-hand side of the equation equals the state's score at the beginning of the period or 1989. Y_1 is included because it is necessary to control for the initial level of the dependent variable (Markus 1979; McAdams 1986; Mooney 1995).

To measure Y_1 and Y_2, an additive index was constructed to measure the number and extent of the legislative ethics restrictions that each state had in place as of 1989 and 1996, respectively. This index score is based on six categories. See above and appendix A for categories, how points are assigned for restrictions in each category, and data sources.

Independent Variables

Political Culture

See appendix B.

Ideology

Ideology is the average of the citizen ideology scores for each state, for 1989 through 1993, calculated using Berry and others' 1997 data (see appendix B for details).

Party Competition

Unified government equals the percentage of the years from 1989 to 1996 that one party held unified control of state government. Data came from *Book of the States*, various years.

The variable *majority party control* equals the average percentage of legislative seats controlled by the party that dominated the legislature (i.e., the party that controlled over 50 percent of the seats), for the years 1989–96. Majority party control is calculated for each biennial session, and the numbers are averaged over the total number of sessions in the period. Data came from the *Book of the States*.

Scandal/Corruption

Scandal was calculated using basically the same scoring method as in chapter 3 and the first half of chapter 4 (see above section and appendix B for details). The one difference in scoring was that extra weight was assigned to sting operations that targeted members of the state legislature, which occurred only during this period out of the three periods examined in this book. The maximum amount of points per scandal in the previous periods was 4, for a scandal involving three or more legislators. Such scandals in most cases involved no more than four legislators. By contrast, the sting operations that occurred in the 1989–96 period involved up to eighteen legislators in a single state, and received substantial and sustained publicity.

Consequently, I counted each sting as worth 8 points, or double the maximum amount of points for any other scandal. *Scandal* here equals the sum of all scandals for all years between 1987 and the first six months of 1996. Each scandal is counted only once. Three sources were used. First, I used the *New York Times Index* (used as described in appendix B). Second, I used the reports from the Department of Justice's *Annual Report to the Congress on the Activities and Operations of the Public Integrity Section* for each year from 1987 through 1996. I relied on the section at the end of each report for incidents involving prosecution of state officials. The third source was the *COGEL Guardian* newsletter, published quarterly by the Council on Governmental Ethics Laws (Los Angeles), for the years 1988–96; 1988 was the first year the newsletter was published. Scandal scores ranged from 0 to 30.

The variable *TPO* equals the traditional party organization score for each state (see appendix B for details). Data came from Mayhew (1986).

Change in Compensation

The variable *change in compensation* equals the change in real biennial compensation for legislators between 1989–90 and 1995–96. Compensation is measured in 1982 dollars. Data came from a data set provided to the author by Morris Fiorina and used in Fiorina 1994. Data for the states not in Fiorina's data set came from the *Book of the States*.

Attorneys in Legislatures

The variable *attorneys* equals the percentage of state legislators (senators and house members) who listed their occupation as attorney. Data came from Bazar (1987) and were calculated for the year 1986.

Policy Diffusion

Diffusion was measured by summing the amount of change in ethics laws for all of a given state's neighbors during the period 1989–95 (see appendix B). Thus each state is assumed to be affected by the aggregate amount of change in all its neighboring states.

Direct Democracy

Initiative process is a dichotomous variable that equals 1 if the state had an initiative process and 0 otherwise. Data came from Ross (1987). See appendix B for details.

Preexisting Laws

Campaign finance laws ranges from 0 to 2. States received 1 point if they had contribution limits on corporations and 1 point if they had contribution limits on unions. States with no limits were scored as 0. Data came from the *Book of the States* and were calculated for the beginning of the period examined here.

Last Passed Laws

Last passed laws controls for the amount of time since a state last enacted a law regulating legislative ethics. The variable was coded 0 if it was between one and five years, as 1 if it was between six and ten years, as 2 if it was eleven years or more, and as 3 if the state never passed a legislative ethics law or legislative ethics rules. The variable is expected to have a positive coefficient because states that have not enacted ethics laws or have not enacted them in a long time should be more likely to enact new laws.

Ordinal Regression and the Analysis of Change in States' Ethics Laws, 1989–96

The dependent variable is construed as ordinal rather than continuous in nature. Forty-seven states are included in the data set. The excluded states are Alaska, Hawaii, and Nebraska. The dependent variable in the ordinal specification takes on three values: $Y = 0$ if there was no change in ethics laws during the period, $Y = 1$ if there was a change less than or equal to 2 points on the additive index, and $Y = 2$ if there was a change greater than 2 in the index. For sixteen states, Y was equal to 0. For sixteen states, it was equal to 1. For fifteen states, it was equal to 2. For purposes of estimating the impact of statistically significant variables in this model, states that scored 2 are considered to have the "strongest" laws (see appendix E, table E.2).

Independent Variables

The independent variables are identical to those used in the linear regression for this time period (see above).

appendix E

Regression Tables for Chapter 4

Table E.1 presents the results of the linear and ordinal regressions for the 1977–88 period. Table E.2 uses the ordinal regression results to show the effect on the probability that a state will experience the maximum amount of change in its ethics laws during this time as key predictors are varied in value. Specifically, it shows the predicted probability that a state will enact the maximum amount of change in its ethics laws during this period $(Y = 2)$, given different values for the independent variables indicated in the left-hand column. All other variables are set at their means. Predicted probabilities are calculated using the coefficients from Model 4 in table 4.2. The formula is $P(Y = 2) = 1 - 1/(1 + e^{-m2} + b_2X_1 + b_3X_2 \ldots)$.

Table E.3 presents the results of the linear and ordinal regressions for the 1989–96 period. Table E.4 uses the ordinal regression results to show the effect on the probability that a state will experience the maximum amount of change in its ethics laws during this time as key predictors are varied in value. Specifically, it shows the predicted probability that a state will enact the maximum amount of change in its ethics laws during this period $(Y = 2)$, given different values for the independent variables indicated in the left-hand column. All other variables are set at their means. Predicted probabilities are calculated using the coefficients from Model 4 in table E.3. The formula is $P(Y = 2) = 1 - 1/(1 + e^{-m2} + b_2X_1 + b_3X_2 \ldots)$.

Table E.1 Explaining Overall Change
in State Legislative Ethics Laws, 1977–88

Variable	Model 1, Linear Regression	Model 2, Linear Regression	Model 3, Ordinal Regression	Model 4, Ordinal Regression
Controls				
Score, 1977	0.680** (.141)	0.660** (.128)		
Last passed laws	0.277 (.256)	0.259 (.231)	1.533** (.468)	1.474** (.420)
Culture/Ideology				
Individualist	0.970 (.890)	0.979* (.470)	−0.088 (1.879)	
Traditionalist	0.179 (.993)		−1.506 (2.095)	
Ideology	0.001 (.022)		−0.046 (.047)	
Party competition				
Unified government	1.628* (.912)	1.597* (.723)	2.888+ (1.784)	3.197* (1.347)
Majority party control	−0.001 (.028)		0.021 (.048)	
Scandal/Corruption				
Scandal	0.128+ (.080)	0.134* (.069)	0.290* (.164)	0.207* (.117)
TPO (traditional party organization)	0.030 (.257)		0.810+ (.562)	0.578* (.297)
Economic self-interest				
Change in compensation	0.027 (.021)	0.029+ (.018)	−0.017 (.039)	
Attorneys	0.033 (.027)	0.037* (.019)	0.014 (.051)	
Policy diffusion				
Neighboring states	0.033 (.050)		0.024 (.112)	
Direct democracy				
Initiative	1.044* (.504)	0.919* (.425)	2.268* (1.149)	2.053* (1.053)
Preexisting laws				
Campaign finance	0.083 (.295)		−0.139 (.591)	
Constant	−1.044 (2.234)	−0.717 (.734)		
Threshold $Y = 0$			5.320+ (4.067)	6.010** (1.858)
Threshold $Y = 1$			6.223+ (4.101)	6.875** (1.935)
Adjusted R^2	0.66	0.71		
Pseudo R^2 (Nagelkerke)			0.57	0.54
−2 log likelihood			55.126	57.05
No. of observations	47	47	47	47

Note: + $p < .10$; * $p < .05$; ** $p < .01$, one-tailed tests. Standard errors in parentheses. Models 1 and 3 include all independent variables. Models 2 and 4 keep only those variables for which the coefficients exceed the standard errors.

Sources: Data for the dependent variable came from state conflict-of-interest statutes and legislative rule books, and *Public Integrity Annual* (Council of State Governments 1996). See appendix D for details on measurement of the dependent and independent variables.

Table E.2   Effects of Changes in Key Variables
on the Predicted Probability of a State Enacting
Maximum Change in Ethics Laws, 1977–88

Variable	*Probability $(Y_2 = 2)$*
Scandal = minimum	.1379
Scandal = maximum	.6610
No initiative	.0566
Initiative	.3333
Unified government = minimum	.0291
Unified government = maximum	.5376

Note: Figures in the right-hand column show the predicted probability that a state will enact the maximum amount of change in its ethics laws during this period $(Y = 2)$, given different values for the independent variables indicated in the left-hand column. All other variables are set at their means. Predicted probabilities are calculated using the coefficients from Model 4 in table E.1, using the formula $P(Y = 2) = 1 - 1/(1 + e^{-m2} + \beta_2 X_1 + \beta_3 X_2 \ldots)$.

Table E.3   Explaining Overall Change in State Legislative Ethics Laws, 1989–96

Variable	Model 1, Linear Regression	Model 2, Linear Regression	Model 3, Ordinal Regression	Model 4, Ordinal Regression
Controls				
Score, 1988	0.608** (.139)	0.597** (.120)		
Last passed laws	−0.354 (.325)	−0.302 (.278)	0.118 (.379)	
Culture/Ideology				
Individualist	−1.399+ (1.010)	−1.118+ (.750)	−2.382+(1.497)	−1.738+ (1.136)
Traditionalist	−0.104 (.967)		0.333 (1.201)	
Ideology	−0.036 (.030)	−0.029+ (.021)	−0.012 (.038)	
Party competition				
Unified government	−0.346 (1.035)		−0.946 (1.326)	
Majority party control	−0.076* (.035)	−0.080** (.028)	−0.060+ (.044)	−0.064* (.035)
Scandal/Corruption				
Scandal	0.233** (.067)	0.213** (.046)	0.234 (.087)	0.185** (.061)
TPO (traditional party organization)	0.529+ (.294)	0.453* (.231)	0.793* (.422)	0.520+ (.323)
Economic self-interest				
Change in compensation	0.002 (.023)		0.026 (.028)	
Attorneys	0.023 (.041)		−0.049 (.051)	
Policy diffusion				
Neighboring states	0.066 (.057)	0.056 (.044)	0.015 (.069)	
Direct democracy				
Initiative	−0.017 (.596)		0.053 (0.732)	0.870 (.770)
Preexisting laws				
Campaign finance	−0.032 (.231)		−0.184 (.284)	
Constant	8.778**(3.063)	8.318**(2.533)		
Threshold $Y = 0$			−4.273 (3.775)	−3.417+ (2.175)
Threshold $Y = 1$			−2.311 (3.728)	−1.554 (2.122)
Adjusted R^2	.69	.73		
Pseudo R^2 (Nagelkerke)			.38	.32
−2 log likelihood			84.127	87.529
No. of observations	47	47	47	47

Note: + $p < .10$; * $p < .05$; ** $p < .01$, one-tailed tests. Standard errors in parentheses. Models 1 and 3 include all independent variables. Models 2 and 4 keep only those variables for which the coefficients exceed the standard errors.

Sources: Data for the dependent variable came from state conflict-of-interest statutes and legislative rule books, and *Public Integrity Annual* (Council of State Governments 1996). See appendix D for details on measurement of the dependent and independent variables.

Table E.4   Effects of Changes in Key Variables on the Predicted Probability of a State Enacting Maximum Change in Ethics Laws, 1989–96

Variable	*Probability ($Y_2 = 2$)*
Scandal = minimum	.2000
Scandal = maximum	.9866
Individualist culture	.1666
Nonindividualist culture	.5370
TPO = minimum	.2700
TPO = maximum	.7487
Majority party control = maximum	.1379
Majority party control = minimum	.5983

Note: TPO = traditional party organization. Figures in the right-hand column show the predicted probability that a state will enact the maximum amount of change in its ethics laws during this period ($Y = 2$), given different values for the independent variables indicated in the left-hand column. All variables other than the variable in the left-hand column are set at their means. Predicted probabilities are calculated using the coefficients from Model 4 in table E.3, using the formula $P(Y = 2) = 1 - 1/(1 + e^{-m2} + \beta_2 X_1 + \beta_3 X_2 \ldots)$.

appendix F

Models and Data Sources for Chapter 5

Event History Analysis of the Authorization
of Independent Ethics Commissions, 1973–96

The Model and the Dependent Variable

Event history analysis, a type of logistic regression, is used to analyze the likelihood of states' authorizing a commission during this time. Forty-six states are included in the data set. The excluded states are Alaska, Hawaii, Louisiana, and Nebraska. Observations are annual, with a state coded as 0 if it does not enact a code in a given year and 1 if it does. Once a state authorizes a commission, it drops out of the data set. The likelihood of commission enactment, or the "hazard rate," is determined by the independent variables in the model. To control for duration dependence, year dummies are included for every year for which data were measured; the first year dummy is excluded and used as the reference category. Data on the establishment of commissions came from the *Campaign Finance, Ethics and Lobby Law Blue Book* (Council on Governmental Ethics Laws 1990, 1993), the *Public Integrity Annual* (Council of State Governments 1996), and state statutes.

Independent Variables

Political Culture

States were divided into three categories corresponding to the classification by Elazar (1970). See appendix B.

Ideology

Ideology is a measure of citizen ideology for each state and year. Source: Berry and others 2001.

Party Competition

Unified government equals 1 if the same party controlled the legislative and executive branches of state government, 0 otherwise. Data are from the Council of State Governments, *Book of the States* (Lexington, Ky.: Council of State Governments, various years).

The variable *majority party control* equals the percentage of legislative seats held by the party that controlled over 50 percent of the seats in the legislature (house and senate combined) in a given year. Source: *Book of the States.*

Scandal/Corruption

Scandal was calculated using the same scoring method used for the analysis of change in ethics laws between 1988 and 1996, described in appendix D (see also appendix B). Data came from three sources. First, I used the *New York Times Index* for 1971–96, searching under each state and "Crime" for each year. Second, the yearly reports by the U.S. Department of Justice, *Annual Report to the Congress on the Activities and Operations of the Public Integrity* Section (Washington, D.C.: U.S. Government Printing Office), were used for 1976–96. I focused on the section on prosecutions of state officials. Finally, I used the quarterly publication *The Guardian,* published by the Council on Governmental Ethics Laws (Los Angeles), for 1988–96. The newsletter was not published before 1988. Scandal scores ranged from 0 to 15.

The variable *TPO* equals the traditional party organization score for each state (see appendix B). The data came from Mayhew (1986).

Compensation

Compensation equals real compensation for legislators for each biennial session and is measured in real (1982) dollars. Data came from a data set provided to the author by Morris Fiorina and used in Fiorina 1994. Data for the states not in Fiorina's data set came from the *Book of the States.*

Attorneys in Legislatures

Attorneys equals the percentage of state legislators (senators and house members) who listed their occupation as attorney. Data came from state *Blue Books* and Bazar (1987). For the years 1973–75, percentages for 1965 were used. For 1976–85, percentages for 1976 were used. For years after 1986, percentages for 1986 were used.

Policy Diffusion

Neighboring states equals the number of neighboring states that had already established an independent commission (Berry and Berry 1990, 1992).

Direct Democracy

Initiative process is a dichotomous variable that equals 1 if the state had an initiative process and 0 otherwise. The data came from Ross (1987). See appendix B for details.

Preexisting Laws

Campaign finance laws ranges from 0 to 2. States received 1 point if they had contribution limits on corporations and 1 point if they had contribution limits on unions in a given year. States with no limits were scored as 0. Data came from the *Book of the States*.

State Wealth

Real per capita income was measured for each state and year, adjusted for inflation using the consumer price index (1982–84 = 100). The data source was the U.S. Department of Commerce, Bureau of the Census, various years.

Bureaucratic Capacity

Bureaucratic capacity was measured as state employment per 10,000 population in October of each previous even-numbered year. The data source was the *Book of the States*, various years.

Gubernatorial Powers

The variable *gubernatorial powers* equals an additive index of gubernatorial powers in four areas: tenure potential, appointive powers, budget powers, and veto powers. The maximum possible score for any state was 20. Data gathered by the *Politics in the American States* series were available for 1969, 1981, and 1989. The scores for 1969 were used for 1973–80, scores for 1981 were used for 1981–88, and the scores for 1989 were used for 1989–96. The data sources were Schlesinger (1971) for the 1969 scores, and Beyle (1983, 1990) for the 1981 and 1989 scores, respectively.

appendix G

Regression Tables for Chapter 5

Table G.1 presents the results of the event history analysis. Because it is difficult to interpret the coefficients in logistic regression, table G.2 presents a more intuitive way of understanding the impact of key explanatory variables. It shows how the probability that a state would authorize an independent commission as the values of key variables (those that are statistically significant in the regression) change. Specifically, it shows the "mean effects," or the difference between the likelihood of commission enactment when a key variable is set at its maximum and its minimum values.

For example, the mean effect of scandal is the difference in the predicted probability of commission enactment for a state that experienced the maximum amount (and severity) of scandals for the data set and a state that experienced no scandals. All other variables are set at their mean values. Mean effects are calculated using the coefficients from Model 2 in table G.1. The formula used to calculate the predicted probabilities is $1/(1 +e^{-L})$, where $L = B_0 + B_1X_1 + B_2X_2. \ldots$

Table G.1   The Authorization of Independent Legislative Ethics Commissions in the American States, 1973–96

Variable	Model 1	Model 2
Culture/Ideology		
Individualist culture	1.293 (1.535)	
Traditionalist culture	−2.338* (1.089)	−1.748* (.744)
Ideology	−0.001 (.022)	
Party competition		
Unified government	0.340 (.637)	
Majority party control	0.023 (.030)	
Scandal/Corruption		
Scandal	0.512** (.132)	0.524** (.123)
TPO (traditional party organization)	−0.813+ (.459)	−0.599* (.233)
Economic self-interest		
Compensation	−0.001 (.018)	
Attorneys	0.032 (0.032)	0.027 (.026)
Policy diffusion		
Neighboring states	1.068** (.411)	0.914* (.374)
Direct democracy		
Initiative	0.291 (.619)	
Preexisting laws		
Campaign finance laws	0.383 (.387)	
Bureaucratic factors		
State wealth	−0.194 (.220)	
Bureaucratic capacity	0.002 (.010)	
Gubernatorial powers	−0.136 (.109)	−0.157+ (0.086)
Year dummies (not presented)	Yes	Yes
Constant	−0.751 (4.422)	−0.332 (1.697)
−2 log likelihood	129.187	133.940
PRE (proportional reduction in error)	.05	.05
Psuedo R^2 (Nagelkerke)	.36	.33
No. of observations	626	626

Note: $+ p < .10$; $* p < .05$; $** p < .01$, one-tailed tests. Standard errors in parentheses. Each model was estimated with a dummy variable for each year (except 1973). Coefficients for the annual dummies are not reported to save space. Model 1 includes all independent variables; Model 2 keeps only those variables for which the coefficients exceed the standard errors. PRE = (errors in predicting the dependent variable, DV, using the modal value of the DV − errors using the model) / errors using the modal value of the DV.

Sources: Data for the dependent variable came from *Campaign Finance, Ethics and Lobby Law Blue Book* (Council on Governmental Ethics Laws 1990, 1993), and *Public Integrity Annual* (Council of State Governments 1996), and state statutes. See appendix F for details on measurement of the dependent and independent variables.

Table G.2   Mean Effects for Key Independent Variables

Variable	Mean Effect (%)
Scandal	71.84
Regional diffusion	1.59
Nontraditionalist culture	0.25
Gubernatorial power	0.59
TPO (traditional party organization)	0.32
Diffusion and nontraditionalist culture	4.17
Diffusion and scandal	97.09

Note: The mean effect represents the difference between the predicted probabilities of ethics commission adoption when the independent variable is at its maximum and minimum values, setting all other variables at their means. For rows with two variables, the mean effect is calculated as the difference between the predicted probabilities when both variables are at the level most and least favorable for commission adoption. Mean effects are calculated using the coefficient estimates of Model 2 in table G.1.

notes

Chapter One

1. Michael Mello, "CVS, R.I's Largest Private Employer, at Center of Probe into Corporate Influence," Associated Press State and Local Wire, February 3, 2004, http://1180-web.lexis-nexis.com.lp.hscl.ufl.edu/universe/document?_m=550397df0327b616ebd1db280f9a4d5b&_docnum=1&wchp=dGLbVzz-zSkVA&_md5=2fdcd6eo77e73e3ffae9f338598a9ad; Noel C. Paul, "As Questions about Conflict of Interest Mount, States Like Rhode Island Consider Making Lawmaking a Full-Time Job," *Christian Science Monitor*, February 5, 2004; Michael Corkery, "Montalbano Proposes to Reinstate Gift Ban," *Providence Journal*, January 27, 2004.

2. Frank Cagle, "Scandals Had Banner Year," *Knoxville News-Sentinel*, December 27, 2003.

3. Fredric U. Dicker, "Pol 'Crook Book' May Be Bribe Firm's Smoking Gun," *New York Post*, February 17, 2003; Celeste Katz, "More Illegal Gifts from Prison Firm," *New York Daily News*, February 23, 2003; Marc Humbert, "Pataki Wants New Ethics Watchdogs for Legislature and Courts," Associated Press State and Local Wire, June 16, 2003, http://80-web.lexis-nexis.com.lp.hscl.ufl.edu/universe/document?_m=95bdd0fd0c94dc9ca764347a8cea59a7&_docnum=1&wchp=dGLbVtz-zSkVA&_md5=9087aa32a98df9fcd0eaec62602f7c43; Tom Precious, "Albany Ethics Overhaul Urged by Watchdogs," *Buffalo News*, January 6, 2004.

4. J. Huffstutter, "Former Illinois Governor Ryan Indicted," *Los Angeles Times*, December 18, 2003; John Patterson, "Lawmakers Approve Sweeping Ethics Bill," *Chicago Daily Herald*, November 21, 2003; Hugo Rojas, Illinois Common Cause President, in discussion with the author, February 11, 2004; Michael Dresser, "Bereano Books Cruise to Host Md. Legislators," *Baltimore Sun*, July 16, 2003; Editorial, "Our Say: Bereano's Latest Idea: A Cruise on the SS Loophole," *Capital-Gazette Communications*, July 20, 2003.

5. Mike Glover, "Key Lawmakers Agree to Revisit Gift Law," Associated Press State and Local Wire, January 30, 2003, http://80-web.lexis-nexis

.com.lp.hscl.ufl.edu/universe/doclist?_m=7f08f11ced0e48461d232f7543db1534 &wchp=dGLbVtz-zSkVA&_md5=2258a5a972ac51f58a5633cdf1c065a3.

6. Martha Stoddard, "Seminar on Scandal Aims at Avoidance," *Omaha World Herald,* January 12, 2004.

7. See the account of development of the professions in William M. Sullivan, *Work and Integrity: The Crisis and Promise of Professionalism in America* (New York: Harper Business, 1995), chap. 1.

8. Governor Thomas Dewey of New York, cited in the *Report of the Special Legislative Commission on Integrity and Ethical Standards in Government to Hon. Thomas E. Dewey, Governor, and to the Legislature of New York* (March 5, 1954), 169.

9. Eleanor D. Glor and Ian Greene, "The Government of Canada's Approach to Ethics: The Evolution of Ethical Government," *Public Integrity* 5 (2003): 39–65; Ian Greene and David Shugarman, *Honest Politics: Seeking Integrity in Canadian Public Life* (Toronto: James Lorimer: 1997); Dennis F. Thompson, *Ethics in Congress* (Washington, D.C.: Brookings Institution Press, 1995); Ronald E. Weber, "The Quality of State Legislative Representation: A Critical Assessment," *Journal of Politics* 61 (1999): 609–27.

10. George C. S. Benson, *Political Corruption in America* (Lexington, Mass.: D.C. Heath, 1978); J. Patrick Dobel, *Public Integrity* (Baltimore: Johns Hopkins University Press, 1999); Ann Marie Donahue, *Ethics in Politics and Government* (New York: H. W. Wilson, 1989); Michael Johnston, *Political Corruption and Public Policy in America* (Monterey, Calif.: Brooks/Cole, 1982); John G. Peters and Susan Welch, "Political Corruption in America; A Search for Definitions and a Theory, or If Political Corruption Is in the Mainstream of American Politics Why Is It Not in the Mainstream of American Politics Research?" *American Political Science Review* 72 (1978): 974–84; Robert N. Roberts and Marion T. Doss, Jr., *From Watergate to Whitewater: The Public Integrity War* (Westport, Conn.: Praeger, 1997); Susan Rose-Ackerman, *Corruption and Government: Causes, Consequences and Reform* (Cambridge: Cambridge University Press, 1999).

11. Christopher J. Anderson and Yuliya V. Tverdova, "Corruption, Political Allegiances, and Attitudes toward Government in Contemporary Democracies," *American Journal of Political Science* 47 (2003): 91–109; Johnston, *Political Corruption and Public Policy in America*; Mitchell A. Seligson, "The Impact of Corruption on Regime Legitimacy: A Comparative Study of Four Countries," *Journal of Politics* 64 (2002): 408–33.

12. Paul R. Abramson, *Political Attitudes in America: Formation and Change* (San Francisco: W. H. Freeman, 1983); Jack Citrin, "Comment: The Political Relevance of Trust in Government," *American Political Science Review* 68 (1974): 973–88; Stephen C. Craig, *The Malevolent Leaders: Popular Discontent in America* (Boulder, Colo.: Westview Press, 1993); Arthur H. Miller, "Political Issues and Trust in Government: 1964–1970," *American Political Science Review* 68 (1974): 951–72; James P. Pfiffner, "Judging Presidential Character," *Public Integrity* 5 (2003): 7–24; Thompson, *Ethics in Congress*; Weber, "Quality of State Legislative Representation."

13. Bradford DeLong and Andrei Shleifer, "Princes and Merchants: Government and City Growth before the Industrial Revolution," *Journal of Law and Economics* 36 (1993): 671–702; Stephen Knack and Philip Keefer, "Institutions and Economic Performance: Cross-Country Tests Using Alternative Institutional Measures," *Economics and Politics* 7 (1995): 207–27; Rafael LaPorta, Florencio Lopez-de Silanes, Andrei Shleifer, and Robert Vishny, *The Quality of Government*, NBER Working Paper 6727 (Cambridge, Mass.: National Bureau of Economic Research, 1998); Paolo Mauro, "Corruption and Growth," *Quarterly Journal of Economics* 110 (1995): 681–712; Douglass North, *Growth and Structural Change* (New York: Norton, 1981).

14. Benson, *Political Corruption in America*.

15. Dennis F. Thompson, *Political Ethics and Public Office* (Cambridge, Mass.: Harvard University Press, 1987), chap. 4; Thompson, *Ethics in Congress*, chap. 1; Herbert Fain, "The Case for a Zero Gift Policy," *Public Integrity* 4 (2002): 61–74; Rebekah Herrick, *Fashioning the More Ethical Representative: The Impact of Ethics Reforms in the U.S. House of Representatives* (Westport, Conn.: Praeger, 2003).

16. Frank Anechiarico and James B. Jacobs, *The Pursuit of Absolute Integrity: How Corruption Control Makes Government Ineffective* (Chicago: University of Chicago Press, 1996); Suzanne Garment, *Scandal: The Crisis of Mistrust in American Politics* (New York: Times Books, 1991); G. Calvin Mackenzie and Michael Hafkin, *Scandal Proof: Do Ethics Laws Make Government Ethical?* (Washington, D.C.: Brookings Institution Press, 2002); Alan Rosenthal, *Drawing the Line: Legislative Ethics in the States* (New York: Twentieth Century Fund, 1996); Susan J. Tolchin and Martin Tolchin, *Glass Houses: Congressional Ethics and the Politics of Venom* (Boulder, Colo.: Westview Press, 2001); though see Herrick, *Fashioning the More Ethical Representative*.

17. Mackenzie and Hafkin, *Scandal Proof*, 177; Donald J. Maletz and Jerry Herbel, "Some Paradoxes of Government Ethics Revisited" (paper presented at 1998 Annual Meeting of the American Political Science Association, Boston), 6.

18. Beth Bazar, *State Legislators' Occupations: A Decade of Change* (Denver: National Conference of State Legislatures, 1987); Herrick, *Fashioning the More Ethical Representative*; Mackenzie and Hafkin, *Scandal Proof*; Alfred Neely IV, "Ethics in Government Laws," in *Ethics in Politics and Government*, ed. Anne Marie Donahue (New York: H. W. Wilson, 1989); Rosenthal, *Drawing the Line*; Beth Rosenson, "Costs and Benefits of Ethics Laws" (paper presented at Conference on Governance and Political Ethics, University of Montreal, Montreal, May 14–15, 2004).

19. See, however, Herrick, *Fashioning the More Ethical Representative*. Kim Quaile Hill, "Democratization and Corruption," *American Politics Research* 31 (2003): 613–31; Mackenzie and Hafkin, *Scandal Proof*; Rosenson, "Costs and Benefits of Ethics Laws."

20. Anechiarico and Jacobs, *Pursuit of Absolute Integrity*, 7; Donald J. Maletz and Jerry Herbel, "Beyond Idealism: Democracy and Ethics Reform," *American Review of Public Administration* 30 (2000): 37, 20.

21. Beth Rosenson, "Why U.S. Senators Voted to Limit Honoraria, 1981–1983" (paper presented at panel on Decision Making in the Modern Senate at Midwest Political Science Association meeting, Chicago, April 25–28, 2002); Beth Rosenson, "Legislative Voting on Ethics Reform in Two States: The Influence of Economic Self-Interest, Ideology and Institutional Power," *Public Integrity* 5 (2003): 205–22.

22. Rosenthal, *Drawing the Line,* 11; Douglas Dales, "Legislators Vote Own Ethics Code," *New York Times,* March 24, 1964.

23. Edmund Beard and Stephen Horn, *Congressional Ethics: The View from the House* (Washington, D.C.: Brookings Institution Press, 1976); Marshall R. Goodman, Timothy Holp, and Eric Rademacher, "State Legislative Ethics: Proactive Reform or Reactive Defense?" (paper presented at 1994 Annual Meeting of Midwest Political Science Association, Chicago); Allan Katz, "The Politics of Congressional Ethics," in *The House at Work,* ed. Joseph Cooper and G. Calvin Mackenzie (Austin: University of Texas Press, 1981); Thompson, *Ethics in Congress.*

24. Marshall R. Goodman, Timothy J. Holp, and Karen M. Ludwig, "Understanding State Legislative Ethics Reform: The Importance of Political and Institutional Culture," in *Public Integrity Annual,* ed. James S. Bowman (Lexington, Ky.: Council of State Governments, 1996); Rosenthal, *Drawing the Line.*

25. Common Cause, "Common Cause Issues Poll," *Common Cause Magazine* (May/June 1991); William G. Mayer, "Public Attitudes on Campaign Finance," in *A User's Guide to Campaign Finance Reform,* ed. Gerald C. Lubenow (Lanham, Md.: Rowman and Littlefield, 2001).

26. Virginia Bradbury, "Government Ethics Reform: The Financial Disclosure Law," Ph.D. diss., Boston College, 1996; Marshall R. Goodman, Timothy Holp, and Eric Rademacher, "Patterns of State Legislative Ethics Reform: Have They Gotten the Message?" (paper presented at 1993 Annual Meeting of American Political Science Association, Washington, D.C.); Goodman, Holp and, Rademacher, "State Legislative Ethics: Proactive Reform or Reactive Defense?"; Goodman, Holp, and Ludwig, "Understanding State Legislative Ethics Reform"; Katz, *Politics of Congressional Ethics;* Rosenthal, *Drawing the Line.*

27. Bradbury, "Government Ethics Reform"; Tom Loftus, "The Road to Ethical Legislatures Isn't Paved with Tougher Laws," in *State Government: CQ's Guide to Current Issues and Activities in 1992–1993,* ed. Thad Beyle (Washington, D.C.: Congressional Quarterly Books, 1992).

28. Goodman, Holp, and Rademacher, "Patterns of State Legislative Ethics Reform"; Goodman, Holp, and Rademacher, "State Legislative Ethics: Proactive Reform or Reactive Defense?"; Goodman et al., "Legislative Ethics: Reform and Reaction in the States"; Goodman, Holp, and Ludwig, "Understanding State Legislative Ethics Reform."

29. Goodman, Holp, and Rademacher, "Patterns of State Legislative Ethics Reform"; Goodman, Holp, and Ludwig, "Understanding State Legislative Ethics Reform."

30. Rosenthal, *Drawing the Line.*

31. Jeffrey M. Berry, *The New Liberalism: The Rising Power of Citizen Groups* (Washington, D.C.: Brookings Institution Press, 1999); Michael McCann, *Taking Reform Seriously: Perspectives on Public Interest Liberalism* (Ithaca, N.Y.: Cornell University Press, 1986); Andrew S. McFarland, *Common Cause: Lobbying in the Public Interest* (Chatham, N.J.: Chatham House Publishers, 1984).

32. McCann, *Taking Reform Seriously*, 76; Richard Hofstadter, *The Age of Reform* (New York: Knopf, 1955), 9; George Mowry, *The California Progressives* (Chicago: Quadrangle Books, 1951), 99.

33. Daniel Elazar, *Cities of the Prairie; The Metropolitan Frontier and American Politics* (New York: Basic Books, 1970); David Nice, "Political Corruption in the American States," *American Politics Quarterly* 11 (1983): 507–17; Michael Johnston, "Corruption and Political Culture in America: An Empirical Perspective," *Publius* 13 (1983): 19–39; Kenneth J. Meier and Thomas M. Holbrook, "I Seen My Opportunities and I Took 'Em:' Political Corruption in the American States," *Journal of Politics* 54 (1992): 135–55.

34. Arthur S. Link and Richard L. McCormick, *Progressivism* (Wheeling, Ill.: Harlan Davidson, 1983); Mowry, *California Progressives*; Clifford W. Patton, *The Battle for Municipal Reform: Mobilization and Attack, 1875 to 1900* (College Park, Md.: McGrath, 1969); Stephen Skowronek, *Building a New American State: The Expansion of National Administrative Capacities, 1877–1920* (Cambridge: Cambridge University Press, 1982); David P. Thelen, *Robert M. LaFollette and the Insurgent Spirit* (Boston: Little, Brown, 1976); Sean M. Theriault, "Patronage, the Pendleton Act, and the Power of the People," *Journal of Politics* 65 (2003): 50–68; Robert Wiebe, *The Search for Order, 1877–1920* (New York: Hill and Wang, 1967).

35. Richard Hofstadter, *The Age of Reform* (New York: Knopf, 1955); Link and McCormick, *Progressivism*; Roberts and Doss, *From Watergate to Whitewater*; Thelen, *Robert M. LaFollette and the Insurgent Spirit.*

36. Marie Gottschalk, *The Shadow Welfare State: Labor, Business and the Politics of Health Care in the United States* (Ithaca, N.Y.: Cornell University Press, 2000); Ellen Immergut, "The Theoretical Core of the New Institutionalism," *Politics and Society* 26 (1998): 5–34; James March and Johan Olsen, "The New Institutionalism: Organizational Factors in Political Life," *American Political Science Review* 78 (1984): 734–49; Walter Powell and Paul J. Di Maggio, eds., *The New Institutionalism in Organizational Analysis* (Chicago: University of Chicago Press; 1991); Kenneth Shepsle, "Studying Institutions: Some Lessons from the Rational Choice Approach," *Journal of Theoretical Politics* 1 (1989): 134–48; Kathleen Thelen and Sven Steinmo, "Historical Institutionalism in Comparative Politics," in *Structuring Politics: Historical Institutionalism in Comparative Analysis*, eds. Sven Steinmo, Kathleen Thelen, and Frank Longstreth (Cambridge: Cambridge University Press, 1992).

37. Barry R. Weingast and William J. Marshall, "The Industrial Organization of Congress; or, Why Legislatures, Like Firms, Are Not Organized as Markets," *Journal of Political Economy* 96 (1998): 132–63; Shepsle, "Studying Institutions."

38. On the impact of compensation at the state level, see Morris P. Fiorina, "Divided Government in the American States: A Byproduct of Legislative Professionalism?" *American Political Science Review* 88 (1994): 304–16; Robert E. Hogan, "Sources of Competition in State Legislative Primary Elections," *Legislative Studies Quarterly* 28 (2003): 103–26; Alan Rosenthal, "Turnover in State Legislatures," *American Journal of Political Science* 18 (1974): 609–16; Peverill Squire, "Legislative Professionalization and Membership Diversity in State Legislatures," *Legislative Studies Quarterly* 17 (1992): 69–79. On the link between pay raises and congressional ethics reform, see Charles H. Stewart III, "Ain't Misbehaving, or, Reflections on Two Centuries of Congressional Corruption" (Center for American Political Studies, Occasional Working Papers, 94–4).

Chapter Two

1. Each state-case consists of a within-state comparison of a failed reform effort and a later, successful reform effort. Thus each case contains two observations. Because there are different values on the dependent variables—the outcomes—and the independent variables (the potential factors that explain the outcomes) within each case, we can apply what John Stuart Mill (*A System of Logic, Rationative and Inductive: Being a Connected View of the Principles of Evidence and the Methods of Scientific Investigation* [Charlottesville, Va.: Ibis Publishing, 1980; originally published 1843]) calls the "method of difference," which attempts to identify the causal factors associated with different outcomes.

2. With congruence procedure, if the outcomes are consistent with what theory predicts, the likelihood of a causal relationship is strengthened. See Alexander George and Timothy J. McKeown, "Case Studies and Theories of Organizational Decision Making," in *Advances in Information Processing in Organizations,* vol. 2, ed. Robert Culam and Richard Smith (Greenwich, Conn.: JAI Press, 1985); Stephen Van Evera, *Guide to Methods for Students of Political Science* (Ithaca, N.Y.: Cornell University Press, 1997). The cases used here are well suited to using congruence procedure because there is large variation in the values of both the outcome or dependent variable, on the one hand, and the explanatory or independent variables, on the other; the variation is also relatively simple to interpret.

3. George C. S. Benson, *Political Corruption in America* (Lexington, Mass.: D.C. Heath, 1978); Marshall R. Goodman, Timothy J. Holp, and Karen M. Ludwig, "Understanding State Legislative Ethics Reform: The Importance of Political and Institutional Culture," in *Public Integrity Annual,* ed. James S. Bowman (Lexington, Ky.: Council of State Governments, 1996); Ari Hoogenboom, "Did Gilded Age Scandals Bring Reform?" in *Before Watergate,* ed. Abraham S. Eisenstadt, Ari Hoogenboom, and Hans L. Trefousse (New York: Brooklyn College Press, 1978); Arthur S. Link and Richard L. McCormick, *Progressivism* (Wheeling, Ill.: Harlan Davidson, 1983); Alan Rosenthal, *Drawing the Line: Leg-*

islative Ethics in the States (New York: Twentieth Century Fund, 1996); Joseph Zimmerman, *Curbing Unethical Behavior in Government* (Westport, Conn.: Greenwood Press, 1994).

4. Anthony Downs, "Up and Down With Ecology: The "Issue-Attention Cycle," *Public Interest* 28 (1972): 38–50; Scott P. Hays and Henry R. Glick, "The Role of Agenda Setting in Policy Innovation: An Event History Analysis of Living-Will Laws," *American Politics Quarterly* 25 (1997): 497–516; John Kingdon, *Agendas, Alternatives and Public Policies* (Boston: Little, Brown, 1984); M. Linsky, *Impact: How the Press Affects Federal Policymaking* (New York: W. W. Norton, 1986); Patrick O'Heffernan, "Mass Media Roles in Foreign Policy," in *Media Power in Politics*, 3rd edition, ed. Doris A Graber (Washington, D.C.: CQ Press, 1994); Everett M. Rogers and James W. Dearing, "Agenda Setting Research: Where Has It Been, Where Is It Going?" in *Communication Yearbook* 11, ed. James A. Anderson (Beverly Hills, Calf.: Sage, 1988).

5. Howard Sacks, "Ethical Standards in the State Legislature," in *Strengthening the States: Essays on Legislative Reform*, ed. Donald G. Herzberg and Alan Rosenthal (New York: Doubleday & Co., 1971); Marshall R. Goodman, Timothy Holp, and Eric Rademacher, "Patterns of State Legislative Ethics Reform: Have They Gotten the Message?" (paper presented at 1993 Annual Meeting of American Political Science Association, Washington, D.C.); Marshall R. Goodman, Timothy Holp, and Eric Rademacher, "State Legislative Ethics: Proactive Reform or Reactive Defense?" (paper presented at 1994 Annual Meeting of Midwest Political Science Association, Chicago).

6. William Bianco, *Trust: Representatives and Constituuents* (Ann Arbor: University of Michigan Press, 1994); John A. Clark, "Congressional Salaries and the Politics of Unpopular Votes," *American Politics Quarterly* 24 (1996): 150–68; Beth Rosenson, "Why U.S. Senators Voted to Limit Honoraria, 1981–1983" (paper presented at panel on Decision Making in the Modern Senate at Midwest Political Science Association meeting, Chicago, April 25–28, 2002).

7. Goodman, Holp, and Ludwig, "Understanding State Legislative Ethics Reform."

8. Stephen Skowronek, *Building a New American State: The Expansion of National Administrative Capacities, 1877–1920* (Cambridge: Cambridge University Press, 1982); David P. Thelen, *Robert M. LaFollette and the Insurgent Spirit* (Boston: Little, Brown, 1976); Robert Wiebe, *The Search for Order, 1877–1920* (New York: Hill and Wang, 1967). Conversely, Ripley and Sundquist argue that lower party competition, in particular as manifested by unified government, may make the passage of legislation easier. See Randall Ripley, *Majority Party Leadership in Congress* (Boston: Little, Brown, 1969); James Sundquist, "Needed: A Political Theory for the New Era of Coalition *Government* in the United States," *Political Science Quarterly* 103 (1988): 613–35.

9. One example is the corrupt elections laws of 1873 in Pennsylvania, which preceded enactment of the secret ballot by eighteen years in that state. The 1873 legislation, which followed media revelations about legislative corruption,

instituted statewide voter registration, required that ballots be numbered, insisted on minority representation at the polls, and provided that contested elections be settled in court. See Ari Hoogenboom, "Did Gilded Age Scandals Bring Reform?" in *Before Watergate*, ed. Abraham S. Eisenstadt, Ari Hoogenboom, and Hans L.Trefousse (New York: Brooklyn College Press, 1978), 132.

10. Lewis L. Gould, *Reform and Regulation in American Politics, 1900–1916* (New York: John Wiley & Sons, 1976), 61. Gould is referring to Republicans in Iowa and Wisconsin who resisted a variety of anticorruption reforms during the first decade of the twentieth century.

11. Virginia Bradbury, "Government Ethics Reform: The Financial Disclosure Law," Ph.D. diss., Boston College, 1996; Tom Loftus, *The Art of Legislative Politics* (Washington, D.C.: CQ Press, 1994); Beth Rosenson, "Legislative Voting on Ethics Reform in Two States: The Influence of Economic Self-Interest, Ideology and Institutional Power," *Public Integrity* 5 (2003): 205–22.

12. On the general influence of governors, see E. Lee Bernick and Charles W. Wiggins, "Executive–Legislative Relations: The Governor's Role as Chief Legislator," in *Gubernatorial Leadership and State Policy*, ed. Eric B. Herzik and Brent W. Brown (Westport, Conn.: Greenwood Press, 1991); Dan Durning, "Education Reform in Arkansas: The Governor's Role in Policymaking," in *Gubernatorial Leadership and State Policy*, ed. Herzik and Brown. On corruption-fighting governors in the Progressive era, see George Mowry, *The California Progressives* (Chicago: Quadrangle Books, 1951), and Thelen, *Robert M. LaFollette and the Insurgent Spirit.* On governors and ethics reform in the 1990s, see Marshall R. Goodman, Timothy Holp, and Eric Rademacher, "State Legislative Ethics: Proactive Reform or Reactive Defense?" (paper presented at 1994 Annual Meeting of Midwest Political Science Association, Chicago).

13. Mowry, *California Progressives*; Thelen, *Robert M. LaFollette and the Insurgent Spirit.*

14. On the competition between the two branches, see Alan Rosenthal, *Governors and Legislators: Contending Powers* (Washington, D.C.: CQ Press, 1990).

15. When using the *New York Times Index* for states outside New York, I looked under the heading for each state and also under the heading "Crime" for each year. When using the *Los Angeles Times*, which has no index, I looked at the front page of each day's paper and also at the "In the State" summary for each day. For the Massachusetts case, I used the indices at the State House Library for the *Boston Globe*, *Boston Herald/Evening Herald*, and *Boston Phoenix*. For each year, I searched under the headings "Corruption," "Politics and Government," "Legislature," and "Governor." For New York, I relied on the *New York Times Index* for each year, looking under the headings "Legislature," "Governor," and "Politics and Government."

16. Data came from a data set provided by Morris Fiorina. See appendix B for more information on the measurement of the compensation variable.

17. Data came from the Council of State Governments, *Book of the States* (Lexington, Ky.: Council of State Governments) for various years.

18. For example, California's average citizen ideology score during its period of reform failure and success combined was 54.93. Massachusetts' score for the similar period was 79.92, and New York's was 66.48. Data came from William D. Berry, Evan J. Ringquist, Richard C. Fording, and Russell L. Hanson, "Measuring Citizen and Government Ideology in the American States, 1960–1993," *American Journal of Political Science* 42 (1997): 337–48; it is available on http://www.pubadm.fsu.edu/archives/. Possible scores range from 0 to 100. Relatively conservative states such as Arizona, Arkansas, and Nebraska never score above 50 for the entire period (1960–93). Conservative states tend to have scores ranging from 0 to 40. The lowest possible score is 1.16 for Mississippi, and the maximum is 93.91 for Massachusetts. California by this measure is the least liberal of the three states, although this is due in part to the fact that ideology is measured for the 1960s, when reform was being considered, and ideology tends to trend upward (in a liberal direction) over the thirty-four-year period.

19. An alternative strategy might have been to do a cross-sectional analysis of state variation in ethics laws. One could look at one state that has very weak legislative ethics regulations and one that has very strong regulations, and then test theories to explain this variation. The problem with this kind of comparison is that in order to understand why two states have very different laws at a given time, it is necessary to understand the history of efforts to enact ethics regulations over a long period prior to that point. Because the first state legislative ethics law was enacted in 1954, to compare two states' ethics laws in the 1980s or 1990s, we must consider each state's actions over a period of decades preceding the point of comparison. By contrast, the case studies here allow for a focus on reform failure and success during more narrowly focused time periods, less than seven years in each case. This allows the use of process-tracing techniques that would be difficult to employ across lengthier periods of time.

20. *Cal. Government Code* § 2-2-8940.

21. Gene Blake, "State Senate Committee Votes Tough Law on Members' Ethics," *Los Angeles Times,* June 24, 1966.

22. Gene Blake, "3 Key Measures Sent to State Senate Floor," *Los Angeles Times,* June 29, 1966. See also the comments of several legislators in Gene Blake, "Legislature Curbs Conflict of Interest," *Los Angeles Times,* July 8, 1966.

23. Gene Blake, "State Legislators: They Serve Too Many Masters?" *Los Angeles Times,* September 15, 1965.

24. It may have been reported on more extensively by the *Sacramento Bee*, however.

25. Blake, "State Legislators: They Serve Too Many Masters?"

26. Blake, "State Legislators: They Serve Too Many Masters?"

27. Gene Blake, "The Financial Resources of California's Legislators," *Los Angeles Times*, Sept. 15, 1965.

28. Editorial, "Legislature: Pay and Ethics," *Los Angeles Times*, September 19, 1965.

29. Editorial, "Legislature: Pay and Ethics"; Don Thomas, "NY Code Sheds Light on Code for Legislators," *Los Angeles Times*, September 19, 1965; "Bill Proposes Code of Ethics for Legislators," *Los Angeles Times*, April 6, 1965; Editorial, "Legislative Reforms Needed," *Los Angeles Times*, June 9, 1965; Editorial, "Bad 'Compromise on Ethics,'" *Los Angeles Times*, June 20, 1966.

30. On the influence of party competition on the passage of the Pendleton Act, see Skowronek, *Building a New American State*. During this era, control of both Congress and the executive branch switched back and forth between the two main parties. Nine years prior to the passage of the Pendleton Act, the Republicans controlled Congress. Two years later, the Democrats were in control, and by 1883 the Republicans had retaken control. Morris Fiorina, Paul Peterson, and Bertram Johnson, *The New American Democracy* (Boston: Allyn Bacon Longman, 2003), 224.

31. Consider, for example, Ohio, where the two parties were tied in the Senate, or South Dakota and Wyoming, where the majority party in the Senate held two- and one-seat advantages, respectively.

32. Sacks, "Ethical Standards in the State Legislature." Because financial disclosure was voluntary for the 1965 *Times* article and most legislators did not choose to provide specific amounts for their outside earnings, we do not know exactly how much legislators stood to lose from the new restrictions. In any event, a 166 percent annual salary increase was a sizable amount.

33. Rosenson, "Why U.S. Senators Voted to Limit Honoraria."

34. Of the thirty members who voted (four senators abstained), thirteen were attorneys. The correlation coefficient for attorneys and support for the bill is only .07, and was not significant at the .10 level. In addition to examining the simple correlation coefficient, I performed a logistic regression that controlled for other factors, which also showed that attorneys were no less likely to support the bill than non-attorneys. The other variables in the regression were (1) members' electoral margin in the last election, (2) a dichotomous measure for whether the member was up for reelection that year (an important variable to control for given the pay-raise component of the bill), (3) a dichotomous measure for occupational status as a business owner, and two measures of institutional power: (4) majority party status, and (5) chairmanship of a committee with above-average seniority for its members. None of the variables in the equation achieved statistical significance. This is most likely due to the fact that there were only twenty-nine observations and six independent variables (complete information was unavailable for one of the thirty who cast a vote on the bill). See California Legislature, *Senate Daily Journal*, July 7, 1966, 1021, for information on how members voted. Members' occupational information came from the *California Blue Book*, 1965–66, 56–62.

35. This is available at http://www.goodbyemag.com/feb/brown.htm. The *Los Angeles Times* accounts of the addresses from 1961 to 1964 show Brown emphasizing educational issues, the development of a rapid transit system, housing, economic development, labor–management relations, natural resources, and election law.

36. Robert M. Blanchard, "Brown Asks Support on Listing Election Costs," *Los Angeles Times*, February 6, 1965.

37. The legislature at that time met for 120 days in odd-numbered years and 30 days for budget sessions in even-numbered years. To consider nonbudgetary issues in an even year, a special session had to be called. See Charles G. Bell and Charles M. Price, *California Government Today* (Homewood, Ill.: Dorsey Press, 1980), 187.

38. E. Lee Bernick, "Gubernatorial Tools: Formal vs. Informal," *Journal of Politics* 41 (1979): 656–64; T. L. Beyle, "Governors," in *Politics in the American States: A Comparative Analysis*, 4th edition, ed. Virginia Gray, Herbert Jacob, and Kenneth Vines (Boston: Little, Brown, 1983); Durning, "Education Reform in Arkansas"; Coleman Ransone, *The American Governorship* (Westport, Conn.: Greenwood Press, 1982).

39. Bernick and Wiggins, "Executive–Legislative Relations," 75.

40. Bell and Price, *California Government Today*, 187, 188.

41. This is available at http://www.rcf.usc.edu/~unruhins/about_jesse_m_unruh.html.

42. Blake, "3 Key Measures Sent to Senate Floor."

43. Gene Blake, "Senate Approves Measures to Modernize State Constitution," *Los Angeles Times*, July 1, 1966; Editorial, "What Does the Senate Want?" *Los Angeles Times*, July 4, 1966.

44. All four Democrats voting no (Miller, Teale, O'Sullivan, and Quick) were committee chairmen. However, every Democrat in the 1965–66 Senate chaired at least one committee. To assess whether the chairs voting no were powerful compared with other chairs voting yes, I considered the relative desirability and power of committee chairmanships. One measure of this power is the average seniority of a committee's members, with higher average seniority indicating a more powerful committee. The first three Democrats who voted no chaired committees with above-average seniority, an indicator that these were powerful committees (*California Blue Book*, 1965–66, 67–68).

45. Blake, "Legislature Curbs Conflict of Interest."

46. Bell and Price, *California Government Today*, 188.

47. Morris P. Fiorina, "Divided Government in the American States: A Byproduct of Legislative Professionalism?" *American Political Science Review* 88 (1994): 304–16.

48. Bell and Price, *California Government Today,* 188.

49. Bradbury, "Government Ethics Reform," 201.

50. Bradbury, "Government Ethics Reform," 48–49.

51. While the Senate Ethics Committee had recommended ten rules changes, all but the two regarding a newly constituted ethics committee and financial disclosure died in committee. Those that never came up for a vote included a $100 annual limit on gifts from each lobbyist to a legislator, fees to lawyer-legislators for representation before state agencies, "no-show" jobs, use of confidential information for financial gain, and all appearances before state agencies where there was a "close economic association" with the person represented. See Bradbury,

"Government Ethics Reform," chap. 4, for a detailed account of the 1977 Senate and House rules changes.

52. While none of these papers published their own indices to coverage prior to the 1980s, the Massachusetts State House Library has an index to coverage by all three papers. I searched for each year under the headings "Corruption," "Politics and Government," "Legislature," and "Governor."

53. Robert J. Anglin, "U.S. Official Sees Corruption in Mass. Government," *Boston Globe*, October 23, 1971.

54. Jonathan Fuerbringer, "Dukakis Says He Inherited Corrupt System," *Boston Globe*, May 7, 1975; Michael Kenney, "Dukakis Backs Off from His 'Legacy of Corruption' Allegation," May 9, 1975.

55. Bradbury, "Government Ethics Reform," 76.

56. These bills were House No. 2008, House No. 4396, and House No. 3577, proposed by Charles Flaherty, John Businger, and Ronald Pina, all liberal Democrats working with Common Cause (see Bradbury, "Government Ethics Reform," 89). See also Editorial, "Financial Disclosure Now," *Boston Globe*, April 24, 1975.

57. Bradbury, "Government Ethics Reform," 90–92.

58. Bradbury, "Government Ethics Reform," 92.

59. Council of State Governments, *Book of the States* (Lexington, Ky.: Council of State Governments), 1974–75 and 1976–77.

60. "House Votes Itself Pay Raise–Hatch Calls It Bad Timing," *Boston Globe*, April 7, 1977.

61. *Book of the States*, 1974–75 and 1976–77.

62. Jeremiah Murphy, "We Will Move Forward," *Boston Globe*, January 11, 1973; Bob Hassett and Bill Duncliffe, "Things That Were Left Unsaid," *Boston Herald*, January 7, 1975; "Governor Promises Balanced Budget," *Boston Globe*, January 8, 1976.

63. Nick King, "Governor Lists Nearly 30 Bills," *Boston Globe*, April 27, 1977.

64. Bradbury, "Government Ethics Reform," 143–46.

65. Bradbury, "Government Ethics Reform," 196.

66. Office of the Governor, *Memorandum on H. 5715*, May 22, 1978. In the end, the House agreed in part with the Senate-Dukakis position. All elected and appointed officials, candidates, and people who held a major policymaking position in state or county government would have to file disclosure reports. People serving without compensation or serving on a governmental board that had no authority to expend public money would be exempted from disclosure. Virginia Bradbury, "Government Ethics Reform," 198–99.

67. Bradbury, "Government Ethics Reform," 153–69.

68. When ethics-in-government proposals go to the ballot, they generally succeed by wide margins. See Thomas E. Cronin, *Direct Democracy: The Politics of Initiative, Referendum and Recall* (Cambridge, Mass.: Harvard University Press,

1989); David Schmidt, *Citizen Lawmakers: The Ballot Initiative Revolution* (Philadelphia: Temple University Press, 1989).

69. Bradbury, "Government Ethics Reform," 183.

70. The preceding account of ethics reform in the House and Senate draws heavily on Bradbury, "Government Ethics Reform," chap. 5.

71. Norman Lockman, "Ethics Bill Headed for Conference," *Boston Globe*, May 16, 1978.

72. Editorial, "Ethical Balancing," *Boston Globe*, April 25, 1978. See also Editorial, "An Ethical Compromise," *Boston Globe*, April 28, 1978.

73. Bradbury, "Government Ethics Reform," 208.

74. Jeffrey Schmaltz, "Victory for Cuomo: Governor Used His Popularity to Get Legislative Accord on Code of Ethics," *New York Times*, July 2, 1987.

75. Robert C. Newman, "New York's New Ethics Law: Turning the Tide on Corruption," *Hofstra Law Review* 16 (1988): 319.

76. *New York Public Officers Law*, § 73.6. Failure to file or filing a false statement would now be punishable by up to $10,000 or a year in prison. The new forms covered not only the finances of legislators themselves but also the finances of their spouses and dependent children. In addition, legislative aides and state employees earning over $30,000 per year were required to file extensive financial disclosure forms.

77. *New York Public Officers Law* § 73.7.

78. See *New York Assembly Bills* 1985, S. 595, A. 715.

79. On the Koppell bill, see *New York Assembly Journal* 1986, 1416–20.

80. Jeffrey Schmaltz, "Cuomo and Senate in Dispute over Inaction on Ethics Bills," *New York Times*, June 26, 1986; *Public Papers of Governor Cuomo*, speech of June 26, 1986, 948.

81. *New York Times Index* for New York State under the headings "Legislature," "Governor," and "Politics and Government."

82. Michael Oreskes, "Prosecutors, Pressing Lindenauer, Warn of an Indictment Next Week," *New York Times*, February 22, 1986; Josh Barbanel, "Charges Assert Parking Bribes of $3.8 Million; 'Racketeering' Depicted in Recent Indictments," *New York Times*, April 11, 1986.

83. Jeffrey Schmaltz, "Final Agreement Reached in Albany on Ethics Bill," *New York Times*, July 1, 1987.

84. Council of State Governments, *Book of the States* (Lexington, Ky.: Council of State Governments, 1986–87).

85. Schmaltz, "Victory for Cuomo."

86. *Book of the States*, 1986–87.

87. Jeffrey Schmaltz, "Cuomo and Senate in Dispute over Inaction on Ethics Bills," *New York Times*, June 27, 1987.

88. Mark A. Uhlig, "Ethics Legislation Faulted By Cuomo; He Warns of Veto," *New York Times*, April 15, 1987; Jeffrey Schmaltz, "A Way of Life Hangs in the Balance as Albany Battles on Ethics," *New York Times*, April 19, 1987.

89. Also exempted from the representation ban were proceedings conducted by the state Tax Commission, Insurance Department, Unemployment
Insurance Appeals Board, Department of Social Services, Department of Labor,
and the Office of Professional Medical Conduct. On the enforcement of the
disclosure provisions, see "Attorney General's Memorandum to Cuomo on
Ethics Bill," *New York Times*, April 15, 1987.

90. Jeffrey Schmaltz, "Albany Accord Helps Proposal for Ethics Bill," *New
York Times*, March 17, 1987.

91. "Transcript of Governor Cuomo's State of the State Address to the Legislature: Cuomo Emphasizes 'Jobs, Justice, Partnership and Drawing on
Resources,'" *New York Times*, January 6, 1983; "Transcript of Cuomo's Address
to the New York Legislature," *New York Times*, January 5, 1984; Maurice Carroll, "Cuomo Plan Seeks Revival of Spirit of the New Deal," *New York Times*,
December 8, 1985; Public Papers of Governor Cuomo, 1985.

92. "Cuomo, in State of State Message, Offers Environment and Job
Plans," *New York Times*, January 9, 1986.

93. Jeffrey Schmaltz, "O'Rourke Is Nominated; Attacks Cuomo Record,"
New York Times, May 30, 1986.

94. Jeffrey Schmaltz, "Cuomo Emphasizes Curb on Spending," *New York
Times,* January 8, 1987.

95. The other two were Wyoming and North Dakota. North Dakota and
Vermont had gift limits, however, under their lobbying statutes. Vermont had
an executive branch ethics code and disclosure requirement, issued in 1988 by
executive order of then-governor Madeline Kunin.

96. Maria Thompson, chair of Common Cause–Vermont, in discussion
with the author, May 1999.

97. *COGEL Guardian,* quarterly newsletter of the Council on Governmental
Ethics (Los Angeles), 1988–96; Department of Justice, *Annual Report to the Congress on the Activities and Operations of the Public Integrity* Section (Washington,
D.C.: U.S. Government Printing Office), 1988–96; *New York Times Index,* listing
for Vermont, 1988–96.

98. Data provided to the author by John Carey.

99. I calculated cumulative scandal scores for each state for the period
1951–96, using data from the *New York Times Index* for all years, Department of
Justice, *Annual Reports* from 1976 to 1996, and the *COGEL Guardian* (Council
on Governmental Ethics, Los Angeles) for 1988 to 1996 (see appendix B for the
scoring of scandals).

100. Marie Gottschalk, *The Shadow Welfare State: Labor, Business and the Politics
of Health Care in the United States* (Ithaca, N.Y.: Cornell University Press, 2000);
Theda Skocpol, "The Limits of the New Deal System and the Roots of Contemporary Welfare Dilemmas," in *The Politics of Social Policy in the United States,* ed.
Margaret Weir, Ann Shola Orloff, and Theda Skocpol (Princeton, N.J.: Princeton
University Press, 1988); R. Kent Weaver and Bert A. Rockman, eds., *Do Institutions Matter?* (Washington, D.C.: Brookings Institution Press, 1993).

Chapter Three

1. Robert S. Allen, ed., *Our Sovereign State* (New York: Vanguard Press, 1949), xxxi; Robert G. Spivack, "New York: Backslider," in *Our Sovereign State*, ed. Allen, 89. The other states covered in the book were California, Georgia, Illinois, Louisiana, Massachusetts, Nebraska, Ohio, Pennsylvania, Texas, Utah, and Wisconsin.

2. Herman A. Lowe, "Pennsylvania: Bossed Cornucopia," in *Our Sovereign State*, ed. Allen, 98–99.

3. Hart Stilwell, "Texas: Owned by Oil and Interlocking Directorates," in *Our Sovereign State*, ed. Allen, 336.

4. Lewis L. Gould, *Reform and Regulation in American Politics, 1900–1916* (New York: John Wiley & Sons, 1976); Stephen Skowronek, *Building a New American State: The Expansion of National Administrative Capacities, 1877–1920* (Cambridge: Cambridge University Press, 1982); Robert Wiebe, *The Search for Order, 1877–1920* (New York: Hill and Wang, 1967); Sean M. Theriault, "Patronage, the Pendleton Act, and the Power of the People," *Journal of Politics* 65 (2003): 50–68.

5. Perhaps the most well known of the Progressive reforms was the Australian or "secret" ballot, which took away parties' control over the voting process, putting it in the hands of ostensibly neutral state officials. Direct democracy reforms included establishment of the initiative option in roughly half the states, an option that allowed voters to bypass states legislatures and make their own laws by majority vote, and recall provisions that gave voters the opportunity to get rid of elected officials before their terms had expired.

6. Richard Allen Baker, "The History of Congressional Ethics," in *Representation and Responsibility: Exploring Legislative Ethics,* ed. Bruce Jennings and Daniel Callahan (New York: Hasting Center, 1985); James D. Carroll and Robert T. Roberts, "'If Men Were Angels': Assessing the Ethics in Government Act of 1978," *Policy Studies Journal* 17 (1988): 435–47; Allan Katz, "The Politics of Congressional Ethics," in *The House at Work*, ed. Joseph Cooper and G. Calvin Mackenzie (Austin: University of Texas Press, 1981); Alan Rosenthal, *Drawing the Line: Legislative Ethics in the States* (New York: Twentieth Century Fund, 1996); David A. Schultz and Robert Maranto, *The Politics of Civil Service Reform* (New York: Peter Lang Publishing, 1998); Andrew Stark, *Conflict of Interest in American Public Life* (Cambridge, Mass.: Harvard University Press, 2000).

7. John Noonan, *Bribes* (Berkeley: University of California Press, 1984), 578; Special Commission on Ethics, Commonwealth of Massachusetts, *Final Report,* June 12, 1995. In 1873, Pennsylvania and New York also revised their constitutions to, respectively, strengthen their bribery statutes with regard to legislators and to prohibit the practice of "special" or "local" bills used with alarming frequency to benefit individual cities, towns, or businesses in return for payoffs to legislators. See Ari Hoogenboom, "Did Gilded Age Scandals Bring Reform?" in *Before Watergate*, ed. Abraham S. Eisenstadt, Ari Hoogenboom, and Hans L. Trefousse (New York: Brooklyn College Press, 1978).

8. Charles H. Stewart III, "Ain't Misbehaving, or, Reflections on Two Centuries of Congressional Corruption" (Center for American Political Studies, Occasional Working Papers, 94-4).

9. Arthur S. Link and Richard L. McCormick, *Progressivism* (Wheeling, Ill.: Harlan Davidson, 1983), 32.

10. "Key Leaders to Confer on Crime," *New York Times*, May 3, 1953; Emanuel Perlmutter, "Routing Thruway Near Track Stirs Yonkers Protest," *New York Times*, October 21, 1953; Charles Grutzner, "Tracks Offer Defense: Hearings Open Today," *New York Times*, October 28, 1953; Emanuel Perlmutter, "Lent Admits Share in Race Concession," *New York Times*, October 15, 1953.

11. Leo Egan, "Dewey Political Future Tied to State Scandals," *New York Times*, October 18, 1953; Editorial, "The Test on Mr. Wicks," *New York Times*, November 16, 1953; New York Times, "Text of the Broadcast by Senator Wicks Regarding His Dealings with Fay," October 19, 1953; Editorial, "The Test on Mr. Wicks," *New York Times*, November 16, 1953; Editorial, "Mr. Wicks Steps Down," November 19, 1953.

12. "Text of Dewey's Annual Message to Legislature Urging Ethics Code for Public Officials," *New York Times*, January 7, 1954; William H. Moore, *The Kefauver Committee and the Politics of Crime, 1950–1952* (Columbia: University of Missouri Press, 1974), 76.

13. "Text of Dewey's Annual Message."

14. Discussion of the 1954 New York law draws on New York Senate Committee on Ethics and Guidance, *State of New York Report and Digest of Pertinent Statutes and Opinions Relating to Integrity and Ethical Standards in Government*, Legislative Document No. 9, 1959.

15. New York Senate Committee on Ethics and Guidance, *State of New York Report and Digest of Pertinent Statutes.*

16. In the wake of a scandal involving misuse of public power by Senate aide Bobby Baker, the U.S. Senate set up a bipartisan ethics committee in 1964 to investigate allegations of improper conduct by senators. The Senate also enacted a code that dealt mainly with the solicitation and use of campaign funds, and also required annual (though not public) disclosure. The House followed with a similar code four years later. On congressional ethics reform during the 1960s, see Congressional Quarterly, *Congressional Ethics: History, Facts and Controversy* (Washington: Congressional Quarterly Books, 1992), 146–47.

17. The only exceptions were for contributions received at fundraisers and for honoraria worth over $300 each.

18. *New Jersey Code* § 52:13D-16; *Maine Code* § 146:19–371, Public Laws 1971; *Louisiana Code* § 42-15-1101; *Utah Code Annotated* § 67-16-12; *Maine Code*, § 146:19–371.

19. Cited in the *Report of the Special Legislative Commission on Integrity and Ethical Standards in Government to Hon. Thomas E. Dewey, Governor, and to the Legislature of New York* (March 5, 1954), 219, 173, 194.

20. Massachusetts Journal of the Senate, Ethics Proposal of Governor John Volpe, March 1, 1961, 1.

21. Specifically, a technique known as event history analysis is used. Observations are annual and states are dropped from the data set after they experience the event in question, in this case passage of an ethics code. Passage of a code is therefore considered to be a nonrepeatable event, a reasonable assumption given that just one state (Massachusetts) enacted and then repealed a code during this time, and the repeal was only partial. The year 1954 is taken as the starting point for the analysis because this is when the first general ethics law that covered legislators was enacted. It is therefore the first year that states were "at risk" of passing such a law. Ending in 1972 means we confine the period to the pre-Watergate years, thereby allowing us to isolate the factors that led states to enact ethics laws prior to the stimulus of this important national event. The data set consists of observations for the forty-eight contiguous states, with the exception of Minnesota and Nebraska, because certain key explanatory variables could not be defined for these two states or for Alaska and Hawaii.

22. Rosenthal, *Drawing the Line*; Dennis F. Thompson, *Ethics in Congress* (Washington, D.C.: Brookings Institution Press, 1995).

23. The factors that explain state ethics statutes are likely to be somewhat different from those that account for state campaign finance laws. Indeed, an exploratory test suggested that the model used here works much better at explaining ethics codes than it does at explaining state limits on political action committee contributions to legislators.

24. Data came from state conflict of interest statutes, legislative rule books, and: Committee on Legislative Rules of the National Legislative Conference, *Conflict of Interest and Related Regulations for State Legislatures* (Lexington, Ky.: Council of State Governments, 1972). The likelihood of code enactment, known as the "hazard rate," is determined by the independent variables. However, we cannot assume that the hazard rate is constant over time. A series of "year dummy" variables is used to control for duration dependence; the first year variable is used as the reference category. The year dummy variables also allow us to control for the possibility that exogenous events, such as the passage of ethics codes in 1967 by the U.S. House and Senate, influenced states' actions. If they did, particular year dummies may be statistically significant. See Nathaniel Beck, Jonathan N. Katz, and Richard Tucker, "Taking Time Seriously: Time-Series-Cross-Section Analysis with a Binary Dependent Variable," *American Journal of Political Science* 42 (1998): 1260–88; Judith Singer and John B. Willett, "It's About Time: Using Discrete-Time Survival Analysis to Study Duration and the Timing of Events," *Journal of Educational Statistics* 18 (1993): 155–95.

25. On party competition and the enactment of legislation, see Duncan Black, *Theory of Committees and Elections* (Cambridge: Cambridge University Press, 1958); Anthony Downs, *An Economic Theory of Democracy* (New York: Harper & Row, 1957); Donald P. Haider-Markel, "Policy Diffusion as a Geographical Expansion of the Scope of Political Conflict: Same Sex Marriage Bans in the 1990s," *State Politics and Policy Quarterly* 1 (2001): 5–26; Thomas M. Holbrook and Emily Van Dunk, "Electoral Competition in the American States," *American Political Science Review* 87 (1993): 955–62; Christopher Z. Mooney and

Mei-Hsien Lee, "Legislating Morality in the American States: The Case of Pre-Roe Abortion Regulation Reform," *American Journal of Political Science* 39 (1995): 599–627; Charles Plott, "A Notion of Equilibrium under Majority Rule," *American Economic Review* 57 (1967): 787–806. On public support for anticorruption laws in particular, see William G. Mayer, "Public Attitudes on Campaign Finance," in *A User's Guide to Campaign Finance Reform*, ed. Gerald C. Lubenow (Lanham, Md.: Rowman and Littlefield, 2001).

26. Schultz and Maranto, *Politics of Civil Service Reform*; Skowronek, *Building a New American State*; David P. Thelen, *Robert M. LaFollette and the Insurgent Spirit* (Boston: Little, Brown, 1976); Robert Wiebe, *The Search for Order, 1877–1920* (New York: Hill and Wang, 1967).

However, Ripley and Sundquist make the opposite argument. These authors assert that it is more difficult to pass legislation under conditions of divided government because it is harder to form coalitions, especially when the policies are the source of some controversy among policymakers. Randall Ripley, *Majority Party Leadership in Congress* (Boston: Little, Brown, 1969); James Sundquist, "Needed: A Political Theory for the New Era of Coalition *Government* in the United States," *Political Science Quarterly* 103 (1988): 613–35. Conversely, scholars such as Mayhew have argued that divided government does not necessarily prevent the enactment of significant legislation. David Mayhew, *Divided We Govern: Party Control, Lawmaking, and Investigations, 1946–1990* (New Haven, Conn.: Yale University Press, 1991).

27. Because both variables measure relative lack of party competition, the coefficients should be negative.

28. James E. Alt and Robert C. Lowry, "Divided Government, Fiscal Institutions and Budget Deficits: Evidence from the States," *American Political Science Review* 88 (1994): 811–28; Charles Barilleaux and Mark E. Miller, "The Political Economy of State Medicaid Policy," *American Political Science Review* 82 (1988): 1088–1107; Gerald Wright Jr., Robert S. Erikson, and John P. McIver, "Public Opinion and Policy Liberalism in the American States," *American Journal of Political Science* 31 (1987): 980–1001.

29. On individual legislator liberalism and support for ethics reform, see Beth Rosenson, "Legislative Voting on Ethics Reform in Two States: The Influence of Economic Self-Interest, Ideology and Institutional Power," *Public Integrity* 5 (2003): 205–22. On Wisconsin and Massachusetts, see Virginia Bradbury, "Government Ethics Reform: The Financial Disclosure Law," Ph.D. diss., Boston College, 1996; Tom Loftus, *The Art of Legislative Politics* (Washington, D.C.: CQ Press, 1994). On public interest groups and liberalism, see Jeffrey M. Berry, *The New Liberalism: The Rising Power of Citizen Groups* (Washington, D.C.: Brookings Institution Press, 1999); Michael McCann, *Taking Reform Seriously: Perspectives on Public Interest Liberalism* (Ithaca, N.Y.: Cornell University Press, 1986).

30. John Kincaid, "Introduction," in *Political Culture, Public Policy and the American States*, ed. John Kincaid (Philadelphia: Center for the Study of Federalism, 1982), 10; Daniel Elazar, *Cities of the Prairie: The Metropolitan Frontier and American Politics* (New York: Basic Books, 1970), 265. Some scholars have sug-

gested that political culture falls on a continuum from traditionalist to individu-alistic to moralistic. See, for example, John Kincaid, "Introduction"; Ira Sharkansky, "The Utility of Elazar's Political Culture," *Polity* 2 (1969): 66–83.

Others contend that individualism and moralism are at opposite ends of the continuum. See, for example, Richard Ellis, *American Political Cultures* (New York: Oxford University Press, 1993). Consensus exists, however, that moralis-tic culture is at one extreme. The model used here is agnostic as to whether individualist or traditionalist culture is "closer" to moralist culture. Moralistic culture is omitted from the regression analysis and is used as the reference cate-gory against which the other two types of culture are compared. The coeffi-cients for the included culture variables should therefore be negative.

31. Frances Stokes Berry and William Berry, "State Lottery Adoptions as Policy Innovations: An Event History Analysis," *American Political Science Review* 84 (1990): 395–415; Frances Stokes Berry and William Berry, "Tax Innovation in the States: Capitalizing on Political Opportunity," *American Journal of Political Science* 36 (1992): 715–42; Virginia Gray, "Innovation in the States: A Diffusion Study," *American Political Science Review* 67 (1973): 1174–85; Haider-Markel, "Policy Diffusion as a Geographical Expansion of the Scope of Political Con-flict"; Scott P. Hays and Henry R. Glick, "The Role of Agenda Setting in Policy Innovation: An Event History Analysis of Living-Will Laws," *American Politics Quarterly* 25 (1991): 497–516; Michael Mintrom, "Policy Entrepreneurs and the Diffusion of Innovation," *American Journal of Political Science* 41 (1997): 738–70; Christopher Z. Mooney and Mei-Hsien Lee, "Legislating Morality in the Amer-ican States"; Christopher Z. Mooney and Mei-Hsien Lee, "The Temporal Diffu-sion of Morality Policy: The Case of Death Penalty Legislation in the American States," *Policy Studies Journal* 27 (1999): 766–80; Jack L. Walker, "The Diffusion of Innovations among the American States," *American Political Science Review* 63 (1969): 880–89.

32. Berry and Berry, "State Lottery Adoptions as Policy Innovations;" Daniel Elazar, *American Federalism: A View from the States* (New York: Thomas Y. Crowell, 1972).

33. Marshall R. Goodman, Timothy J. Holp and Karen M. Ludwig, "Understanding State Legislative Ethics Reform: The Importance of Political and Institutional Culture," in *Public Integrity Annual*, ed. James S. Bowman (Lex-ington, Ky.: Council of State Governments, 1996); Rosenthal, *Drawing the Line.*

34. David W. Allen, "Corruption, Scandal and the Political Economy of Adopting Lobbying Policies," *Public Integrity* 1 (2001): 13–42.

35. George C. S. Benson, *Political Corruption in America* (Lexington, Mass.: D.C. Heath, 1978); Gould, *Reform and Regulation*; Richard Hofstadter, *The Age of Reform* (New York: Knopf, 1955); Hoogenboom, "Did Gilded Age Scandals Bring Reform?"; Link and McCormick, *Progressivism*; Stewart III, "Ain't Misbe-having."

36. Link and McCormick, *Progressivism,* 32.

37. Frank R. Baumgartner and Bryan D. Jones, *Agendas and Instability in American Politics* (Chicago: University of Chicago Press, 1993); Anthony Downs,

"Up and Down With Ecology: The "Issue-Attention Cycle,'" *Public Interest* 28 (1972), 38–50; Hays and Glick, "Role of Agenda Setting in Policy Innovation"; John Kingdon, *Agendas, Alternatives and Public Policies* (Boston: Little, Brown, 1984).

38. R. Douglas Arnold, *The Logic of Congressional Action* (New Haven, Conn.: Yale University Press, 1990); Lawrence Mohr, "Determinants of Innovation in Organizations," *American Political Science Review* 63 (1969): 111–26.

39. Alfred Neely IV, "Ethics in Government Laws," in *Ethics in Politics and Government,* ed. Anne Marie Donahue (New York: H. W. Wilson, 1989); Beth Rosenson, "Why U.S. Senators Voted to Limit Honoraria, 1981–1983" (paper presented at panel on Decision Making in the Modern Senate at Midwest Political Science Association meeting, Chicago, April 25–28, 2002); Rosenson, "Legislative Voting on Ethics Reform in Two States"; Rosenthal, *Drawing the Line.*

40. Charles A. Beard, *An Economic Interpretation of the Constitution of the United States* (New York: Free Press, 1986); Henry Chappell, "Conflict of Interest and Congressional Voting: A Note," *Public Choice* 37 (1981): 331–36; Calvin Jillson and Cecil Eubanks, "The Political Structure of Constitution Making: The Federal Convention of 1787," *American Journal of Political Science* 28 (1984): 435–58; Robert McGuire and Robert Ohsfeldt, "Public Choice Analysis and the Ratification of the Constitution," in *The Federalist Papers and the New Institutionalism,* ed. Bernard Grofman and Donald Wittman (New York: Agathon Press, 1989).

41. Morris P. Fiorina, "Divided Government in the American States: A Byproduct of Legislative Professionalism?" *American Political Science Review* 88 (1994): 304–16; Robert E. Hogan, "Sources of Competition in State Legislative Primary Elections," *Legislative Studies Quarterly* 28 (2003): 103–26; Beth Rosenson, "Costs and Benefits of Ethics Laws" (paper presented at the Conference on Governance and Political Ethics, University of Montreal, Montreal, May 14–15, 2004); Alan Rosenthal, "Turnover in State Legislatures," *American Journal of Political Science* 18 (1974): 609–16; Peverill Squire, "Legislative Professionalization and Membership Diversity in State Legislatures," *Legislative Studies Quarterly* 17 (1992): 69–79.

42. John A. Clark, "Congressional Salaries and the Politics of Unpopular Votes," *American Politics Quarterly* 24 (1996): 150–68; Marshall R. Goodman, Timothy Holp, and Eric Rademacher, "Patterns of State Legislative Ethics Reform: Have They Gotten the Message?" (paper presented at 1993 Annual Meeting of American Political Science Association, Washington, D.C.); Rosenson, "Why U.S. Senators Voted to Limit Honoraria"; Rosenthal, *Drawing the Line;* Stewart, "Ain't Misbehaving"; Sandra Williams, *Conflict of Interest: The Ethical Dilemma in Politics* (London: Gower, 1985). In 1853, members were banned from representing clients before any federal agencies. In 1977, the congressional ethics codes were passed, placing a variety of restrictions on legislators. In 1983 and 1989, Congress enacted honoraria and other outside income limits. On the history of federal ethics laws, see Congressional Quarterly, *Congressional Ethics,* chap. 11.

43. Ann O'M. Bowman and Richard Kearney, *The Resurgence of the States* (Englewood Cliffs, N.J.: Prentice Hall, 1986); David Hedge, *Governance and the Changing American States* (Boulder, Colo.: Westview Press, 1998); William Pound, "State Legislative Careers: Twenty-Five Years of Reform," in *Changing Patterns in State Legislative Careers,* ed. Gary F. Moncrief and Joel A. Thompson (Ann Arbor: University of Michigan Press, 1992); Rosenthal, *Drawing the Line*; Howard Sacks, "Ethical Standards in the State Legislature," in *Strengthening the States: Essays on Legislative Reform,* ed. Donald G. Herzberg and Alan Rosenthal (New York: Doubleday & Company, 1971).

44. Rosenson, "Legislative Voting on Ethics Reform in Two States."

45. Bradbury, "Government Ethics Reform"; Thomas E. Cronin, *Direct Democracy: The Politics of Initiative, Referendum and Recall* (Cambridge, Mass.: Harvard University Press, 1989); Elisabeth Gerber, *The Populist Paradox* (Princeton, N.J.: Princeton University Press, 1999); David Schmidt, *Citizen Lawmakers: The Ballot Initiative Revolution* (Philadelphia: Temple University Press, 1989); Caroline J. Tolbert, "Changing Rules for State Legislatures: Direct Democracy and Governance Policies," in *Citizens as Legislators: Direct Democracy in the United States,* ed. Shaun Bowler, Todd Donovan, and Caroline J. Tolbert (Columbus: Ohio State University Press, 1998); Ronald E. Weber, "The Quality of State Legislative Representation: A Critical Assessment," *Journal of Politics* 61 (1999): 609–27.

46. Tolbert, "Changing Rules for State Legislatures."

47. Marie Gottschalk, *The Shadow Welfare State: Labor, Business and the Politics of Health Care in the United States* (Ithaca, N.Y.: Cornell University Press, 2000); Ann Shola Orloff, "The Political Origins of America's Belated Welfare State," in *The Politics of Social Policy in the United States,* ed. Margaret Weir, Ann Shola Orloff, and Theda Skocpol (Princeton, N.J.: Princeton University Press, 1988); Theda Skocpol, "The Limits of the New Deal System and the Roots of Contemporary Welfare Dilemmas," in *The Politics of Social Policy in the United States,* ed. Weir, Orloff, and Skocpol; R. Kent Weaver and Bert A. Rockman, eds., *Do Institutions Matter?* (Washington, D.C.: Brookings Institution Press, 1993).

48. The discussion in the text is based on Model 2 in table C.1. There is no difference between the two models used, as measured by a chi-squared log-likelihood test. Therefore I use the more parsimonious model–the one with the fewest variables, which keeps only those variables from Model 1 for which the coefficients equaled or exceeded their standard errors–as the final model and the basis for discussion.

49. William H. Moore, *The Kefauver Committee and the Politics of Crime, 1950–1952* (Columbia: University of Missouri Press, 1974), chaps. 4–7.

50. Sean Nicholson-Crotty, David A. Peterson, and Lawrence Grossback, "A Unified Theory of Policy Diffusion" (paper presented at Annual Meeting of American Political Science Association, Boston, 2002).

51. I am grateful to Alan Rosenthal for this point.

52. The reason for this has to do with the nonlinear nature of the curve in logistic regression, which resembles an S-shape.

53. Dewey was instrumental in the enactment of the 1954 New York Code. Volpe pushed for the 1961 code in Massachusetts. For Volpe's proposed bill, see *Massachusetts Journal of the Senate*, 1961, 1. For the legislation that was enacted in May 1961, see Massachusetts Legislative Documents, House No. 3202.

54. Massachusetts, which repealed its 1961 financial disclosure law the following year, is the only exception, and it is actually only a partial exception because the state added other ethics restrictions, notably a gift limit, in 1962 when it eliminated mandatory disclosure.

55. For example, Maine in 1961 put in place via legislative resolution a vague, one-paragraph code. The code began with a typical, generic statement about the need to uphold the trust placed in public officeholders. It went on to state simply that "No state legislator will accept any employment which can possibly impair his independence and integrity of judgment nor will he exercise his position of trust to secure unwarranted privileges for himself or for others." The code concludes with a sentence urging state legislators to be "ever mindful of the ordinary citizen who might otherwise be unrepresented, and . . . endeavor conscientiously to pursue the highest standards of legislative conduct." No penalties for violation are included nor is any enforcement mechanism—not even censure or other forms of discipline by either body of the legislature—mentioned. *Maine Code*, § 146:19–371, Public Laws 1971.

56. On California, see *California Codes* § 2-2-8920. In New Jersey, representation was limited in cases relating to workers' compensation and proceedings before the Division of Civil Rights and the Public Employment Relations Commission. *New Jersey Rev. Stat.* § 52:13D-16. In Connecticut, thirteen agencies were listed, such as the department of motor vehicles, gaming policy board, and liquor control board. See *Connecticut Gen. Stat* § 1–10.

57. Robert M. Stern, "Ethics in the States," in *Representation and Responsibility*, ed. Jennings and Callahan, 254; Memoirs of J. Q. Adams, quoted in California Fair Political Practices Commission, *Legislators as Advocates before State Agencies: Avoiding Conflicts of Interest* (Sacramento, January 12, 1981), 12.

58. Wisconsin Ethics Board, *Officials' Receipt of Food, Drink, Favors, Services, etc.*, July 1992. With regard to New York, although the 1964 law did not limit food or beverages, it did ban gifts "in the form of money, service, loan, travel, entertainment, hospitality, thing or promise . . . under circumstances in which it could be reasonably inferred that the gift was intended to influence (the legislator), or could reasonably be expected to influence him, in the performance of his duties. The limit was increased to $75 in the 1987 revision of the ethics law. See *New York Public Officers Law*, § 73-4. On the Kentucky law, see Committee on Legislative Rules of the National Legislative Conference, *Conflict of Interest and Related Regulations for State Legislatures.*

59. Committee on Legislative Rules of the National Legislative Conference, *Conflict of Interest and Related Regulations for State Legislatures.*

60. There is one fewer category than for the index shown in chapter 1, because one of the components measured there, honoraria limits, did not exist in the 1954–72 period. See appendix A for the scoring of the index.

61. The dependent variable can alternately be construed as essentially con-tinuous in nature, thus necessitating a linear model, or as ordinal, requiring an ordinal regression. Using an ordinal specification addresses the criticism that the dependent variable is not truly continuous and is best seen as ordinal in nature (Greene 1990) and also the fact that it trends upward over time (see appendix B for details on how the linear regression model used here addresses these issues). Ordinal regression eliminates the main problems associated with these criticisms. First, it does not require the assumption that the difference between $Y = 0$ and $Y = 1$ is the same as the difference between $Y = 1$ and $Y = 2$. Second, because of how the dependent variable is measured for the ordinal specification, the fact that it trends upward over time is no longer significant.

62. Specifically, table C.4 uses the ordinal regression results to show the effects on the probability that a state will experience the maximum amount of change in its ethics laws when the values of key predictors are varied, in a man-ner similar to the calculation of "mean effects" for binary logistic regression. The discussion in the text focuses on the common results of the two different types of models used in the regression analysis.

63. Editorial, "Two Masters at Albany," *New York Times*, August 10, 1963.

64. Charles Grutzner, "Criticism Grows over Bank Cruise," *New York Times*, October 16, 1963; "Two Masters at Albany," *New York Times*, August 10, 1963; "Home from the Sea," *New York Times*, October 25, 1963; "For Legislative Integrity," *New York Times*, March 9, 1964; and "Watchful of the Public Inter-est," *New York Times*, March 19, 1964.

65. John Silbey, "Albany Is Cool to Ethics Report," *New York Times*, March 10, 1964.

66. Silbey, "Albany Is Cool to Ethics Report"; Grutzner, "Watchful of the Public Interest."

67. The first bill would remove the existing exemptions from the represen-tation ban for the Department of Taxation and Division of Corporations as well as the Court of Claims. The second bill would revamp the existing system of ethics oversight for legislators. At the time, oversight was in the hands of the legislative ethics committees in each house and an advisory commission within the attorney general's office composed of the standing members of the legisla-tive ethics committees plus the dean of the Albany Law School and president of the New York Bar Association. The proposed commission would replace the existing advisory commission. It would consist of seven members, all nonlegis-lators, three to be appointed by the governor and four by the legislature. Thus legislators would still retain a hand, and indeed a weighty hand, in the commis-sion. Its only power would be to issue nonbinding advisory opinions, and only certain public officials—not the general public—could request opinions. For *Times* coverage of the votes, see Douglas Dales, "Legislators Vote Own Ethics Code," *New York Times*, March 24, 1964, and Sydney Schanberg, "Ethics Mea-sures Lose in Assembly in Narrow Votes," *New York Times*, May 5, 1965.

68. Sydney Schanberg, "Assembly, in Switch, Votes to Tighten Code of Ethics," *New York Times*, May 25, 1965. Quantitative analysis of who switched

sides yielded some interesting results. Those who switched from opposition to support were more likely to be chairmen of committees, and to have more years of service in the legislature. Multivariate regression on the initial vote showed that chairmanship of a committee and more years of seniority predicted a greater likelihood of opposition. On the second vote, chairmanship and seniority no longer had a statistically significant influence on members' votes. This suggests that the opposition of these members was neutralized by the newspaper pressure. Members from liberal districts—those with a higher vote percentage for the state Liberal Party—were also more likely to support the final bill than other members, whereas district liberalism had not been a significant predictor of support on the final bill. Members' responses to the newspaper pressure may therefore have been mediated by the perceived interest of the issue to their constituents; liberal constituents were presumably perceived by legislators as more supportive of ethics reform. Lawyer-legislators were still more likely than other members to oppose the bill even after the newspaper reported the roll call on the first bill. Being a lawyer had a negative and statistically significant impact on support for ethics reform in both votes. Thus lawyer-legislators appeared to be relatively impervious to the media pressure.

69. Schanberg, "Assembly, in Switch, Votes to Tighten Code of Ethics."

70. Schanberg, "Ethics Measures Lose in Assembly in Narrow Votes."

71. In other words, scandals may be endogenous to the extent that the stronger a state's ethics laws are, the more scandals that may be reported. This problem is partially resolved by controlling for the level of a state's ethics laws at the beginning of the period. However, if strengthening of the laws *during* a given period influences the number of scandals during that period, an endogeneity problem arises in which the error term will be correlated with the dependent variable.

72. Forty-six observations is a small number for employing this technique. Nevertheless, I used as an instrument the number of *federal* indictments and convictions of state legislators, governors, and other statewide officials. Data came from the same sources as for the scandal variable (see appendix B). The first-stage regression of the scandal variable on the instrument yielded an adjusted R^2 value of .50. This variable is not influenced by change in state conflict-of-interest laws. It is not a perfect instrumental variable because it is really just one part of the actual scandal variable itself, the part that is uncorrelated with the error term for the dependent variable. A better instrumental variable might have been the number of U.S. attorneys for each state during the period examined, but this information was not available. The instrumented scandal variable was still statistically significant in both the linear and ordinal regressions, although the significance level dropped to .05 and .10, respectively. In the second-stage regression, none of the other substantive results were changed, although the significance level of some key variables fell.

73. Interestingly, Michigan has consistently lagged behind other professionalized legislatures in the stringency of its ethics laws. As of 1996, Michigan still

stood out in its failure to require any financial disclosure from legislators, putting it with a handful of states such as Idaho and Vermont. Michigan's relatively weak legislative ethics laws relative to other states with professionalized legislatures may be due to the fact that Michigan has had relatively fewer scandals compared with states such as Illinois, Massachusetts, and New York.

Chapter Four

1. Alan Rosenthal, *Drawing the Line: Legislative Ethics in the States* (New York: Twentieth Century Fund, 1996); Dennis F. Thompson, *Ethics in Congress* (Washington, D.C.: Brookings Institution Press, 1995); Joseph Zimmerman, *Curbing Unethical Behavior in Government* (Westport, Conn.: Greenwood Press, 1994).

2. See Rosenthal, *Drawing the Line,* chap. 1. On the Kentucky sting and its consequences, see Penny M. Miller, *Kentucky Politics and Government* (Lincoln: University of Nebraska Press, 1994), 326–28. On the West Virginia sting operation and its consequences, see Richard Brisbin, *West Virginia Politics and Government* (Lincoln: University of Nebraska Press, 1994), 25–26.

3. The other eight were Indiana, Nebraska, Nevada, Ohio, Oregon, South Carolina, South Dakota, and Tennessee.

4. *Tennessee Statutes* § 3–6-108.

5. *Pennsylvania Const. Stat. tit* § 65§401 to § 65§413.

6. Because the first state limits on honoraria were enacted in 1974, this factor was not included in the index for the pre-Watergate period.

7. See also note 61 to chapter 3 for details on the two types of models used and the difference between them. Minnesota, which was not included in the pre-Watergate analysis, switched from a nonpartisan to a partisan legislature by the beginning of this period, allowing for calculation of variables such as majority party control and unified government. Nebraska still had a nonpartisan legislature, so those variables could not be calculated and Nebraska was omitted again from the analysis. Hawaii and Alaska were also omitted again.

8. The rationale for including this control variable is that states that have recently strengthened their legislative ethics laws will probably be less likely to enact additional strengthening changes in the immediate future. By contrast, states that have not enacted any new restrictions for legislators recently should be more likely to enact new laws, all else equal. In other words, recent passage of new ethics regulations will reduce the pressure on legislators to enact such restrictions, whereas if a long time has passed since the state's ethics laws have been strengthened, this may create more pressure to do so. Also, as explained in appendix D, a control variable is added for the strength of a state's laws at the beginning of the period (this variable had dropped out of the equation in the models of chapter 3 because it equaled zero for all states).

9. Two linear regressions and two ordinal regressions were used. The first of each type of regression uses all the independent variables; the second of each

type keeps only those variables for which the coefficient equaled or exceeded the standard error. The discussion in the text focuses on the common results of Models 2 and 4 (see table E.1 in appendix E).

10. Specifically, table E.2 uses the ordinal regression results to show the effects on the probability that a state will experience the maximum amount of change in its ethics laws when the values of key predictors are varied, in a manner similar to the calculation of "mean effects" for binary logistic regression. Appendix E explains how these effects are calculated.

11. Arthur Maass, "U.S. Prosecution of State and Local Officials for Political Corruption: Is the Bureaucracy Out of Control in a High-Stakes Operation Involving the Constitutional System?" *Publius* 17 (1987): 195, 201.

12. Maass, "U.S. Prosecution of State and Local Officials," 206. For additional treatments of federal prosecution of corruption under the Mail Fraud Act and other federal laws beginning in the 1970s, see Alan Ehrenhalt, "Justice and Ambition," *Governing*, September 1989, 38–44; Suzanne Garment, *Scandal: The Crisis of Mistrust in American Politics* (New York: Times Books, 1991); and John Noonan, *Bribes* (Berkeley: University of California Press, 1984), 584–601.

13. A pattern of racketeering activity requires two acts of racketeering within ten years. See Maass, "U.S. Prosecution of State and Local Officials," 210–12, for a discussion of RICO and its use by federal prosecutors.

14. U.S. Department of Justice, *Report to Congress on the Activities and Operations of the Public Integrity Section for 1982* (Washington, D.C.: U.S. Government Printing Office, 1982), 16–17; U.S. Department of Justice, *Report to Congress on the Activities and Operations of the Public Integrity Section for 1985* (Washington, D.C.: U.S. Government Printing Office, 1985), 30.

15. The Pennsylvania "ghost-payrolling" scheme was later revealed to be more extensive than initially thought. Federal prosecutors ultimately obtained convictions of the former majority leader of the Senate, a current state senator, and a former state senator, in addition to the original state senator who was indicted. See *New York Times Index*, 1978, and U.S. Department of Justice, *Report to Congress on the Activities and Operations of the Public Integrity Section for 1980* (Washington, D.C.: U.S. Government Printing Office, 1980), 12. On the Louisiana scandal, see *New York Times Index*, 1976, under Louisiana. On the Missouri scandal, see *New York Times Index*, 1979, under Missouri.

16. Edward T. Pound, "Abscam Jury Testimony Said to Back Jenrette," *New York Times*, March 15, 1980.

17. U.S. Department of Justice, *Report to Congress on the Activities and Operations of the Public Integrity Section for 1987* (Washington, D.C.: U.S. Government Printing Office, 1987), 26.

18. As discussed in note 71 of chapter 3, there is a potential concern about the endogeneity of scandal. Again, I applied an instrumental variables approach to address this problem. The instrument used was the number of federal indictments and convictions of state legislators, governors, and other statewide officials. Data came from the same sources as for the scandal variable (see appendix

D). The first-stage regression of the scandal variable on the instrument yielded an adjusted R^2 value of .79. The instrumented scandal variable was still significant at the .05 level in both the linear and ordinal specifications.

19. Randall Ripley, *Majority Party Leadership in Congress* (Boston: Little, Brown, 1969); James Sundquist, "Needed: A Political Theory for the New Era of Coalition Government in the United States," *Political Science Quarterly* 103 (1988): 613–35.

20. One example is Wisconsin. Tom Loftus, the former Democratic speaker of the Assembly, writes, "I came to the Wisconsin legislature in 1976 with a class of reformers determined to restore the public confidence in government shaken by Watergate. Led by Governor Patrick J. Lucey, we passed the most sweeping changes in the way elections were conducted and government was operated since Fighting Bob LaFollette and the Progressives threw out the party bosses early in this century." Tom Loftus, "The Road to Ethical Legislatures Isn't Paved with Tougher Laws," in *State Government: CQ's Guide to Current Issues and Activities in 1992–1993*, ed. Thad Beyle (Washington, D.C.: Congressional Quarterly Books, 1992), 104.

21. Kenneth J. Meier and Thomas M. Holbrook, "'I Seen My Opportunities and I Took 'Em': Political Corruption in the American States," *Journal of Politics* 54 (1992): 150.

22. Elder Witt, "Is Government Full of Crooks or Are We Just Better at Finding Them?" *Governing* 2 (September 1989): 33–38. See also Dale Krane and Stephen D. Shaffer, *Mississippi Government and Politics* (Lincoln: University of Nebraska Press, 1996), 234.

23. See Common Cause, *Common Cause Fights for Good State Government: Histories of Common Cause State Organizations Prepared on the Occasion of the Twentieth Anniversary of Common Cause*, September 1990, no page number; Carol W. Lewis, "A Review of Provisions of Conflict of Interest," *COGEL* Guardian (Council on Governmental Ethics, Los Angeles), December 1991, 8–9.

24. Common Cause, *Common Cause Fights for Good State Government.*

25. While the compensation variable was positively signed and marginally significant in the linear specification, it was negatively signed and insignificant in the ordinal specification. The culture variable was significant only in the linear model. There, individualistic culture had the opposite effect from that of the pre-Watergate period.

26. Data for this variable came from Jonathan Siegel's survey published in Andrew McFarland, *Public Interest Lobbies: Decision Making on Energy* (Washington, D.C.: American Enterprise Institute, 1984), 53. The top five states were Vermont, Massachusetts, Connecticut, California, and Maryland. The bottom five were Mississippi, Alabama, South Carolina, Louisiana, and Arkansas.

27. The variable proved insignificant in both the linear and ordinal specifications.

28. These new restrictions are not considered in the regression analysis, however, because they are best characterized as campaign finance regulations rather than as ethics or conflict regulations, as defined in this book.

29. The Senate had always lagged behind the House in its regulation of honoraria. A brief history of congressional honoraria regulation is as follows: The first law to regulate honoraria at the federal level was the 1974 Federal Elections Campaign Act. Then in 1977, the U.S. House and Senate passed ethics codes that limited outside earned income to 15 percent of members' salaries and lowered the ceiling on allowable annual honoraria to $10,000 and on allowable individual honoraria to $1,000. In 1979, the Senate voted to delay the limit for four years, allowing senators to keep $2,000 per speech and up to $25,000 total per year. The early 1980s also saw attempts in the Senate to roll back the honoraria limits. In 1981 the Senate repealed the $25,000 limit entirely by a two-vote margin. The House, frustrated by the disparity between the two bodies on this matter, responded by raising its ceiling on outside earnings from 15 to 30 percent. See Congressional Quarterly, *Congressional Ethics: History, Facts and Controversy* (Washington, D.C.: Congressional Quarterly Books, 1992), chap. 11, for a history of congressional honoraria limits.

With regard to Durenberger and Wright, the Senate Ethics Committee found that Durenberger used a book he wrote as a "mechanism to evade the statutory limitations on honoraria." At the time, honoraria for senators were restricted to 30 percent of members' salaries. See Dennis Thompson, *Ethics in Congress* (Washington, D.C.: Brookings Institution Press, 1995), 34. Similarly, Speaker Wright resigned in 1989 after the House Ethics Committee determined that his practice of selling his book to lobbyists was intended as an "overall scheme to evade the House outside earned income limits," in particular the limit on honoraria. See Congressional Quarterly, *Congressional Ethics*, 23.

30. In Maryland, the proposal passed the state Senate but failed in the House. In Tennessee, the proposal was considered in the Senate during debate over the legislative rules, but no action was taken on the proposal because "senators believed that fees for their participation at meetings were an important perquisite of office." See Council of State Governments, *COGEL Blue Book* (Lexington, Ky.: Council of State Governments, 1988), 143, 151.

31. Tennessee's was also only for the Senate. See Tennessee Legislative Rules.

32. See Congressional Quarterly, *Congressional Ethics*, 155.

33. Massachusetts lawmakers enacted the gift ban as part of the state election law, leaving intact the section of the conflict-of-interest statute that restricts gifts from lobbyists to $100. In 1999, Common Cause of Massachusetts was trying to eliminate this discrepancy in the law by having lawmakers include the ban in the conflict of interest statutes, replacing the existing $100 limit. A special state commission established to suggest changes to the state ethics laws recommended that this change be made. See Commonwealth of Massachusetts, *Final Report, Special Commission on Ethics,* June 12, 1995. On Florida, Ohio, and Texas, see Rosenthal, *Drawing the Line*, 113.

34. James Browning, executive director of Maryland Common Cause, in discussion with the author, February 3, 2004.

35. Joyce Bullock, "In Search of the Toughest State Ethics Law," *State Government News*, May 1994, 34–37; Elaine Stuart, "Trail of Smears," *State Government News*, May 1994, 22–33; Marshall R. Goodman, Timothy J. Holp, and Karen M. Ludwig, "Understanding State Legislative Ethics Reform: The Importance of Political and Institutional Culture," in *Public Integrity Annual*, ed. James S. Bowman (Lexington, Ky.: Council of State Governments, 1996); Rosenthal, *Drawing the Line.*

36. The one difference is in the measurement of the scandal variable. I give extra points to states in which the legislature was the target of a sting operation designed to expose legislators accepting a bribe, because this type of scandal is arguably qualitatively different from other scandals that involved more than one legislator (Rosenthal, *Drawing the Line*). See appendix D for details on the measurement of the scandal variable.

37. Specifically, table E.4 uses the ordinal regression results to show how changing values of the key independent variables affect the probability that a state will experience the maximum amount of change in its ethics laws, in a manner similar to the calculation of "mean effects" for binary logistic regression.

38. An instrumental variables approach was again used to address the potential endogeneity of the scandal variable. The instrument used was the number of federal indictments and convictions of state legislators, governors, and other statewide officials. Data came from the same sources as for the scandal variable (see appendix D). The first-stage regression of the scandal variable on the instrument yielded an adjusted R^2 value of .25. In both the linear and the ordinal regression, the instrumented scandal variable was still significant at the .01 level. The significance level of some other key variables did decline when the instrumental variables approach was used.

39. *COGEL Guardian* (Council on Governmental Ethics, Los Angeles), March 1996, 17; Robert N. Roberts and Marion T. Doss, *From Watergate to Whitewater: The Public Integrity War* (Westport, Conn: Praeger Press, 1997), 93; Rosenthal, *Drawing The Line*, chapter 1.

40. National Conference of State Legislatures, *The State of State Legislative Ethics* (Denver: National Conference of State Legislatures, 2002), 41; Rosenthal, *Drawing the Line*, chapter 1. See also the accounts in the reports by the U.S. Department of Justice, *Report to Congress on the Activities and Operations of the Public Integrity Section* (Washington D.C.: Government Printing Office), 1989–95, as well as accounts in the *COGEL Guardian* (Council on Governmental Ethics, Los Angeles) for 1988 to 1996.

41. See Linda Wagar and Elaine S. Knapp, "The Truth about Ethics," in *State Government, CQ's Guide to Current Issues and Activities, 1992–93*, ed. Thad Beyle (Washington: Congressional Quarterly Books, 1992), 157.

42. Amy E. Young, "In the States," *Common Cause Magazine* (May/June 1991), 41.

43. Common Cause/Michigan newsletter, 1993–96; Karen Hansen, "The Pulitzer Prize, *The Detroit News* and Us," *State Legislatures*, July 1994, 45; Carol

W. Lewis, "A Review of Provisions of Conflict of Interest," *COGEL Guardian* (Council on Governmental Ethics, Los Angeles), December 1991, 8.

44. Common Cause, *Common Cause Fights for Good State Government,* no page number.

45. See Rosenthal, *Drawing the Line,* 185–94.

46. See *New York Times Index,* 1990, under Texas, and *COGEL Guardian* (Council on Governmental Ethics, Los Angeles), April 1991, 22.

47. See Congressional Quarterly, *State Government: CQ's Guide to Current Issues and Activities, 1995–1996* (Washington, D.C.: Congressional Quarterly Books, 1996), 111. See also *COGEL Guardian* (Council on Governmental Ethics, Los Angeles), December 1991 and June 1994. For changes in Alabama law, see *Ala. Code* § 36–25-1 through 36–25-30.

48. Globe Spotlight Series, "Caucus in the Carribean: Flaherty, Political Friends Enjoy Secret Spree with Lobbyists," *Boston Globe,* May 24, 1993; *COGEL Guardian* (Council on Governmental Ethics, Los Angeles), June 1994, 13.

49. Andrea Estes, "Ethics Panel Calls Halt to Politicians' Ticket Perk," *Boston Globe,* January 16, 2004.

50. For a discussion of the Wisconsin scandal, see Tom Loftus, *The Art of Legislative Politics* (Washington, D.C.: CQ Press, 1994), 147–65, and Jeffrey L. Katz, "Sipping From the Cup of Corruption," *Governing* 5 (November 1991), 28. For resulting changes in the state's conflict of interest laws, see Wisconsin Statutes, § 19.41 to § 19.58.

51. Hansen, "Pulitzer Prize, *The Detroit News* and Us."

52. It proved to be statistically insignificant in both model specifications.

53. Since the mid-1980s, it has proven extremely difficult for legislators to push through increases in their salaries. While voters are rarely enthusiastic about raising legislative salaries, it seems that the 1990s were a time of particular recalcitrance. This recalcitrance appears to be part of a broader trend in antilegislator sentiment during this period, which is evident in the passage of term limits for state legislators in twenty-three states between 1990 and 1994 (data provided by U.S. Term Limits). Even in states that have compensation commissions, public outcry against proposed raises stymied most attempts during the 1989–96 period to keep salaries in line with inflation. California's compensation commission is the only one in the nation that can approve pay raises without public, legislative, or gubernatorial oversight. See Charles Mahtesian, "When the Voters Freeze Your Pay," *Governing* 7 (December 1993), 34–39. Some legislatures, such as those in Texas and Rhode Island, have responded to voters' opposition to raising salaries with considerable ingenuity, increasing indirect forms of pay such as pensions while leaving direct compensation untouched. After Texas voters refused in 1989 to approve a constitutional amendment that would have tripled legislators' salaries from a relatively low $7,200, a House member pushed through an amendment lowering the age at which former lawmakers could collect their pensions. Between 1989 and 1993 in Texas, the expense per diem—which legislators can adjust without consulting

the electorate–nearly tripled from $35 to $80. After Pennsylvania's House speaker unsuccessfully floated the idea of a pay raise in 1992, the House Rules Committee just weeks later in a closed-door meeting also passed a resolution to raise per diem expenses significantly, to the highest level of any state (see Mahtesian). Other state legislatures also scaled back the length of their sessions where voters were unwilling to raise their salaries; for example, Louisiana and Pennsylvania both did so in 1993.

54. Rosenthal, *Drawing the Line.*

55. The National Conference of State Legislatures groups state legislatures into three categories. Category 1 states are full-time, with relatively high pay, large staff, and stable membership. These include California, New York, and Illinois. Category 3 states are part time and poorly paying, with small staff and high turnover; these include the above-mentioned states. Category 2 states are hybrids which fall in between the other two groups; examples from this group are Nebraska, Missouri, and Maryland. (Data provided by National Conference of State Legislatures, 1997).

56. Doris Sue Wong, "Common Cause to Drop Drive to Limit Clout of PAC Money," *Boston Globe,* June 17, 1994.

57. Jack Wardlaw and Bill Walsh, "Ethics Bill Approved Nearly Unanimously," *Louisiana Times-Picayune*, April 20, 1996.

58. *COGEL Guardian* (Council on Governmental Ethics, Los Angeles), June 1991, 21.

Chapter Five

1. Brooks Jackson, *Broken Promise: Why the Federal Election Commission Failed* (New York: Twentieth Century Fund, 1990); Frederick M. Hermann, "Bricks without Straw: The Plight of Governmental Ethics Agencies in the United States," in *Public Integrity Annual,* ed. James S. Bowman (Lexington, Ky.: Council of State Governments, 1996); Russell L. Williams, "Controlling Ethical Practices through Laws and Rules: Evaluating the Florida Commission on Ethics," in *Public Integrity Annual,* ed. Bowman.

2. National Conference of State Legislatures, *The State of State Legislative Ethics* (Denver: National Conference of State Legislatures, 2002), 8–11.

3. Dennis Thompson, *Ethics in Congress* (Washington, D.C.: Brookings Institution Press, 1995).

4. Marc Humbert, "Pataki Wants New Ethics Watchdogs for Legislature and Courts," Associated Press State and Local Wire, June 16, 2003, http://80-web.lexis-nexis.com.lp.hscl.ufl.edu/universe/document?_m=95bdd0fd0c94dc9ca764347a8cea59a7&_docnum=1&wchp=dGLbVtz-zSkVA&_md5=9087aa32a98df9fcd 0eaec62602f7c43; Tom Precious, "Albany Ethics Overhaul Urged by Watchdogs," *Buffalo News,* January 6, 2004; Fredric U. Dicker, "Pol 'Crook Book' May Be Bribe Firm's Smoking Gun," *New York Post,*

February 17, 2003; Celeste Katz, "More Illegal Gifts from Prison Firm," *New York Daily News*, February 23, 2003.

5. Matthew D. McCubbins, Roger G. Noll, and Barry R.Weingast, "Administrative Procedures as Instruments of Political Control," *Journal of Law, Economics, and Organization* 3 (1987): 243–77; Terry M. Moe, "An Assessment of the Positive Theory of 'Congressional Dominance,'" *Legislative Studies Quarterly* 12 (1987): 475–520; Barry R. Weingast and Mark J. Moran, "Bureaucratic Discretion or Congressional Control? Regulatory Policymaking by the Federal Trade Commission," *Journal of Political Economy* 91 (1983): 769–800.

6. Robert M. Stern, "Ethics in the States," in *Representation and Responsibility: Exploring Legislative Ethics*, ed. Bruce Jennings and Daniel Callahan (New York: Plenum Press, 1985); Christopher Schwarz, "Ethics: Passing Judgment or Passing the Buck?" *State Government News*, February 1994, 11–13; Thompson, *Ethics in Congress*; Donald J. Maletz and Jerry Herbel, "Some Paradoxes of Government Ethics Revisited" (paper presented at Annual Meeting of American Political Science Association, Boston, 1998); W. J. Michael Cody and Richardson R. Lynn, *Honest Government: An Ethics Guide for Public Service* (Westport, Conn.: Greenwood, 1992); though see Donald J. Maletz and Jerry Herbel, "Beyond Idealism: Democracy and Ethics Reform," *American Review of Public Administration* 30 (2000): 19–45; Williams, "Controlling Ethical Practices Through Laws and Rules," for a more critical view of the commissions.

7. Thompson, *Ethics in Congress*, 159.

8. Stern, "Ethics in the States."

9. Bill Shluter, former chairman of the New Jersey Joint Legislative Committee on Ethics Standards, quoted in Schwarz, "Ethics: Passing Judgment or Passing the Buck?" 11. The counsel for the New Jersey Legislative Joint Ethics Committee said that in a recent five-year period, the committee had only investigated legislators three times for violating state conflict-of-interest laws, and in none of the cases were fines levied (counsel for the New Jersey Legislative Joint Ethics Committee in discussion with the author, summer 1997).

10. Thompson, *Ethics in Congress*, 160, 161. For an additional argument in favor of independent ethics commissions, see Ronald E. Weber, "The Quality of State Legislative Representation: A Critical Assessment," *Journal of Politics* 61 (1999): 609–27.

11. Robert J. Huckshorn, "Who Gave It? Who Got It? The Enforcement of Campaign Finance Laws in the States," *Journal of Politics* 47 (1985): 773–89; Schwarz, "Ethics: Passing Judgment or Passing the Buck?"; David Ensign, "Reforming Public Integrity Laws in an Era of Declining Trust," in *Book of the States, 1996–97 Edition* (Lexington, Ky.: Council of State Governments, 1996).

12. On the Office of Government Ethics, see James D. Carroll and Robert T. Roberts, "'If Men Were Angels': Assessing the Ethics in Government Act of 1978," *Policy Studies Journal* 17 (winter 1988–89): 435–47.

13. Thompson, *Ethics in Congress*.

14. Hermann, "Bricks without Straw."

15. Hawaii, Alaska, Nebraska, and Louisiana are not included in the data set, the first three for the same reason that they were excluded from the analysis of the other chapters: certain key variables were undefined. Hawaii has a commission with limited jurisdiction over the state's legislative ethics laws. Nebraska also has an independent commission that monitors legislative ethics. Alaska does not. Louisiana is excluded from the analysis because its creation of an independent commission predated the beginning of the study period by nine years, making it something of an anomaly, not part of the broader trend seen during the post-Watergate period. Data came from the Council on Governmental Ethics Laws, *Campaign Finance, Ethics and Lobby Law Blue Book* (Lexington, Ky.: Council on Governmental Ethics Laws, 1990, 1993); *Public Integrity Annual,* ed. Bowman; and state statutes.

16. Because the dependent variable is dichotomous, a type of analysis known as event history analysis is used. States that established a commission are coded as 1. Those that did not, choosing instead a weaker enforcement mechanism (legislative ethics committees, secretary of state, or attorney general), are coded as 0. Observations are annual and states are dropped from the risk set for years after they establish a commission. I control for possible time dependence by using dummy variables for the individual years, with the first year excluded and used as the reference category.

Nonstraightforward cases were coded as follows: Michigan was dropped from the data set in 1975, even though the commission established then was later declared unconstitutional. California was dropped from the data set in 1974 when it authorized a commission, even though legislators took away its jurisdiction over legislators' ethics in 1996. Also, some states first established a commission with jurisdiction over legislators' financial disclosure only but later granted authority over their standards of conduct. I coded these states 1 in the year they granted the second type of authority and zero prior to that year. Finally, I excluded the two states, Vermont and Wyoming, that had no legislative ethics or disclosure laws on the books during the entire study period. Logically, it makes no sense for a state to set up an independent commission if there are no ethics laws to enforce. If a state enacted an ethics law during the study period, as fourteen of them did, it was added to the data set for that year and the following years.

17. She finds that while political culture and party competition are significant explanatory factors in both cases, legislative staffing is significant only for explaining variation in the stringency of the lobby law index, while pay per session is significant only in explaining enforcement. See Cynthia Opheim, "Explaining the Differences in State Lobby Regulation," *Western Political Quarterly* 44 (1991): 405–41.

18. Consider for example, the annual budget for several ethics commissions as of 2002. The budget for the Arkansas Ethics Commission was $549,710; for the Connecticut Ethics Commission, it was $883,000. For the Oklahoma Ethics Commission, it was $533,730. These figures include ethics

enforcement for a wide range of public officials, not just legislators, and also enforcement for a wide range of functions, because some commissions also enforce lobby laws. None of the commissions had a budget over $1 million. See National Conference of State Legislatures, *State of State Legislative Ethics*, 112–14.

19. James E. Alt and Robert C. Lowry, "Divided Government, Fiscal Institutions and Budget Deficits: Evidence from the States," *American Political Science Review* 88 (1994): 811–28; Charles Barrilleaux and Ethan Bernick, "Explaining States' Treatment of the 'Deserving Poor': A Model of Supplemental Security Income Supplements, 1990–1996" (paper presented at the Annual Meeting of the American Political Science Association, Boston, 1998); Thomas R. Dye, *Politics, Economics and the Public* (Chicago: Rand McNally, 1966); Virginia Gray, "The Socioeconomic and Political Context of States," in *Politics in the American States*, ed. Virginia Gray, Herbert Jacob, and Robert Albritton (New York: HarperCollins, 1990); Sung-Don Hwang and Virginia Gray, "External Limits and Internal Determinants of State Public Policy," *Western Political Quarterly* 44 (1991): 277–99.

20. Margaret Weir, Ann Shola Orloff, and Theda Skocpol, "Introduction: Understanding American Social Politics," in *The Politics of Social Policy in the United States*, ed. Margaret Weir, Ann Shola Orloff, and Theda Skocpol (Princeton, N.J.: Princeton University Press, 1988).

21. E. Lee Bernick and Charles W. Wiggins, "Executive–Legislative Relations: The Governor's Role as Chief Legislator," in *Gubernatorial Leadership and State Policy*, ed. Eric B. Herzik and Brent W. Brown (Westport, Conn.: Greenwood Press, 1991); T. L. Beyle, "Governors," in *Politics in the American States: A Comparative Analysis*, 4th edition, ed. Virginia Gray, Herbert Jacob and Kenneth Vines (Boston: Little Brown, 1983); T. L. Beyle, "Governors," in *Politics in the American States: A Comparative Analysis*, 5th edition, ed. Virginia Gray, Herbert Jacob, and Robert Albritton (Glenview, Ill.: Scott, Foresman, 1990); Dan Durning, "Education Reform in Arkansas: The Governor's Role in Policymaking," in *Gubernatorial Leadership and State Policy*, ed. Eric B. Herzik and Brent W. Brown (Westport, Conn.: Greenwood Press, 1991); James A. Schlesinger, "Politics of the Executive," in *Politics in the American States*, 2nd edition, ed. Herbert Jacob and Kenneth Vines (Boston: Little, Brown, 1971).

22. Frances Stokes Berry and William Berry, "State Lottery Adoptions as Policy Innovations: An Event History Analysis," *American Political Science Review* 84 (1990): 395–415; Frances Stokes Berry and William Berry, "Tax Innovation in the States: Capitalizing on Political Opportunity," *American Journal of Political Science* 36 (1992): 715–42; Christopher Z. Mooney and Mei-Hsien Lee, "Legislating Morality in the American States: The Case of Pre-Roe Abortion Regulation Reform," *American Journal of Political Science* 39 (1995): 599–627.

23. One possible explanation for this surprising finding is that a high degree of ongoing corruption may reflect greater acceptance of corruption and hence a smaller impetus to enact clean government legislation. In other words,

TPO (traditional party organization) scores, used as a proxy for ongoing corruption, may reflect a state's political culture in a similar but not identical way to the Elazar measure of culture. Thus the measure would pick up public tolerance for corruption in a way not fully measured by the Elazar typology. Still, the results are at odds with the findings for chapters 3 and 4, suggesting that this factor is inconsistent in its impact on ethics policy.

24. McCubbins, Noll, and Weingast, "Administrative Procedures as Instruments of Political Control"; Moe, "Assessment of the Positive Theory of 'Congressional Dominance'"; Weingast and Moran, "Bureaucratic Discretion or Congressional Control?"

25. See, for example, Moe, "Assessment of the Positive Theory of 'Congressional Dominance'" on the National Labor Relations Board. Not only who appoints, but also the particular features of the appointments process, affect agency action. For example, the Federal Election Commission (FEC) was hobbled from the outset by the fact that although its members are presidentially appointed, half its members must be from one party and the others must be from the other party. This is a design that virtually ensures gridlock and conflict. In the case of the FEC, the way that members are appointed clearly matters for what they can and will do (Jackson, *Broken Promise*). In the case of the independent state ethics commissions, there is generally no such restriction regarding the party of those appointed to serve, but there is a wide range in terms of who has the power to appoint members.

26. Hawaii, Louisiana, and Nebraska, which are not included in the event history data set, are included here. Michigan, where the commission was declared unconstitutional right after it was established, is not included.

27. In most states with commissions, either the governor or legislative leaders appoint the members. In Arkansas, however, one member is appointed by the attorney general and one by the lieutenant governor; the remaining three are appointed by the governor, Senate president, and speaker of the House, respectively. In Nebraska, four are appointed by the governor and four by the secretary of state, and the ninth is the secretary of state himself. In Mississippi, two of the eight members are appointed by the governor, two by the lieutenant governor, two by the judiciary, and two by legislators. Even in those states where nonlegislators make all the appointments, the Senate generally has the power to confirm gubernatorial appointments, so this independence is not absolute.

28. McCubbins, Noll, and Weingast, "Administrative Procedures as Instruments of Political Control"; see also Weingast and Moran, "Bureaucratic Discretion or Congressional Control?" on appointments and budgetary control.

29. Linda Wagar and Elaine S. Knapp, "The Truth about Ethics," in Congressional Quarterly, *State Government, CQ's Guide to Current Issues and Activities, 1992–93,* ed. Thad Beyle (Washington, D.C.: Congressional Quarterly Books, 1992).

30. Earl S. Mackey, "Dismantling the Kentucky Legislative Ethics Law," *Public Integrity* 5 (2003): 152; Earl Mackey, "Ethics Laws and Legislative Independence," in *Public Integrity Annual,* ed. Bowman.

31. Bruce Landis, "Ethics Panel Promises More Bite," *Providence Journal,* Februrary 1, 2004; Steve Cross, chief of investigations for the Rhode Island Ethics Commission, in discussion with the author, February 20, 2004.

32. Council on Government Ethics Laws, *Ethics 1994: Events, Issues and Trends* (Los Angeles: Council on Government Ethics Laws, 1995); *COGEL Guardian* (Council on Governmental Ethics, Los Angeles), June 1996, 18.

33. See Virginia Bradbury, "Government Ethics Reform: The Massachusetts Financial Disclosure Law," Ph.D. diss., Boston College, 1996, 156, with respect to the Massachusetts State Ethics Commission.

34. One rare exception was Missouri, where the state Supreme Court in 1991 struck down an initial ballot question regarding an independent commission. The question was then changed to address the issues raised in the court case. *COGEL Guardian* (Council on Governmental Ethics, Los Angeles), February 1991, 18.

35. Common Cause, *Common Cause Conflict of Interest Legislation in the States* (Washington, D.C.: Common Cause, 1990), 17.

36. Bradbury, "Government Ethics Reform," 211. Bradbury argues that the Court's unanimous decision that the commission lacked jurisdiction over certain parts of the law was a good one, because the commission in her opinion had "strayed" from its statutory mandate and expanded unreasonably upon its original domain.

37. *COGEL Guardian* (Council on Governmental Ethics, Los Angeles), June 1991, 27; *COGEL Guardian* (Council on Governmental Ethics, Los Angeles), December 1993, 18; *COGEL Guardian* (Council on Governmental Ethics, Los Angeles), February 1994, 16.

38. *COGEL Guardian* (Council on Governmental Ethics, Los Angeles), August 1990, 20.

39. Russell L. Williams, "Controlling Ethical Practices through Laws and Rules," 66; Texas Public Citizen Press Release, April 16, 2003; Noreen Gillespie, "Committee Proposes Changes to Ethics Laws," *Associated Press State & Local Wire,* January 16, 2004, http://80-web-lexis-nexis.com.lp.hscl.ufl.edu/universe/document?_m=5905ff2b2991194a48b89ee750aafa13&_docnum=1& wchp=dGLbVzz-zSkVb&_md5=900a992a734087fe6749bb64539b5d7e.

Chapter Six

1. Frank R. Baumgartner and Bryan D. Jones, *Agendas and Instability in American Politics* (Chicago: University of Chicago Press, 1993).

2. Vincent G. Moscardelli, Moshe Haspel, and Richard S. Wike, "Party Building through Campaign Finance Reform: Conditional Party Government in the 104th Congress," *Journal of Politics* 60 (1998): 691–704; David A. Schultz

and Robert Maranto, *The Politics of Civil Service Reform* (New York: Peter Lang Publishing, 1998); Stephen Skowronek, *Building a New American State: The Expansion of National Administrative Capacities, 1877–1920* (Cambridge: Cambridge University Press, 1982).

3. Everett M. Rogers and James W. Dearing, "Agenda Setting Research: Where Has It Been, Where Is It Going?" Reprinted in Doris A. Graber, *Media Power in Politics*, 4th edition, ed. Doris A. Graber (Washington, D.C.: C.Q. Press, 2000), 79; John Kingdon, *Agendas, Alternatives and Public Policies* (Boston: Little, Brown, 1984), 103; Baumgartner and Jones, *Agendas and Instability in American Politics*, 20.

4. *New York Times Index*, 1986 and 1987, under the heading "New York State, Politics and Government."

5. Kevin McDermott, "Illinois House OKs Overhaul of Ethics Standards," *St. Louis Post-Dispatch*, November 21, 2003.

6. R. Douglas Arnold, *The Logic of Congressional Action* (New Haven, Conn.: Yale University Press, 1990).

7. Common Cause, "Common Cause Issues Poll," *Common Cause Magazine*, May/June 1991; William G. Mayer, "Public Attitudes on Campaign Finance," in *A User's Guide to Campaign Finance Reform*, ed. Gerald C. Lubenow (Lanham, Md.: Rowman and Littlefield, 2001).

8. Benjamin Ginsberg and Martin Shefter, *Politics by Other Means: The Declining Importance of Elections in America* (New York: Basic Books, 1990); Susan J. Tolchin and Martin Tolchin, *Glass Houses: Congressional Ethics and the Politics of Venom* (Boulder, Colo.: Westview Press, 2001).

9. Hugo Rojas, director of Illinois Common Cause, in discussion with the author February 11, 2004. See also http://www.ilcampaign.org/issues/ethics/ethicsProposal.asp for details on the 2003 law.

10. National Conference of State Legislatures, *The State of State Legislative Ethics* (Denver: National Conference of State Legislatures: 2002), 46.

11. Editorial, "Our Say; Bereano's Latest Idea: A Cruise on the SS Loophole," *The Capital*, July 20, 2003; Michael Dresser, "Bereano Books Cruise to Host Md. Legislators," *Baltimore Sun*, July 16, 2003.

12. National Conference of State Legislatures, *State of State Legislative Ethics*, 133.

13. On the Federal Election Commission as toothless tiger, see Brooks Jackson, *Broken Promise: Why the Federal Election Commission Failed* (New York: Twentieth Century Fund, 1990).

14. G. Calvin Mackenzie and Michael Hafkin, *Scandal Proof: Do Ethics Laws Make Government Ethical?* (Washington, D.C.:, Brookings Institution Press, 2002), 44. Watergate did lead, however, to campaign finance reform in the form of the 1974 Federal Election Campaign Act.

15. Mackenzie and Hafkin, *Scandal Proof*; Alan Rosenthal, *Drawing the Line: Legislative Ethics in the States* (New York: Twentieth Century Fund, 1996).

16. Mike Glover, "Key Lawmakers Agree to Revisit Gift Law," Associated Press State & Local Wire, January 30, 2003, http://80-web.lexis-nexis.

com.lp.hscl.ufl.edu/universe/doclist?_m=7f08f11ced0e48461d232f7543db1534 &wchp=dGLbVtz-zSkVA&_md5=2258a5a972ac51f58a5633cdf1c065a3.

17. Beth Rosenson, "Legislative Voting on Ethics Reform in Two States: The Influence of Economic Self-Interest, Ideology and Institutional Power," *Public Integrity* 5 (2003): 205–22.

18. Rosenson, "Legislative Voting on Ethics Reform in Two States."

19. Illinois Campaign for Political Reform, press release, August 26, 2003.

20. This backlash is evidenced by Congress' decision in 1999 not to authorize the independent counsel statute, which critics argued had been unduly politicized and led to wasteful expenditure of taxpayer money.

21. Susan Levine, "Legislative Ethics Data Find Outlet on Internet," *Washington Post*, January 13, 2004; Bart Jansen, "Complaints about Ethics Bill Threaten Its Toughest Provisions," Associated Press State & Local Wire, February 17, 1999, http://80-web-lexis-nexis.comlp.hscl.ufl.edu/universe/ document? _m=d99f503ac66104d7198f357a318ae1d&_docnum=1&wchp= dGLbVzz-zSkVb&md5=af43c29de713ed96ae838f9cc5ea080d.

22. National Conference of State Legislatures, *State of State Legislative Ethics*, 33, 46.

23. Frank Anechiarico and James B. Jacobs, *The Pursuit of Absolute Integrity: How Corruption Control Makes Government Ineffective* (Chicago: University of Chicago Press, 1996); Mackenzie and Hafkin, *Scandal Proof*; Donald J. Maletz and Jerry Herbel, "Beyond Idealism: Democracy and Ethics Reform," *American Review of Public Administration* 30 (2000): 19–45; Beth Rosenson, "Costs and Benefits of Ethics Laws" (paper presented at Conference on Governance and Political Ethics, University of Montreal, Montreal, May 14–15, 2004).

24. Dennis F. Thompson, *Political Ethics and Public Office* (Cambridge, Mass.: Harvard University Press, 1987). See also Michael Josephson, "Ethics Legislation: Problems and Potential," in *The State of State Legislative Ethics*, by National Conference of State Legislatures (Denver: National Conference of State Legislatures, 2002); and Maletz and Herbel, "Beyond Idealism," on how ethics laws aim too low and trivialize the concept of political ethics.

25. National Conference of State Legislatures, *State of State Legislative Ethics*, 23–29.

references

Abramowitz, Alan I. 1988. Explaining Senate Election Outcomes. *American Political Science Review* 82: 385–403.

———. 1991. Incumbency, Campaign Spending and the Decline of Competition in U.S. House Elections. *Journal of Politics* 53: 34–56.

Abramson, Paul R. 1983. *Political Attitudes in America: Formation and Change.* San Francisco: W. H. Freeman.

Allen, David W. 2001. Corruption, Scandal and the Political Economy of Adopting Lobbying Policies. *Public Integrity* 1: 13–42.

Allen, Robert S., ed. 1949. *Our Sovereign State.* New York: Vanguard Press.

Alt, James E., and Robert C. Lowry. 1994. Divided Government, Fiscal Institutions and Budget Deficits: Evidence from the States. *American Political Science Review* 88: 811–28.

Amenta, Edwin, and Theda Skocpol. 1988. Redefining the New Deal: World War II and the Development of Social Provision in the United States. In *The Politics of Social Policy in the United States*, ed. Margaret Weir, Ann Shola Orloff, and Theda Skocpol. Princeton, N.J.: Princeton University Press.

Anderson, Christopher J., and Yuliya V. Tverdova. 2003. Corruption, Political Allegiances, and Attitudes toward Government in Contemporary Democracies. *American Journal of Political Science* 47: 91–109.

Anechiarico, Frank, and James B. Jacobs. 1996. *The Pursuit of Absolute Integrity: How Corruption Control Makes Government Ineffective.* Chicago: University of Chicago Press.

Arnold, R. Douglas. 1990. *The Logic of Congressional Action.* New Haven, Conn.: Yale University Press.

Baker, Richard Allen. 1985. The History of Congressional Ethics. In *Representation and Responsibility: Exploring Legislative Ethics,* ed. Bruce Jennings and Daniel Callahan. New York: Hasting Center.

Banducci, Susan A., and Jeffrey A. Karp. 1994. Electoral Consequences of Scandal and Reapportionment in the 1992 House Elections. *American Politics Quarterly* 22: 3–26.

Barrilleaux, Charles, and Ethan Bernick. 1998. Explaining States' Treatment of the Deserving Poor: A Model of Supplemental Security Income Supplements, 1990–1996. Paper presented at Annual Meeting of American Political Science Association, Boston.

Barrilleaux, Charles, Thomas Holbrook, and Laura Langer. 1998. Parties, Elections and the American Welfare States. Unpublished manuscript.

Barrilleaux, Charles, and Mark E. Miller. 1988. The Political Economy of State Medicaid Policy. *American Political Science Review* 82: 1088–1107.

Bartlett, Robert V. 1979. The Marginality Hypothesis: Electoral Insecurity, Self-Interest and Voting Behavior. *American Politics Quarterly* 7: 498–508.

Baumgartner, Frank R., and Bryan D. Jones. 1993. *Agendas and Instability in American Politics.* Chicago: University of Chicago Press.

Bazar, Beth. 1987. *State Legislators' Occupations: A Decade of Change.* Denver: National Conference of State Legislatures.

Beard, Charles A. 1986. *An Economic Interpretation of the Constitution of the United States.* New York: Free Press.

Beard, Edmund, and Stephen Horn. 1976. *Congressional Ethics: The View from the House.* Washington, D.C.: Brookings Institution Press.

Beck, Nathaniel, Jonathan N. Katz, and Richard Tucker. 1998. Taking Time Seriously: Time-Series-Cross-Section Analysis with a Binary Dependent Variable. *American Journal of Political Science* 42: 1260–88.

Bell, Charles G., and Charles M. Price. 1980. *California Government Today.* Homewood, Ill.: Dorsey Press.

Benson, George C. S. 1978. *Political Corruption in America.* Lexington, Mass.: D. C. Heath.

Bernick, E. Lee. 1979. Gubernatorial Tools: Formal vs. Informal. *Journal of Politics* 41: 656–64.

Bernick, E. Lee, and Charles W. Wiggins. 1991. Executive–Legislative Relations: The Governor's Role as Chief Legislator. In *Gubernatorial Leadership and State Policy*, ed. Eric B. Herzik and Brent W. Brown. Westport, Conn.: Greenwood Press.

Berry, Frances Stokes, and William Berry. 1990. State Lottery Adoptions as Policy Innovations: An Event History Analysis. *American Political Science Review* 84: 395–415.

———. 1992. Tax Innovation in the States: Capitalizing on Political Opportunity. *American Journal of Political Science* 36: 715–42.

Berry, Jeffrey M. 1999. *The New Liberalism: The Rising Power of Citizen Groups.* Washington, D.C.: Brookings Institution Press.

Berry, William D., Evan J. Ringquist, Richard C. Fording, and Russell L. Hanson. 1997. Measuring Citizen and Government Ideology in the American States, 1960–1993. *American Journal of Political Science* 42: 337–48. Available at http://www.pubadm.fsu.edu/archives/.

———. 2001. Measuring Citizen and Government Ideology in the United States. ICPSR Study 1208. Available at http://www.icpsr.umich.

Beyle, T. L. 1983. Governors. In *Politics in the American States: A Comparative Analysis*, 4th edition, ed. Virginia Gray, Herbert Jacob, and Kenneth Vines. Boston: Little, Brown.

———. 1990. Governors. In *Politics in the American States: A Comparative Analysis*, 5th edition, ed. Virginia Gray, Herbert Jacob, and Robert Albritton. Glenview, Ill.: Scott, Foresman.

Bianco, William. 1994. *Trust: Representatives and Constituents.* Ann Arbor: University of Michigan Press.

Black, Duncan. 1958. *Theory of Committees and Elections.* Cambridge: Cambridge University Press.

Bowman, Ann O'M., and Richard Kearney. 1986. *The Resurgence of the States.* Englewood Cliffs, N.J.: Prentice Hall.

Bradbury, Virginia. 1996. Government Ethics Reform: The Massachusetts Financial Disclosure Law. Ph.D. diss., Boston College.

Brisbin, Richard. 1994. *West Virginia Politics and Government.* Lincoln: University of Nebraska Press.

Bullock, Joyce. 1994. In Search of the Toughest State Ethics Law. *State Government News,* May, 34–37.

California Fair Political Practices Commission. 1981. *Legislators as Advocates before State Agencies: Avoiding Conflicts of Interest.* Sacramento: Fair Political Practices Commission.

Carroll, James D., and Robert T. Roberts. 1988. "If Men Were Angels": Assessing the Ethics in Government Act of 1978. *Policy Studies Journal* 17: 435–47.

Chappell, Henry. 1981. Conflict of Interest and Congressional Voting: A Note. *Public Choice* 37: 331–36.

Citrin, Jack. 1974. Comment: The Political Relevance of Trust in Government. *American Political Science Review* 68: 973–88.

Clark, John A. 1996. Congressional Salaries and the Politics of Unpopular Votes. *American Politics Quarterly* 24: 150–68.

Clausen, Aage R. 1973. *How Congressmen Decide.* New York: St. Martin's Press.

Cody, W. J. Michael, and Richardson R. Lynn. 1992. *Honest Government: An Ethics Guide for Public Service.* Westport, Conn.: Praeger.

Common Cause. 1990. *Common Cause Conflict of Interest Legislation in the States.* Washington, D.C.: Common Cause.

———. 1991. Common Cause Issues Poll. *Common Cause Magazine,* May/June.

Commonwealth of Massachusetts. 1995. *Final Report of the Special Commission on Ethics.* Boston: Commonwealth of Massachusetts.

Congressional Quarterly. 1992. *Congressional Ethics: History, Facts and Controversy.* Washington, D.C.: Congressional Quarterly Books.

Converse, Philip E. 1967. The Concept of a Normal Vote. In *Elections and the Political Order,* ed. Angus Campbell, P. E. Converse, Warren Miller, and Donald E. Stokes. New York: John Wiley & Sons.

Council on Governmental Ethics Laws. 1988, 1990, 1993. *Campaign Finance, Ethics and Lobby Law Blue Book.* Lexington, Ky.: Council on Governmental Ethics Laws.

———. 1995. *Ethics 1994: Events, Issues and Trends.* Los Angeles: Council on Governmental Ethics Laws.

Council of State Governments. 1996. *Public Integrity Annual,* ed. James S. Bowman. Lexington, Ky.: Council of State Governments.

Craig, Stephen C. 1993. *The Malevolent Leaders: Popular Discontent in America.* Boulder, Colo.: Westview Press.

Cronin, Thomas E. 1989. *Direct Democracy: The Politics of Initiative, Referendum and Recall.* Cambridge, Mass.: Harvard University Press.

DeLeon, Peter. 1993. *Thinking about Political Corruption.* Armonk, N.Y.: M. E. Sharpe.

DeLong, Bradford, and Andrei Shleifer. 1993. Princes and Merchants: Government and City Growth before the Industrial Revolution. *Journal of Law and Economics* 36: 671–702.

Dimock, Michael A., and Gary C. Jacobson. 1995. Checks and Choices: The House Bank Scandal's Impact on Voters in 1992. *Journal of Politics* 57:1143–59.

Dobel, J. Patrick. 1999. *Public Integrity.* Baltimore: Johns Hopkins University Press.

Donahue, Ann Marie. 1989. *Ethics in Politics and Government.* New York: H. W. Wilson.

Downs, Anthony. 1957. *An Economic Theory of Democracy.* New York: Harper & Row.

———. 1972. Up and Down with Ecology: The Issue-Attention Cycle. *Public Interest* 28: 38–50.

Durning, Dan, 1991. Education Reform in Arkansas: The Governor's Role in Policymaking. In *Gubernatorial Leadership and State Policy,* ed. Eric B. Herzik and Brent W. Brown. Westport, Conn.: Greenwood Press.

Dye, Thomas R. 1966. *Politics, Economics and the Public.* Chicago: Rand McNally.

Ehrenhalt, Alan. 1989. Justice and Ambition. *Governing,* September, 38–44.

Elazar, Daniel. 1970. *Cities of the Prairie: The Metropolitan Frontier and American Politics.* New York: Basic Books.

———. 1972. *American Federalism: A View from the States.* New York: Thomas Y. Crowell.

Ellis, Richard. 1993. *American Political Cultures.* New York: Oxford University Press.

Ensign, David. 1996. Reforming Public Integrity Laws in an Era of Declining Trust. In *Book of the States, 1996–97 Edition.* Lexington, Ky.: Council of State Governments.

Erikson, Robert S. 1978. Constituency Opinion and Congressional Behavior: A Reexamination of the Miller-Stokes Representation Data. *American Journal of Political Science* 22: 511–35.

Erikson, Robert S., Gerald C. Wright, and John P. McIver. 1993. *Statehouse Democracy: Public Opinion and Policy in the American States.* Cambridge: Cambridge University Press.

Fain, Herbert. 2002. The Case for a Zero Gift Policy. *Public Integrity* 4: 61–74.

Fiorina, Morris P. 1973. Electoral Margins, Constituency Influence, and Policy Moderation: A Critical Assessment. *American Politics Quarterly* 1: 478–98.

———. 1989. *Congress: Keystone of the Washington Establishment.* 2nd ed. New Haven, Conn.: Yale University Press.

———. 1994. Divided Government in the American States: A Byproduct of Legislative Professionalism? *American Political Science Review* 88: 304–16.

Fiorina, Morris, Paul Peterson, and Bertram Johnson. 2003. *The New American Democracy.* Boston: Allyn Bacon Longman, 224.

Fisher, Louis. 1999. Starr's Record as Independent Counsel. *PS: Political Science and Politics* 32: 546–49.

Florida Commission on Ethics and the Florida House of Representatives. 1987. *The Florida Commission on Ethics: Its History, Evolution and Future.* Tallahassee: Florida Commission on Ethics and the Florida House of Representatives.

Garment, Suzanne. 1991. *Scandal: The Crisis of Mistrust in American Politics.* New York: Times Books.

George, Alexander. 1979. Case Studies and Theory Development: The Method of Structured, Focused Comparison. In *Diplomacy: New Approaches in History, Theory and Policy,* ed. Paul Lauren. New York: Free Press.

George, Alexander, and Timothy J. McKeown. 1985. Case Studies and Theories of Organizational Decision Making. In *Advances in Information Processing in Organizations,* vol. 2, ed. Robert Culam and Richard Smith. Greenwich, Conn.: JAI Press.

Gerber, Elisabeth. 1999. *The Populist Paradox.* Princeton, N.J.: Princeton University Press.

Ginsberg, Benjamin, and Martin Shefter. 1990. *Politics by Other Means: The Declining Importance of Elections in America.* New York: Basic Books.

Glick, Henry R. 1992. *The Right to Die.* New York: Columbia University Press.

Glor, Eleanor D., and Ian Greene. 2003. The Government of Canada's Approach to Ethics: The Evolution of Ethical Government. *Public Integrity* 5: 39–65.

Goodman, Marshall R., Timothy J. Holp, and Karen M. Ludwig. 1996. Understanding State Legislative Ethics Reform: The Importance of Political and Institutional Culture. In *Public Integrity Annual,* ed. James S. Bowman. Lexington, Ky.: Council of State Governments.

Goodman, Marshall R., Timothy Holp, Louis Martin, and Eric Rademacher. 1994. Legislative Ethics: Reform and Reaction in the States. Paper presented at Annual Meeting of American Political Science Association, New York.

Goodman, Marshall R., Timothy Holp, and Eric Rademacher. 1993. Patterns of State Legislative Ethics Reform: Have They Gotten the Message? Paper presented at the Annual Meeting of American Political Science Association, Washington, D.C.

———. 1994. State Legislative Ethics: Proactive Reform or Reactive Defense? Paper presented at Annual Meeting of Midwest Political Science Association, Chicago.

Gottschalk, Marie. 2000. *The Shadow Welfare State: Labor, Business and the Politics of Health Care in the United States.* Ithaca, N.Y.: Cornell University Press.

Gould, Lewis L. 1976. *Reform and Regulation: American Politics, 1900–1916.* New York: John Wiley & Sons.

Gray, Virginia. 1973. Innovation in the States: A Diffusion Study. *American Political Science Review* 67: 1174–85.

———. 1990. The Socioeconomic and Political Context of States. In *Politics in the American States,* ed. Virginia Gray, Herbert Jacob, and Robert Albritton. New York: HarperCollins.

Greene, Ian, and David Shugarman. 1997. *Honest Politics: Seeking Integrity in Canadian Public Life.* Toronto: James Lorimer.

Greene, William H. 1990. *Econometric Analysis.* New York: Macmillan.

Grumm, John. 1971. The Effects of Legislative Structure on Legislative Performance. In *State and Urban Politics,* ed. Richard I. Hofferbert and Ira Sharkansky. Boston: Little, Brown.

Haider-Markel, Donald P. 2001. Policy Diffusion as a Geographical Expansion of the Scope of Political Conflict: Same Sex Marriage Bans in the 1990s. *State Politics and Policy Quarterly* 1: 5–26.

Hall, Richard L. 1991. Participation, Abdication, and Representation in Congressional Committees. In *Congress Reconsidered,* 5th edition, ed. Lawrence C. Dodd and Bruce I. Oppenheimer. Washington, D.C.: Congressional Quarterly Books.

Hansen, Karen. 1994. The Pulitzer Prize, *The Detroit News* and Us. *State Legislatures,* July, 5.

Hays, Scott P., and Henry R. Glick. 1997. The Role of Agenda Setting in Policy Innovation: An Event History Analysis of Living-Will Laws. *American Politics Quarterly* 25: 497–516.

Hedge, David. 1998. *Governance and the Changing American States.* Boulder, Colo.: Westview Press.

Hermann, Frederick M. 1996. Bricks without Straw: The Plight of Governmental Ethics Agencies in the United States. In *Public Integrity Annual,* ed. James S. Bowman. Lexington, Ky.: Council of State Governments.

Herrick, Rebekah. 2003. *Fashioning the More Ethical Representative: The Impact of Ethics Reforms in the U.S. House of Representatives.* Westport, Conn.: Praeger.

Hibbing, John R. 1983. Washington on 75 Dollars a Day: Members of Congress Voting on Their Own Tax Break. *Legislative Studies Quarterly* 8: 219–30.

Hill, Kim Quaile. 2003. Democratization and Corruption. *American Politics Research* 31: 613–31.

Hofstadter, Richard. 1955. *The Age of Reform.* New York: Knopf.

Hogan, Robert E. 2003. Sources of Competition in State Legislative Primary Elections. *Legislative Studies Quarterly* 28: 103–26.

Holbrook, Thomas M., and Emily Van Dunk. 1993. Electoral Competition in the American States. *American Political Science Review* 87: 955–62.

Hoogenboom, Ari. 1978. Did Gilded Age Scandals Bring Reform? In *Before Watergate,* ed. Abraham S. Eisenstadt, Ari Hoogenboom, and Hans L. Trefousse. New York: Brooklyn College Press.

Huckshorn, Robert J. 1985. Who Gave It? Who Got It? The Enforcement of Campaign Finance Laws in the States. *Journal of Politics* 47: 773–89.

Hwang, Sung-Don, and Virginia Gray. 1991. External Limits and Internal Determinants of State Public Policy. *Western Political Quarterly* 44: 277–99.

Immergut, Ellen. 1998. The Theoretical Core of the New Institutionalism. *Politics and Society* 26: 5–34.

Jackson, Brooks. 1990. *Broken Promise: Why the Federal Election Commission Failed.* New York: Twentieth Century Fund.

Jackson, John E., and John W. Kingdon. 1992. Ideology, Interest Group Scores, and Legislative Votes. *American Journal of Political Science* 36: 805–23.

Jillson, Calvin, and Cecil Eubanks. 1984. The Political Structure of Constitution Making: The Federal Convention of 1787. *American Journal of Political Science* 28: 435–58.

Johnston, Michael. 1982. *Political Corruption and Public Policy in America*. Monterey, Calif.: Brooks/Cole.

———. 1983. Corruption and Political Culture in America: An Empirical Perspective. *Publius* 13: 19–39.

Jones, Charles. 1968. Joseph G. Cannon and Howard W. Smith: An Essay on the Limits of Leadership in the House of Representatives. *Journal of Politics* 30: 617–46.

Josephson, Michael. 2002. Ethics Legislation: Problems and Potential. In *The State of State Legislative Ethics*. Denver: National Conference of State Legislatures.

Katz, Allan. 1981. The Politics of Congressional Ethics. In *The House at Work*, ed. Joseph Cooper and G. Calvin Mackenzie. Austin: University of Texas Press.

Katz, Jeffrey L. 1991. Sipping from the Cup of Corruption. *Governing*, November, 28–29.

Kennedy, Peter. 1993. *A Guide to Econometrics*. 2nd ed. Cambridge, Mass.: MIT Press.

Killea, Lucy, and Bob Kirscht. 1993. Should Revolving Doors Be Closed for Legislators? *State Government News*, April, 10–11.

Kincaid, John. 1982a. Introduction. In *Political Culture, Public Policy and the American States*, ed. John Kincaid. Philadelphia: Center for the Study of Federalism.

———. 1982b. Political Culture and the Quality of Urban Life. In *Political Culture, Public Policy and the American States*, ed. John Kincaid. Philadelphia: Center for the Study of Federalism.

King, Gary, Robert Keohane, and Sidney Verba. 1994. *Designing Social Inquiry*. Princeton, N.J.: Princeton University Press.

Kingdon, John. 1984. *Agendas, Alternatives and Public Policies*. Boston: Little, Brown.

———. 1989. *Congressmen's Voting Decisions*. 3rd ed. Ann Arbor: University of Michigan Press.

Knack, Stephen, and Philip Keefer. 1995. Institutions and Economic Performance: Cross-Country Tests Using Alternative Institutional Measures. *Economics and Politics* 7: 207–27.

Krane, Dale, and Stephen D. Shaffer. 1996. *Mississippi Government and Politics*. Lincoln: University of Nebraska Press.

Krauss, Ellis S., and Jon Pierre. 1993. Targeting Resources for Industrial Change. In *Do Institutions Matter?* ed. R. Kent Weaver and Bert A. Rockman. Washington, D.C.: Brookings Institution Press.

Krehbiel, Keith. 1991. *Information and Legislative Information*. Ann Arbor: University of Michigan Press.

Kuklinski, James. 1977. District Competitiveness and Legislative Roll-Call Behavior: A Reassessment of the Marginality Hypothesis. *American Journal of Political Science* 21: 627–38.

————. 1978. Electoral Margins, District Homogeneity, and the Responsiveness of Legislators. In *Accountability in Urban Society*, ed. S. Greer, R. Hedlund, and J. Gibson. Beverly Hills, Calif.: Sage.

Kultgen, John. 1988. *Ethics and Professionalism*. Philadelphia: University of Pennsylvania Press.

LaPorta, Rafael, Florencio Lopez-de Silanes, Andrei Shleifer, and Robert Vishny. 1998. *The Quality of Government*. NBER Working Paper 6727. Cambridge, Mass.: National Bureau of Economic Research.

Lewis, Carol W. 1991. A Review of Provisions of Conflict of Interest. *COGEL Guardian*, December, 8–9.

Lichter, S. Robert, and Daniel R. Amundson. 1994. Less News Is Worse News. In *Congress, the Press and the Public*, ed. Thomas E. Mann and Norman J. Ornstein. Washington, D.C.: American Enterprise Institute.

Lijphart, Arend. 1971. Comparative Politics and the Comparative Method. *American Political Science Review* 65: 682–93.

Link, Arthur S., and Richard L. McCormick. 1983. *Progressivism*. Wheeling, Ill.: Harlan Davidson.

Linsky, M. 1986. *Impact: How the Press Affects Federal Policymaking*. New York: W. W. Norton.

Loftus, Tom. 1992. The Road to Ethical Legislatures Isn't Paved with Tougher Laws. In *State Government: CQ's Guide to Current Issues and Activities in 1992–1993*, ed. Thad Beyle. Washington, D.C.: Congressional Quarterly Books.

————. 1994. *The Art of Legislative Politics*. Washington, D.C.: CQ Press.

Lutz, James M. 1987. Regional Leadership Patterns in the Diffusion of Public Policies. *American Politics Quarterly* 15: 387–98.

Maass, Arthur. 1987. U.S. Prosecution of State and Local Officials for Political Corruption: Is the Bureaucracy Out of Control in a High-Stakes Operation Involving the Constitutional System? *Publius* 17: 195–230.

Mackenzie, G. Calvin, and Michael Hafkin. 2002. *Scandal Proof: Do Ethics Laws Make Government Ethical?* Washington, D.C.: Brookings Institution Press.

Mackey, Earl. 1996. Ethics Laws and Legislative Independence. In *Public Integrity Annual*, ed. James S. Bowman. Lexington, Ky.: Council of State Governments.

————. 2003. Dismantling the Kentucky Legislative Ethics Law. *Public Integrity* 5: 152.

Mahtesian, Charles. 1993. When the Voters Freeze Your Pay. *Governing*, December, 34–39.

Maletz, Donald J., and Jerry Herbel. 1998. Some Paradoxes of Government Ethics Revisited. Paper presented at Annual Meeting of American Political Science Association, Boston.

————. 2000. Beyond Idealism: Democracy and Ethics Reform. *American Review of Public Administration* 30: 19–45.

March, James, and Johan Olsen. 1984. The New Institutionalism: Organizational Factors in Political Life. *American Political Science Review* 78: 734–49.

Markus, Gregory B. 1979. *Analyzing Panel Data*. Beverly Hills, Calif.: Sage.

Mauro, Paolo. 1995. Corruption and Growth. *Quarterly Journal of Economics* 110: 681–712.

Mayer, William G. 2001. Public Attitudes on Campaign Finance. In *A User's Guide to Campaign Finance Reform*, ed. Gerald C. Lubenow. Lanham, Md.: Rowman and Littlefield.

Mayhew, David R. 1975. *Congress: The Electoral Connection.* New Haven, Conn.: Yale University Press.

———. 1986. *Placing Parties in American Politics.* Princeton, N.J.: Princeton University Press.

———. 1991. *Divided We Govern: Party Control, Lawmaking, and Investigations, 1946–1990.* New Haven, Conn.: Yale University Press.

McAdams, John. 1986. Alternatives for Dealing with Error in the Variables: An Example Using Panel Data. *American Journal of Political Science* 30: 256–78.

McCann, Michael. 1986. *Taking Reform Seriously: Perspectives on Public Interest Liberalism.* Ithaca, N.Y.: Cornell University Press, 1986.

McCubbins, Matthew D., Roger G. Noll, and Barry R. Weingast. 1987. Administrative Procedures as Instruments of Political Control. *Journal of Law, Economics, and Organization* 3: 243–77.

McFarland, Andrew S. 1984. *Public Interest Lobbies: Decision-Making on Energy.* Washington, D.C.: American Enterprise Institute.

———. 1984. *Common Cause: Lobbying in the Public Interest.* Chatham, N.J.: Chatham House Publishers.

McGuire, Robert, and Robert Ohsfeldt. 1989. Public Choice Analysis and the Ratification of the Constitution. In *The Federalist Papers and the New Institutionalism*, ed. Bernard Grofman and Donald Wittman. New York: Agathon Press.

Meier, Kenneth J., and Thomas M. Holbrook. 1992. "I Seen My Opportunities and I Took 'Em": Political Corruption in the American States. *Journal of Politics* 54: 135–55.

Mill, John Stuart. 1980 (originally published 1843). *A System of Logic, Rationative and Inductive: Being a Connected View of the Principles of Evidence and the Methods of Scientific Investigation.* Charlottesville, Va.: Ibis Publishing.

Miller, Arthur H. 1974. Political Issues and Trust in Government: 1964–1970. *American Political Science Review* 68: 951–72.

———. 1999. Sex, Politics and Public Opinion: What Political Scientists Really Learned from the Clinton-Lewinsky Scandal. *PS: Political Science and Politics* 32: 721–28.

Miller, Penny M. 1994. *Kentucky Politics and Government.* Lincoln: University of Nebraska Press.

Miller, Warren E., and Donald E. Stokes. Constituency Influence in Congress. *American Political Science Review* 57: 45–56.

Mintrom, Michael. 1997. Policy Entrepreneurs and the Diffusion of Innovation. *American Journal of Political Science* 41: 738–70.

Moe, Terry M. 1987a. An Assessment of the Positive Theory of "Congressional Dominance." *Legislative Studies Quarterly* 12: 475–520.

————. 1987b. Interests, Institutions, and Positive Theory; The Politics of the NLRB. *Studies in American Political Development* 2: 236–99.

————. 2003. The Presidency and the Bureaucracy: The Presidential Advantage. In *The Presidency and the Political System*, ed. Michael Nelson. Washington, D.C.: CQ Press.

Mohr, Lawrence. 1969. Determinants of Innovation in Organizations. *American Political Science Review* 63: 111–26.

Mooney, Christopher. 1995. Citizens, Structures, and Sister States: Influences on State Legislative Professionalism. *Legislative Studies Quarterly* 20: 47–67.

Mooney, Christopher Z., and Mei-Hsien Lee. 1995. Legislating Morality in the American States: The Case of Pre-Roe Abortion Regulation Reform. *American Journal of Political Science* 39: 599–627.

————. 1999. The Temporal Diffusion of Morality Policy: The Case of Death Penalty Legislation in the American States. *Policy Studies Journal* 27: 766–80.

Moore, William H. 1974. *The Kefauver Committee and the Politics of Crime, 1950-1952*. Columbia: University of Missouri Press.

Moscardelli, Vincent G., Moshe Haspel, and Richard S. Wike. 1998. Party Building through Campaign Finance Reform: Conditional Party Government in the 104th Congress. *Journal of Politics* 60: 691–704.

Mowry, George. 1951. *The California Progressives*. Chicago: Quadrangle Books.

National Conference of State Legislatures. 2002. *The State of State Legislative Ethics*. Denver: National Conference of State Legislatures.

Neely, Alfred, IV. 1989. Ethics in Government Laws. In *Ethics in Politics and Government*, ed. Anne Marie Donahue. New York: H. W. Wilson.

Newman, Robert C. 1988. New York's New Ethics Law: Turning the Tide on Corruption. *Hofstra Law Review* 16: 319–44.

Nice, David. 1983. Political Corruption in the American States. *American Politics Quarterly* 11: 507–17.

Nicholson-Crotty, Sean, David A. Peterson, and Lawrence Grossback. 2002. A Unified Theory of Policy Diffusion. Paper presented at Annual Meeting of American Political Science Association, Boston.

Noonan, John. 1984. *Bribes*. Berkeley: University of California Press.

North, Douglass. 1981. *Growth and Structural Change*. New York: W. W. Norton.

O'Heffernan, Patrick. 1994. Mass Media Roles in Foreign Policy. In *Media Power in Politics*, 3rd edition, ed. Doris A Graber. Washington, D.C.: CQ Press.

Opheim, Cynthia. 1991. Explaining the Differences in State Lobby Regulation. *Western Political Quarterly* 44: 405–19.

Orloff, Ann Shola. 1988. The Political Origins of America's Belated Welfare State. In *The Politics of Social Policy in the United States*, ed. Margaret Weir, Ann Shola Orloff, and Theda Skocpol. Princeton, N.J.: Princeton University Press.

Parker, Glenn R. 1992. The Distribution of Honoraria Income in the United States Congress: Who Gets Rents in Congress and Why? *Public Choice* 73: 167–81.

Patton, Clifford W. 1969. *The Battle for Municipal Reform: Mobilization and Attack, 1875 to 1900*. College Park, Md.: McGrath.

Peters, John G., and Susan Welch. 1978. Political Corruption in America; A Search for Definitions and a Theory, or If Political Corruption Is in the Mainstream of American Politics Why Is It Not in the Mainstream of American Politics Research? *American Political Science Review* 72: 974–84.

Pffifner, James P. 2003. Judging Presidential Character. *Public Integrity* 5: 7–24.

Plott, Charles. 1967. A Notion of Equilibrium under Majority Rule. *American Economic Review* 57: 787–806.

Polsby, Nelson, 1968. The Institutionalization of the U.S. House of Representatives. *American Political Science Review* 62: 144–68.

Poole, Keith T., and Howard Rosenthal. 1991. Patterns of Congressional Voting. *American Journal of Political Science* 35: 228–78.

Pound, William. 1992. State Legislative Careers: Twenty-Five Years of Reform. In *Changing Patterns in State Legislative Careers,* ed. Gary F. Moncrief and Joel A. Thompson. Ann Arbor: University of Michigan Press.

Powell, Walter W., and Paul J. Di Maggio, eds. 1991. *The New Institutionalism in Organizational Analysis.* Chicago: University of Chicago Press.

Price, H. Douglas. 1977. Career and Committees in the American Congress: The Problem of Structural Change. In *The History of Parliamentary Behavior,* ed. William O. Ayedelotte. Princeton, N.J.: Princeton University Press.

Ranney, Austin. 1971. *Politics in the American States,* 2nd edition, ed. Herbert Jacob and Kenneth N. Vines. Boston: Little, Brown.

Ransone, Coleman. 1982. *The American Governorship.* Westport, Conn.: Greenwood Press.

Report of the Special Legislative Commission on Integrity and Ethical Standards in Government to Hon. Thomas E. Dewey, Governor and to the Legislature of NY (March 5, 1954).

Ripley, Randall. 1969. *Majority Party Leadership in Congress.* Boston: Little, Brown.

Roberts, Robert N., and Marion T. Doss, Jr. 1997. *From Watergate to Whitewater: The Public Integrity War.* Westport, Conn.: Praeger Press.

Rogers, Everett M., and James W. Dearing. 1988. Agenda Setting Research: Where Has It Been, Where Is It Going? In *Communication Yearbook* 11, ed. James A. Anderson. Beverly Hills, Calif.: Sage.

Rohde, David. 1991. *Parties and Leaders in the Postreform House.* Chicago: University of Chicago Press.

Rose-Ackerman, Susan. 1999. *Corruption and Government: Causes, Consequences and Reform.* Cambridge: Cambridge University Press.

Rosenson, Beth. 2002. Why U.S. Senators Voted to Limit Honoraria, 1981–1983. Paper presented at panel on Decision Making in the Modern Senate at the Midwest Political Science Association meeting, Chicago.

———. 2003. Legislative Voting on Ethics Reform in Two States: The Influence of Economic Self-Interest, Ideology and Institutional Power. *Public Integrity* 5: 205–22.

———. 2004. Costs and Benefits of Ethics Laws. Paper presented at Conference on Governance and Political Ethics, University of Montreal, Montreal, May 14–15.

Rosenthal, Alan. 1974. Turnover in State Legislatures. *American Journal of Political Science* 18: 609–16.

———. 1990. *Governors and Legislators: Contending Powers.* Washington, D.C.: CQ Press.

———. 1996. *Drawing the Line: Legislative Ethics in the States.* New York: Twentieth Century Fund.

Ross, Michael. 1987. *State and Local Politics and Policy* . Englewood Cliffs, N.J.: Prentice Hall.

Ruhil, Anirudh V. S. 2003. Urban Armageddon or Politics as Usual? The Case of Municipal Civil Service Reform. *American Journal of Political Science* 47: 159–70.

Rundquist, Barry S., Gerald S. Strom, and John G. Peters. 1977. Corrupt Politicians and Their Electoral Support: Some Experimental Observations. *American Political Science Review* 71: 954–63.

Sacks, Howard. 1971. Ethical Standards in the State Legislature. In *Strengthening the States: Essays on Legislative Reform*, ed. Donald G. Herzberg and Alan Rosenthal. New York: Doubleday.

Savage, Robert. 1978. Policy Innovativeness as a Trait of American States. *Journal of Politics* 40: 212–23.

Schlesinger, James A. 1971. Politics of the Executive. In *Politics in the American States*, 2nd edition, ed. Herbert Jacob and Kenneth Vines. Boston: Little, Brown.

Schmidt, David. 1989. *Citizen Lawmakers: The Ballot Initiative Revolution.* Philadelphia: Temple University Press.

Schultz, David A., and Robert Maranto. 1998. *The Politics of Civil Service Reform.* New York: Peter Lang Publishing.

Schwarz, Christopher. 1994. Ethics: Passing Judgment or Passing the Buck? *State Government News*, February, 11–13.

Seligson, Mitchell A. 2002. The Impact of Corruption on Regime Legitimacy: A Comparative Study of Four Countries. *Journal of Politics* 64: 408–33.

Sharkansky, Ira. 1969. The Utility of Elazar's Political Culture. *Polity* 2: 66–83.

Shepsle, Kenneth. 1989. Studying Institutions: Some Lessons from the Rational Choice Approach. *Journal of Theoretical Politics* 1: 134–48.

Shepsle, Kenneth, and Barry R. Weingast. 1979. Structure-Induced Equilibrium and Legislative Choice. *Public Choice* 37: 503–19.

———. 1987. The Institutional Foundation of Committee Power. *American Political Science Review* 81: 85–104.

———. 1994. Positive Theories of Congressional Institutions. *Legislative Studies Quarterly* 19: 149–80.

Singer, Judith, and John B. Willett. 1993. It's About Time: Using Discrete-Time Survival Analysis to Study Duration and the Timing of Events. *Journal of Educational Statistics* 18: 155–95.

Skocpol, Theda. 1988. The Limits of the New Deal System and the Roots of Contemporary Welfare Dilemmas. In *The Politics of Social Policy in the United States,* ed. Margaret Weir, Ann Shola Orloff, and Theda Skocpol. Princeton, N.J.: Princeton University Press.

Skowronek, Stephen. 1982. *Building a New American State: The Expansion of National Administrative Capacities, 1877-1920.* Cambridge: Cambridge University Press.

Sonner, Molly W., and Clyde Wilcox. 1999. Forgiving and Forgetting: Public Support for Bill Clinton during the Lewinsky Scandal. *PS: Political Science and Politics* 32: 554–57.

Squire, Peverill. 1992. Legislative Professionalization and Membership Diversity in State Legislatures. *Legislative Studies Quarterly* 17: 69–79.

Stark, Andrew. 2000. *Conflict of Interest in American Public Life.* Cambridge, Mass.: Harvard University Press.

Stern, Robert M. 1985. Ethics in the States. In *Representation and Responsibility: Exploring Legislative Ethics,* ed. Bruce Jennings and Daniel Callahan. New York: Plenum Press.

Stewart, Charles H, III. 1994. Ain't Misbehaving, or, Reflections on Two Centuries of Congressional Corruption. Center for American Political Studies. Occasional Working Papers, 94–4.

Stuart, Elaine. 1994. Trail of Smears. *State Government News,* May, 22–33.

Sullivan, William M. 1995. *Work and Integrity: The Crisis and Promise of Professionalism in America.* New York: Harper Business.

Sundquist, James. 1988. Needed: A Political Theory for the New Era of Coalition Government in the United States. *Political Science Quarterly* 103: 613–35.

Thelen, David P. 1976. *Robert M. LaFollette and the Insurgent Spirit.* Boston: Little, Brown.

Thelen, Kathleen, and Sven Steinmo. 1992. Historical Institutionalism in Comparative Politics. In *Structuring Politics: Historical Institutionalism in Comparative Analysis,* ed. Sven Steinmo, Kathleen Thelen, and Frank Longstreth. Cambridge: Cambridge University Press.

Theriault, Sean M. 2003. Patronage, the Pendleton Act, and the Power of the People. *Journal of Politics* 65: 50–68.

Thompson, Dennis F. 1987. *Political Ethics and Public Office.* Cambridge, Mass.: Harvard University Press.

———. 1995. *Ethics in Congress.* Washington, D.C.: Brookings Institution Press.

Tolbert, Caroline J. 1998. Changing Rules for State Legislatures: Direct Democracy and Governance Policies. In *Citizens as Legislators: Direct Democracy in the United States,* ed. Shaun Bowler, Todd Donovan, and Caroline J. Tolbert. Columbus: Ohio State University Press.

Tolchin, Susan J., and Martin Tolchin. 2001. *Glass Houses: Congressional Ethics and the Politics of Venom.* Boulder, Colo.: Westview Press.

Van Evera, Stephen. 1997. *Guide to Methods for Students of Political Science.* Ithaca, N.Y.: Cornell University Press.

Wagar, Linda, and Elaine S. Knapp. 1992. The Truth about Ethics. In *State Government, CQ's Guide to Current Issues and Activities, 1992–93*, ed. Thad Beyle. Washington, D.C.: Congressional Quarterly Books.

Walker, Jack L. 1969. The Diffusion of Innovations among the American States. *American Political Science Review* 63: 880–89.

Weaver, R. Kent, and Bert A. Rockman, eds. 1993. *Do Institutions Matter?* Washington, D.C.: Brookings Institution Press, 1993.

Weber, Ronald E. 1999. The Quality of State Legislative Representation: A Critical Assessment. *Journal of Politics* 61: 609–27.

Weingast, Barry R., and William J. Marshall. 1988. The Industrial Organization of Congress; or, Why Legislatures, Like Firms, Are Not Organized as Markets. *Journal of Political Economy* 96: 132–63.

Weingast, Barry R., and Mark J. Moran. 1983. Bureaucratic Discretion or Congressional Control? Regulatory Policymaking by the Federal Trade Commission. *Journal of Political Economy* 91: 769–800.

Weir, Margaret, Ann Shola Orloff, and Theda Skocpol. 1988. Introduction: Understanding American Social Politics. In *The Politics of Social Policy in the United States*, ed. Margaret Weir, Ann Shola Orloff, and Theda Skocpol. Princeton, N.J.: Princeton University Press.

Wiebe, Robert. 1967. *The Search for Order, 1877–1920.* New York: Hill and Wang.

Wilkerson, John D. 1990. Reelection and Representation in Conflict: The Case of Agenda Manipulation. *Legislative Studies Quarterly* 15: 263–82.

Williams, Russell L. 1996. Controlling Ethical Practices through Laws and Rules: Evaluating the Florida Commission on Ethics. In *Public Integrity Annual*, ed. James S. Bowman. Lexington, Ky.: Council of State Governments.

Williams, Sandra. 1985. *Conflict of Interest: The Ethical Dilemma in Politics.* London: Gower.

Wilson, Woodrow. 1882. Government by Debate. Unpublished manuscript. Cited in H. Douglas Price. 1977. Career and Committees in the American Congress: The Problem of Structural Change. In *The History of Parliamentary Behavior*, ed. William O. Ayedelotte. Princeton, N.J.: Princeton University Press.

Witt, Elder. 1989. Is Government Full of Crooks or Are We Just Better at Finding Them? *Governing* 2 (Sept. 1989): 33–38.

Wright, Gerald C., Jr., Robert S. Erikson, and John P. McIver. 1987. Public Opinion and Policy Liberalism in the American States. *American Journal of Political Science* 31: 980–1001.

Young, Amy E. 1991. In the States. *Common Cause Magazine*, May/June, 41.

Zimmerman, Joseph. 1994. *Curbing Unethical Behavior in Government.* Westport, Conn.: Greenwood Press.

index

The letter *t* following a page number denotes a table.